International Political Economy Series

General Editor: **Timothy M. Shaw**, Professor of Commonwealth Governance and Development, and Director of the Institute of Commonwealth Studies, School of Advanced Study, University of London

Titles Include:

Leslie Elliott Armijo (*editor*)
FINANCIAL GLOBALIZATION AND DEMOCRACY IN EMERGING MARKETS

Robert Boardman
THE POLITICAL ECONOMY OF NATURE
Environmental Debates and the Social Sciences

Jörn Brömmelhörster and Wolf-Christian Paes (*editors*)
THE MILITARY AS AN ECONOMIC ACTOR
Soldiers in Business

Gordon Crawford
FOREIGN AID AND POLITICAL REFORM
A Comparative Analysis of Democracy Assistance and Political Conditionality

Matt Davies
INTERNATIONAL POLITICAL ECONOMY AND MASS COMMUNICATION
IN CHILE
National Intellectuals and Transnational Hegemony

Martin Doornbos
INSTITUTIONALIZING DEVELOPMENT POLICIES AND RESOURCE STRATEGIES
IN EASTERN AFRICA AND INDIA
Developing Winners and Losers

Fred P. Gale
THE TROPICAL TIMBER TRADE REGIME

Meric S. Gertler and David A. Wolfe
INNOVATION AND SOCIAL LEARNING
Institutional Adaptation in an Era of Technological Change

Anne Marie Goetz and Rob Jenkins
REINVENTING ACCOUNTABILITY
Making Democracy Work for the Poor

Mary Ann Haley
FREEDOM AND FINANCE
Democratization and Institutional Investors in Developing Countries

Keith M. Henderson and O. P. Dwivedi (*editors*)
BUREAUCRACY AND THE ALTERNATIVES IN WORLD PERSPECTIVES

Jomo K.S. and Shyamala Nagaraj (*editors*)
GLOBALIZATION VERSUS DEVELOPMENT

Angela W. Little
LABOURING TO LEARN
Towards a Political Economy of Plantations, People and Education in Sri Lanka

John Loxley (*editor*)
INTERDEPENDENCE, DISQUILIBRIUM AND GROWTH
Reflections on the Political Economy of North–South Relations at the Turn of
the Century

Don D. Marshall
CARIBBEAN POLITICAL ECONOMY AT THE CROSSROADS
NAFTA and Regional Developmentalism

Susan M. McMillan
FOREIGN DIRECT INVESTMENT IN THREE REGIONS OF THE SOUTH AT
THE END OF THE TWENTIETH CENTURY

S. Javed Maswood
THE SOUTH IN INTERNATIONAL ECONOMIC REGIMES
Whose Globalization?

James H. Mittelman and Mustapha Pasha (*editors*)
OUT FROM UNDERDEVELOPMENT
Prospects for the Third World (Second Edition)

Lars Rudebeck, Olle Törnquist and Virgilio Rojas (*editors*)
DEMOCRATIZATION IN THE THIRD WORLD
Concrete Cases in Comparative and Theoretical Perspective

Benu Schneider (*editor*)
THE ROAD TO INTERNATIONAL FINANCIAL STABILITY
Are Key Financial Standards the Answer?

Howard Stein (*editor*)
ASIAN INDUSTRIALIZATION AND AFRICA
Studies in Policy Alternatives to Structural Adjustment

International Political Economy Series
Series Standing Order ISBN 0–333–71708–2 hardcover
Series Standing Order ISBN 0–333–71110–6 paperback
(*outside North America only*)

You can receive future titles in this series as they are published by placing a standing order.
Please contact your bookseller or, in case of difficulty, write to us at the address below with
your name and address, the title of the series and one of the ISBNs quoted above.

Customer Services Department, Macmillan Distribution Ltd, Houndmills, Basingstoke,
Hampshire RG21 6XS, England

The South in International Economic Regimes

Whose Globalization?

S. Javed Maswood
Department of International Business & Asian Studies
Griffith Business School
Griffith University, Brisbane, Australia

337. 09172
M42 N

First published in 2006 by
PALGRAVE MACMILLAN
Houndmills, Basingstoke, Hampshire RG21 6XS and
175 Fifth Avenue, New York, N.Y. 10010
Companies and representatives throughout the world.

PALGRAVE MACMILLAN is the global academic imprint of the Palgrave Macmillan division of St. Martin's Press, LLC and of Palgrave Macmillan Ltd. Macmillan® is a registered trademark in the United States, United Kingdom and other countries. Palgrave is a registered trademark in the European Union and other countries.

ISBN 13: 978–1–4039–9713–5 hardback
ISBN 10: 1–4039–9713–6 hardback

This book is printed on paper suitable for recycling and made from fully managed and sustained forest sources.

A catalogue record for this book is available from the British Library.

Library of Congress Cataloging-in-Publication Data

Maswood, Syed Javed.
        The South in international economic regimes : whose globalization? / S. Javed Maswood.
            p. cm.
        Includes bibliographical references and index.
        ISBN 1–4039–9713–6 (cloth)
            1. International trade. 2. International economic relations.
        3. Developing countries—Foreign economic relations. 4. Developing countries—Commerce. 5. Developing countries—Economic conditions.
        I.Title.

HF1379.M378 2006
337'.09172'4—dc22   2005044519

10 9 8 7 6 5 4 3 2 1
15 14 13 12 11 10 09 08 07 06

Printed and bound in Great Britain by
Antony Rowe Ltd, Chippenham and Eastbourne

To Nadia, Naveed, and Nasser

Contents

List of Tables

List of Abbreviations

AIDS	acquired immune deficiency syndrome
AMF	Asian Monetary Fund
APEC	Asia Pacific Economic Cooperation
ARVs	anti-retroviral medicines
ASEAN	Association of South-East Asian Nations
CAFTA	Central American Free Trade Agreement
CAP	Common Agricultural Policy (EU)
CEA	Council of Economic Advisors
DSB	Dispute Settlement Body (WTO)
EU	European Union
FDI	foreign direct investment
GATS	General Agreement on Trade in Services
GATT	General Agreement on Tariffs and Trade
GDP	gross domestic product
GSP	generalized system of preferences
G-8	Group of Eight
G-20	Group of Twenty
HIV	human immunodeficiency virus
IBRD	International Bank for Reconstruction and Development (World Bank)
ILO	International Labour Organization
IMF	International Monetary Fund
IT	Information and Technology
ITO	International Trade Organization
MAI	multilateral agreement on investment
MDGs	Millennium Development Goals
MFA	Multi-Fiber Agreement
MFN	most favoured nation
MNCs	multinational corporations
NAFTA	North American Free Trade Agreement
NGOs	non-governmental organizations
ODA	official development assistance
OECD	Organization for Economic Cooperation and Development
OMA	Orderly Marketing Agreement
PTA	preferential trade agreement
SARS	severe acute respiratory syndrome

SDT	special and differential treatment
TPM	trigger price mechanism
TRAA	Trade Related Adjustment Assistance
TRIMs	trade related investment measures
TRIPs	trade related intellectual property
UK	United Kingdom
UN	United Nations
UNCTAD	UN Conference on Trade and Development
UNDP	UN Development Program
US	United States of America
VER	voluntary export restraint
WDM	World Development Movement
WHO	World Health Organization
WTO	World Trade Organization

Acknowledgments

I began researching and writing this book while in Washington and completed it when I returned to Brisbane. Many individuals have contributed to the making of this book and I would like to acknowledge their help and support. In Washington, I am grateful to Aaditya Mattoo of the World Bank for giving generously of his time and for putting me in touch with several other individuals. Others at the World Bank who helped with the research include Kym Anderson, Will Martin, Gianni Zanini, and John Nash. In Geneva, I met and interviewed a number of individuals, including Patrick Low and Jayashree Watal at the World Trade Organization. They both agreed to sit down with me for extensive discussions on the Doha Round agenda and helped me reach a better understanding of the process. Two developing country representatives to the WTO also agreed to lengthy interviews and I would like to thank Faizel Ismail, Head of the South African Delegation to the WTO and Ambassador Toufiq Ali, the Bangladesh Representative to the WTO. Carsten Fink at the World Bank office in Geneva was also very helpful and I would like to thank him for his generosity. At the Food and Agriculture Office in Geneva, Panos Konandreas kindly explained the intricacies of agriculture trade and I am grateful to him also for providing me with copies of his papers.

Tim Shaw, editor of the IPE series read a draft of the manuscript and offered numerous helpful suggestions, as did the anonymous referees. Their help has contributed, I hope, to a much-improved book.

Finally, I owe a deep debt of gratitude to my family. My wife did not suffer through the process of preparing this manuscript; she was an integral part of it. Nadia provided invaluable research input and encouragement. She accompanied me on my travels and the interview rounds, and looked after our two boys. Nasser and Naveed had free run of the WTO corridors while I did my interviews. My youngest son Nasser also spent much of his infancy sitting on my lap while I tackled the keyboard with one finger. His distractions made this book a joyful experience.

1
Introduction

Structure and outline

This book focuses on international economic regimes, their impact on developing countries and contemporary negotiations spearheaded by developing countries to create structures and rules, or regimes that are relatively fair and equitable. In a large and diverse group, it is near impossible to devise structures that optimize the interests of all and at best there can be a balance between the interests and needs of developed countries and those of developing countries. Categorizing countries in two groups is conventional and useful even though we cannot overlook the diversity within each group, especially the latter that includes the high-income developing countries to the least developed countries and many groups in between.

The starting assumption here is that rules that were formulated at the end of the Second World War have failed developing countries and their aspirations. These rules were products of negotiations among developed countries with minimal input from developing countries. The early marginalization of developing countries continued in the ensuing decades and helps explain their relatively passivity in, for example, trade negotiations. Issues that were important to developed countries dominated the agenda of the first seven trade negotiating rounds of the General Agreement on Tariffs and Trade (GATT) and developing countries stood largely on the sidelines. The passive involvement of developing countries changed to active engagement in the Doha Round, a transition prompted, first, by their integration in the global economy through structural adjustment programs of the International Monetary Fund (IMF) and the World Bank and, second, by a consequent desire to shape emerging rules and norms of engagement that do not discriminate against their developmental aspirations as has been the case in the past.

Borrowing on regime theory, I argue that regimes, in general, advance interests of the select few powerful countries and of the hegemonic architect. Regimes are, however, not created complete or perfect, as a consequence of bounded rationality and inability to design for unforeseen and unpredictable developments. Over time, changing circumstances and new developments produce ad hoc and arbitrary modifications and adaptations but these changes do not alter the basic foundation on which regimes are established. As such inequities built into regimes at the inception remain largely in place, preserving the position of the privileged. International economic regimes, then and now, continue to impede the capacity of a large number of developing countries to fulfil a fair distribution of economic benefit or to achieve their developmental goals. This is not to deny however, that some developing countries have recorded envious growth rates in recent decades, particularly China and India and the original Asian tiger economies of South Korea, Taiwan, Singapore and Hong Kong.

Despite some success stories, international trade and economic systems have lacked equity. Developing countries are confronted by numerous obstacles to exports, such as quantitative export restrictions, tariff escalation on agricultural commodities, and subsidies in Organization for Economic Cooporation and Development (OECD) countries that also undermine production in developing countries. These have impeded the capacity of developing countries to fully utilize trade opportunities to advance their developmental goals.

This particular statement of the problem is not incontrovertible and it might be argued that the exceptions listed earlier adequately demonstrate that developing countries can successfully implement export-led growth strategies. Proponents of globalization see the charges of inequity and unfairness leveled at rules and institutions created by the developed countries after the Second World War as mischievous. For example, Jagdish Bhagwati, a leading economist, writes:

> As far as the charges of hypocrisy, double standards, and unfair trade that are passionately leveled today at . . . international institutions and also at the rich nations . . . [by Oxfam and by the World Bank among others] these beliefs and allegations are often little more than rubbish.[1]

If nothing else, Bhagwati is a useful reminder that passion is not limited to those who oppose globalization. Bhagwati brings a near religious zeal to his defense of economic globalization. In an ideal world, his assertions would be understandable because developing countries indeed are guilty of, for instance, higher levels of protectionism than developed countries and tend also to skirt around regulatory frameworks claiming a right to special and differential treatment (SDT). Their benefits from participating in a global economy are indeed, to some extent contingent on domestic reforms and improved policy cultures. However, systemic factors cannot be ignored and we need to remember that international economic exchange takes place not in an ideal world but in a world influenced and shaped by political considerations. Economic inequalities are not entirely attributable to global economic forces but they are not inconsequential. In an ideal world, as *Global Monitoring Report 2005* of the World Bank suggests, "developing countries would obtain about one-third of the global gain from freeing all merchandise trade, well above their one-fifth share of global GDP."[2] That, however, is an unlikely scenario but if it could be achieved it will lead to significant reduction of the large and growing income differential that exists across the North–South divide. Globalization itself may be value-neutral but rules and structures that give it form and purpose are purposely skewed.

Remarking on regulatory frameworks, Bernard Hoekman of the World Bank writes that for developing countries to benefit, it is necessary to get "the [multilateral] rules right."[3] Domestic rules and policies also matter but unless systemic bias and inequities are removed, the problems confronting developing countries will not have been resolved. The focus in this book is on multilateral rules. The economic approach to multilateral rules has been to concentrate on the logic of free trade, which in itself is convincing enough but has proved politically impractical since its introduction into economic thinking. Instead, this book adopts a political economy approach to understand why rules are constructed the way they are, how developing countries might advance their own agenda, and pitfalls along the way.

In the context of redressing existing systemic inequities, developing countries also have a unique window of opportunity. In the past their demands for a fair deal in the international economy had produced little real change but they now have a historic opportunity to influence the supply of new regulatory structures for the emerging global economy. With the start of the Doha Round of trade negotiations, developed western countries signaled a readiness to inject more balance into redesigned regimes for a global economy. They did this when they agreed to launch the Doha Round as the "development round" in order to overcome resistance from some developing countries to a new trade round. The post-Seattle context also was a factor in such a designation of the Doha Round.

The window of opportunity is no guarantee that developing countries will achieve their objectives. While developed countries have agreed to factor in developing country interests, in principle, their readiness in practice to accept necessary modifications during actual negotiations has been well short of initial rhetorical pronouncements. There are a number of obstacles that impedes the pursuit of justice, including the fact that in a unipolar world, the United States (US) effectively exercises global policy leadership. The US government through its global reach and influence largely creates global rules and principles and yet as a surrogate global government, it is accountable only to the citizens of the US. This harsh reality complicates the task of establishing rules that are fair and balanced, from a global perspective. To push forward with their heightened expectations, some developing countries, in turn, formed the Group of Twenty (G-20) to act as a common lobbying group but its immediate result was stalemate at the Cancun meeting of the World Trade Organization (WTO). If multilateral negotiations fail there is always a danger of descent into bilateralism but there is reason enough to assume that both developed and developing countries will seek to avert a complete collapse of multilateral agencies and institutions.

Since the collapse of the Cancun meeting, both developed and developing countries have demonstrated a readiness to find common ground and develop solutions that are mutually acceptable. This led to the July Framework Agreement after about a year of quiet diplomacy. The final outline of settlement is not entirely certain but Chapter 8 will evaluate the achievements of the G-20 in Doha Round negotiations to introduce greater balance into the trade regime.

Certainly, no compromise agreement will satisfy all developing countries, given the disparity of material conditions. Thus, for example, while textile quotas were phased out by developed countries at the end of 2004, as negotiated in the Uruguay Round of GATT negotiations and as demanded by most developing countries, the result will benefit a few large textile manufacturers, like China and India, but might be detrimental to many other smaller developing countries that established an indigenous textile industry behind quota protection of the Multi-Fiber Agreement (MFA), such as Sri Lanka, Bangladesh, Mauritius and so on. Similarly any agreement that the G-20 is able to influence in the Doha Round will provide differential benefits to its membership and to the larger group of developing countries.

Given that the final bargain will have differential benefits in absolute terms, a measure of success or failure of G-20 will depend on *processes* that are put in place and whether these inhibit or facilitate development. Essentially, the main evaluative criteria of any new regime will be whether they introduce an international equivalence of equal opportunity and affirmative action regulations. This is over and above expectations that the Doha Round Agreement will not be as demanding on developing countries as was the Uruguay Round Agreement.

As far as structure of the book is concerned, the first chapter sets out the nature of international economic regimes and globalization. I look at the rise of globalization and compare contemporary globalization to its nineteenth-century counterpart. I then look at how nineteenth-century and twentieth-century globalization differed in terms of providing developmental opportunities to a larger number of countries before looking, more closely, at how developing countries have been marginalized in the postwar structures of international economic exchange. Chapter 2 is a theory and begins with a discussion of regime theory and their rational design. I then consider the likelihood that negotiations will produce a paradigm shift in the way benefits are distributed across regime members. This brings in the role of non-governmental organizations (NGOs) and negotiating coalitions such as the G-20. The remaining chapters contain empirical case studies and Chapter 8 will look at how we might evaluate the success or failure of G-20 in achieving its challenging goals.

Globalization—an Introduction

Globalization is a broadly defined phenomenon that has influenced most aspects of society, economics, politics and culture such that events in one part of the world have consequences in remote parts. Even the so-called closed societies were not insulated from external forces. The collapse of Soviet Union and the East European command economies was a result largely of prolonged economic and political failure but also due to increased public awareness of conditions beyond the iron curtain. Despite state obsession to quarantine western and liberal political and economic norms, the task was made harder by the relative ease with which foreign information and media permeated these closed societies.

Similarly, while the ease of international travel has been a boon to economic globalization, it also facilitated the global spread of Severe Acute Respiratory Syndrome (SARS) in 2003. Without the large-scale flow of peoples across national boundaries, it might have been possible to contain the outbreak to its source in southern China. The epidemic not only spilled over into the immediate neighborhood but a large number of SARS cases were diagnosed as far away as Toronto, Canada.

However, even acknowledging that global forces can be observed in many fields of human activity, economic globalization is still much more developed than societal, political or cultural globalization. Indeed, while many countries welcome economic globalization, they remain wary of cultural globalization because of the loss, whether implied or real, of national cultural values.

Economic globalization marks a qualitative shift in international political economy and yet has crept up almost unannounced in the last two decades. In hindsight, it is tempting to trace its lineage to postwar economic and trade liberalization but economic globalization was not an intended target of the architects of postwar economic liberalism. Moreover, while the GATT, the IMF and the World Bank (IBRD) had considerable success in liberalizing international economic exchange they can be credited only with creating conditions for shallow economic interdependence and integration. Contemporary globalization is a far more revolutionary process underpinned not simply by trade but also by the emergence of global production networks and global manufacturing. In some areas, globalization has compromised the ability of national governments to independently manage their national economies and, at the same time, made it imperative for governments to try and enhance national economic competitiveness. Understood in these terms, globalization cannot be explained as a logical and natural progression of postwar economic liberalism alone.

Nor is globalization a simple restoration of economic norms from an earlier period. Some have observed a basic continuity with the system of free trade that had emerged in the mid-nineteenth century but which was disrupted by economic nationalism in the early twentieth century. It may be tempting to conceptualize contemporary globalization in terms of a world restored but the parallels are superficial. Attempts to establish a pattern of continuity serve only to mask the radical global transformation since around the mid-1980s. The "naysayers" however deny that globalization marks a new departure opting instead to compare it to trade liberalization and "globalization" of the nineteenth and early twentieth century. Kenneth Waltz, for instance, in his 1999 James Madison Lecture repeated his assertion from 1970 that the world in 1999 was less interdependent than is usually supposed and that globalizers had underestimated the extent to which the new resembled the old. He continued to argue that in international trade flows, the world was no more globalized than what it was a hundred years earlier and that even financial markets at the turn of the "previous century were at least as integrated as they are now."[4]

This position has credibility only if we rely on statistical measures of trade dependence but is misleading because it ignores the emergence of new global production structures based on the quantum leap in communications and information technology. The "nothing new under the sun" approach is misleading as well because production and the economic base have profound consequences for other aspects of human society. And, to the extent that production structures have evolved, globalization is a much wider phenomenon.

At the same time, globalization is not a reality in being, but a process in becoming. It is not even a globally uniform process. Kratochwil cautions, "we should not be misled by our own rhetoric . . . we should be aware that the impact varies tremendously. The 'market' might be more global for the Organization for Economic Cooperation and Development (OECD) countries, but other regions, such as Africa, might now be less systematically connected to this world than before."[5] Importantly though, globalization is not a continuation of the past although there are elements that can be traced to earlier times in history.

Contemporary globalization is unlike any commonly understood variant of economic liberalization. For instance, it includes but is much more than a world defined in terms of relatively free flow of goods and services. Trade growth has exceeded gross domestic product (GDP) growth for much of the postwar period and this is usually attributed to the liberalizing successes of the GATT and the Bretton Woods regime.[6] One perspective on globalization might be to portray it as a natural progression and logical end of economic liberalization and of economic interdependence. As such, globalization might be the end of economic history, much as Francis Fukuyama[7] portrayed the triumph of democracy as representing the logical culmination of political evolution.

Multilateral institutions have played a key role as vehicles of economic liberalization. The GATT lowered barriers to trade among its contracting parties while the IMF and the World Bank were instrumental in exchange and financial liberalization, and deregulatory reforms. A measure of trade liberalization is the reduction of industrial trade tariffs from around 60 percent after the Second World War to less than 5 percent on average at the end of the 1990s. Tariffs, of course, are not the only trade restricting measures but GATT also helped dismantle and streamline many non-tariff barriers, including discriminatory regulatory and standards regime. Together these have had a tremendous impact on trade flows globally, which increased at a rate faster than global output. In 2001, total global trade in goods and services was US$6 trillion. Financial liberalization began considerably later but has had a substantially greater impact on international capital flows. Apart from a rapid increase in short-term capital flows, foreign direct investment (FDI) flows also increased from around US$200 billion in 1990 to more than US$1.1 trillion in 2000.[8]

Globalization however means more and is characterized by the emergence of global production structures. Apart from historically low barriers to trade (in terms of tariff and non-tariff barriers to trade in manufactured goods) and increased capital flows (as a result of financial liberalization), economic globalization is unparalleled in the way production is globally networked. Here, it should be noted that while globalization is partially the "unplanned child"[9] of the Bretton Woods bargain, it is also, interestingly, a result of opposite, illiberal, tendencies in international political economy. Liberalization was not the only, or even the initial impetus to the emergence of global production structures, because foreign consumption demand can just as easily be met with exports as with local production in export markets. Japan played a critical role in establishing global production networks and this was spurred on initially by American neo-protectionism, even if success of the strategy eventually depends on maintaining liberal trade to protect firms from disruptions in intra-firm trade.

Neo-protectionism in the 1970s and 1980s forced corporations to develop alternative strategies to circumvent obstacles to their international operations and export profile. A significant result of neo-protectionism was the establishment of global production networks that altered the landscape of manufacturing activities. Previously, production was largely organized within national economic boundaries and products represented a specific nationality but, as a result of global production structures, production is globally organized and products have ambiguous national identities. Essential to these developments were the revolutionary advances in information and communications technology. These have also produced a greater sharing of knowledge across and through all strata of societies and cultures. Without technological advances and instantaneous communication across vast distances, it would have been impossible to establish and then to maintain global production networks. But technology provides only the necessary condition. A primary catalyst for globalization was the rise of neo-protectionism in the 1980s. Thus, paradoxically, economic globalization has been a product of forces that are in stark contrast to its consequences.

Moreover, in highlighting the influence of neo-protectionism in deepening economic integration,[10] it is important to acknowledge also the role of Japanese foreign investments in the 1980s and 1990s. Tracing globalization in part to neo-protectionism is not historically unique since trade disruptions have always motivated the global spread of business. It was trade disruption during the First World War that sparked and spread industrialization in Latin American countries and again, during the protectionist interlude between the two world wars, foreign investment expanded to compensate for loss of access to overseas markets. Rising tariff level was the main reason for 40 percent of the 34 investment decisions analyzed by Geoffrey Jones.[11] Even so, globalization today is unlike the global spread of business in the nineteenth or twentieth centuries. Contemporary globalization is centered on the notion of production networks that have weakened national economic identities.

Global production networks can be understood, first, in terms of cross-national ownership of production activities and, second, as networks of spatially distributed manufacturing of parts and components for finished products. Ownership has become globalized with, for instance, the automobile industry restructured around an intricate network of equity ownership including that between Daimler-Chrysler and Mitsubishi and between Toyota and General Motors. More elaborate is the sourcing of parts and components from around the world, resulting in the emergence of globalized companies and globalized production, where it is difficult to clearly establish national identities.

Neo-protectionism was a strategic American response to the dual problem of safeguarding declining industries and alleviating chronic trade deficits. The rules of international trade devised at the end of the Second World War assumed that the US would enjoy trade surpluses for some considerable time as it was the only remaining industrial power. However, as a result of expenditures associated with President Johnson's Great Society Program and overseas military commitments including the war in Vietnam, the American trade balance was in deficit by the late 1960s. In the 1970s, trade deficits were compounded by additional threats to core industries, such as automobile and steel, as a result of a Japanese export surge. The prospect of de-industrialization fuelled protectionist sentiments and forced the American government to respond with neo-protectionist "gray area"[12] measures to limit imports from Japan in order to allow domestic industries the breathing space to recover and regroup.

In the mid-1970s, the US government negotiated an Orderly Marketing Agreement (OMA) to limit Japanese exports of color television sets. This however failed to protect domestic television manufacturers, which were ultimately forced to relocate their operations to countries where production, that is labor, costs were a fraction of costs in the US. Another gray area measure was the Trigger Price Mechanism (TPM), which gave US steel manufacturers relief from increasing Japanese imports. The TPM did not entirely reverse the competitive decline of American steel industry and had to be supplemented with additional bailout measures and assistance, including limits on import competition. American commitment to the steel industry can be largely attributed to its strategic role in civil and defense-related manufacturing sectors.

These neo-protectionist measures culminated in the American decision, in the early 1980s, to require Japanese car manufacturers to exercise voluntary export restraint (VER). Japanese car exports to the US had surged following a quadrupling of oil prices in 1973 and while consumers embraced the more fuel-efficient Japanese cars, US manufacturers rapidly lost market shares and profitability. Under pressure both from manufacturers and labor unions worried at the prospect of massive job losses, the US government initiated bilateral talks to limit Japanese exports and thereby to provide US car manufacturers a breathing space and guaranteed market share to assist with their plans to modernize production processes in order to compete with Japan in the domestic market. Japanese manufacturers resisted American pressure to stem the flow of exports and the dispute festered for several years before the US government threatened unilateral sanctions against imported Japanese cars. Eventually, the dispute was resolved when Japanese manufacturers agreed "voluntarily" to limit their exports to the US. An unintended consequence of the VER was that it initiated a process that ultimately transformed global production structures, given the nature of Japanese foreign investment patterns and strategies.

Prior to the VER agreement in the early 1980s, Japanese car manufacturers had been reluctant to invest in manufacturing facilities overseas, preferring to meet foreign demand with exports from Japan. Manufacturers were concerned that foreign production would compromise their competitive advantage because of presumed difficulties in transplanting also their just-in-time inventory control system and quality control practices in foreign markets. But with quantitative restrictions on exports, car manufacturers had a choice of either establishing production facilities in restricted markets or relinquishing market share. Rather than cede market shares, all major car manufacturers quickly established plants in North America. This was one of the intended objectives of the US in demanding export restraint but criticisms remained of Japanese manufacturing in the US, which relied on many parts and materials imported from Japan. This reduced the total benefit of local manufacturing for the US economy.

Later in the decade, sustained and substantial appreciation of the Yen against the Dollar following the Plaza Accord of September 1985 rendered Japanese exports more expensive. Threatened by loss of export markets, car manufacturers and other export-oriented industries in Japan shifted their manufacture and procurement of parts to low cost production centers in other East Asian countries. This led to the establishment of a regional production network[13] and the relocation of industries to cheaper production platforms in East Asia. Beginning with fears of de-industrialization in the US, neo-protectionism and the Plaza Accord raised the specter of "hollowing out" of industries within Japan. The fear was exaggerated but regionalized production became a precursor to global production structures, as the practice spread and was embraced by manufacturers in other countries.

Japan's regional production networks or alliances replicated the domestic *keiretsu* structure of Japanese corporations, a development that Hatch and Yamamura identified as regionalization of the Japanese economy. The integration of regional economies around a Japanese core began in the late 1980s in the context of currency revaluation and the ensuing search for cheaper production platforms in order to remain internationally competitive. The process accelerated after the Japanese economic bubble burst in the early 1990s. Regionalization was encouraged by the Japanese government as a way for firms and banking institutions to remain profitable in the post-bubble period by investing in the growth economies of East Asia. The expectation was that regional profits would pay for debt write-offs domestically. After a long period of abstention from direct economic linkages, bar normal trade flows, Japanese firms invested extensively in East Asia. The government encouraged but could not, of course, compel all the firms that ultimately established regional production networks to engage in regional FDI. The flood of foreign investment can be attributed in part to a herding mentality of capitalists, and to the noticeable tendency of Japanese firms to emulate their competitors, not only in the production profile but also in production methods. Michael Porter described this in terms of a so-called absence of strategic management in Japanese firms that engage in competition more by becoming like their competitors than by establishing a distinct identity and survival strategy. Porter identified the absence of strategy as one of the sources of economic malaise in Japan in the 1990s and recommended a complete reform of the nature of inter-firm competition in Japan in order to overcome the lingering post-bubble economic crisis.

In a few short years, production had been regionalized with new production bases in regional countries dependent on the import of parts and capital goods from Japan and, in turn, supplying local, Japanese and third country consumers with finished consumer goods. The single largest host of Japanese investments in the region is China but even in Thailand, by 1994, about 7 percent of total workforce was employed in Japanese firms.[14]

Internal reform, however, proved difficult and Japanese firms, encouraged by the government, tried instead to restore their economic health by searching profit and growth opportunities in the region. Parts of the Asia-Pacific region became a practical extension of the Japanese economy as Japanese firms set up a web of production networks and subsidiaries not only to meet local demand but also home demand in Japan and third country export demand. As parts of the region were "Japanized," Hatch and Yamamura also observed that by the late 1990s the Japanese economy had undergone a dramatic shift. An aggressive domestic reform program might have revolutionized the Japanese economy but instead it emerged as far more regionalized.[15] It may have been a softer option for Japanese firms until, that is, the collapse of East Asian economic bubble in 1997. The regionalization drive did not help the task of strengthening the base of the domestic economy but certainly aided the globalization project.

Regionalization and later globalization of production networks are examples of how capitalism has continued to evolve in response to shifting environmental conditions. The development of global production networks was subsequent to earlier adaptive responses, such as *redistribution* and *reorganization*. Schaeffer writes that redistribution became a feature of capitalist development between 1945 and the 1970 when European countries and Japan re-industrialized, generally at the expense of American industrial development. Reorganization became a noticeable trend in the 1980s and 1990s and was distinguished first by an increased incidence of mergers and acquisitions and second by the introduction of new production technologies that led to job losses and downsizing.[16]

Economic globalization is a process that is linking national economies into a nearly seamless web of global unity. There is continuing debate about whether the final stage of complete economic integration will be realized in the foreseeable future but that is the hope of globalizers who envision a "world without walls."[17] But notions that economic globalization will produce political and cultural homogenization are fanciful. Indeed, Huntington[18] celebrates the end of Cold War ideological confrontation with the caution that future conflicts might draw upon cultural and civilizational differences between Western, Confucian and Islamic societies. He finds that civilizational values have become more deeply embedded in human psyche and is troubled by our demonstrable failure to tolerate alternative value systems and by the tendency of the powerful countries to try and force a realignment of value systems to reflect their values. During the Cold War period, the same missionary zeal was present as well but held in check by the bipolar political structure. In the contemporary period, the possibility of conflict may even be greater since there is nothing to constrain the only remaining superpower.

As an emerging reality, globalization has its ardent advocates and diehard detractors. Critics rail against its assumed negative consequences on social welfare, environment, state, equality, and distribution of benefits. Some denounce globalization and find succor in the natural human dislike for change. It is certain that globalization and deep economic integration has reduced the policy autonomy and independence for national governments, as well as eroded the postwar consensus on state welfarism, if not by choice by the necessity of enhancing international competitiveness. There is little debate that globalization has come at the expense of the national welfare state. The state has reduced its socio-economic functions opting to, instead, rely on market forces to promote welfare targets. The demise of the welfare state has become necessary in order for economies to position themselves to compete in a global economy with improved costs structure and market incentives. As such, governments have privatized and deregulated to strengthen the market impulse and scaled back the safety nets associated with welfare states. In broad terms, national managerial autonomy and authority may have diminished but it would be a great leap of faith, however, to assert that the state system is approaching obsolescence.

Nonetheless, national economies will be buffeted by events and developments in seemingly distant and remote parts of the world. Globalization also means that a crisis in one country can easily spill over to affect neighboring countries, as happened in 1997 when speculative attacks on the Thai Baht triggered a financial crisis not only in Thailand but also across the East Asian region. Moreover, apart from the contagion effects of economic globalization, globalization of financial capital, through liberalization of capital accounts transaction, may even be blamed for instigating crises. The East Asian financial crisis may have been staved off if these countries had embarked on liberalization in a more prudent and cautious manner than the model advocated by the IMF of rapid liberalization and removal of capital controls.

Economic globalization and trade opportunities, however, should not be associated only with negative and deleterious consequences. Its proponents celebrate efficiency gains, economies of scale and growth. Globalization can also be a powerful catalyst for growth and welfare. For example, East Asian economies replicated the postwar Japanese economic miracle by actively engaging the global economy and using trade to enhance their growth potential, in the decades prior to 1997.

Criticisms of globalization

Economic globalization is unlikely to be matched by any similar political evolution dissolving political borders. The state system will endure for the foreseeable future and national political leaders will, with less autonomy, authority and control, preside over national economies constrained by international forces. Thus, while political borders may endure, irreversible forces of global production, economic exchange and capital flows will continue to erode economic segmentation. National political leaders will have less control over the performance of domestic economies even though they may continue to be held accountable by their electorates and which may influence their political fortunes. In this context, the political challenge is to ensure that global linkages do not impose disproportionate costs and that benefits override the loss of direct influence. It is a situation that demands that governments respond seriously to the challenge of rule making for the global economy so that their own interests are protected from the egregious behavior of others.

Depending on the structure of rules, globalization can either be an intensely exploitative arrangement or a tool for promoting development and growth. It can reproduce the imperialism of free trade, or trade and global market forces can be harnessed for their growth potential, especially in developing countries. At present, while many governments, especially in developed countries, and multilateral agencies extol the virtues of globalization, the negative externalities of globalization have received considerable attention and, consequently, in both developed and developing countries, there are strong negative views about globalization and its consequences. Some of the criticisms are deserved while others are misguided. In the former category is the protest movement that decries globalization as entrenching the privileges of the few while impoverishing the majority and sacrificing consumer rights for the sake of corporate empowerment. This criticism relates to the rules and regulatory biases that have prevented globalization from benefiting a greater number of countries, when clearly globalization need not be conceptualized as a zero-sum-game.

In the latter category are concerns, especially in advanced countries, that globalization has instigated a "race to the bottom," as a result of competitive pressures from low cost developing countries. In May 2003, *Time* magazine ran a cover story on the shrinking paycheck of American workers. The report chronicled the misfortunes of a growing number of American workers who find themselves compelled to accept lower wages. This was attributed, of course in part, to deteriorating economic conditions at home but also to pressure from cheaper production centers in developing countries. Competition for some workers had come from such unlikely places as India where a call center operator, for instance, earned about ten percent of operators in the US. Not surprisingly, in 2000, approximately 27,000 jobs in the information and technology (IT) industries were transferred abroad by American firms. It is estimated that by 2015, a cumulative total of 472,000 IT jobs will move to overseas locations.

In March 2004, *Time* magazine carried yet another cover story on outsourcing of American jobs and reported that by 2015 a cumulative total of 3.3 million jobs were likely to leave the country. Firms have discovered that they can increase shareholder value by outsourcing and achieving cost reductions. Between 1998–2000, American firms were able to achieve cost savings of about US$8 billion by outsourcing some of their activities to developing countries.[19] The downside is that not enough new jobs are being created to compensate for job losses and retraining schemes have failed most workers caught in the trap. Anticipating a resurgence of protectionist sentiments, Alan Greenspan, Chairman of the US Federal Reserve Board cautioned that, "Protectionism will do little to create jobs, and if foreigners retaliate we will surely lose jobs. We need to discover the means to enhance the skills of our work force and to further open markets here and abroad."[20]

The same phenomenon of outsourcing can also be observed in other industrial economies. Many large firms have also devolved their account-ing and computing requirements to developing countries, which offer attractive costs savings. With instantaneous communications many global firms have discovered that such positions can easily be farmed out to distant places to improve corporate competitiveness and profitability.

In general the loss of employment as a result of globalization has not been very significant in developed countries. However, a rapidly changing economic environment has forced individuals to accept the possibility that they may have to change careers several times in their lifetime. In the past, a chosen occupation would often be a lifetime vocation. Studies in the US have shown that as far as adaptability and flexibility are concerned, individuals with advanced educational qualifications are more adaptive to change than those with high school qualifications. It is not surprising therefore that the better educated tend to be more supportive of globalization since they have less to fear from it.[21]

Critics of globalization associate the export of jobs with a race to the bottom that will progressively erode hard-won worker rights and wage structures in developed countries to the levels of developing countries. Yet, rather than become alarmist about this development, it is important to note, as mentioned earlier, that there has not been a flood of companies relocating out of developed countries, nor a net job loss. Indeed the US was, until very recently, the largest recipient of FDI in the world, something that cannot be explained by the race to the bottom thesis. Moreover, while the race to the bottom thesis implies a shrinking of income inequalities between developed and developing countries, this gap has actually widened in the globalization period.

To the extent that some economic activities have been relocated to low-cost countries, this is only an example of a global division of labor based on competitive and cost structures, a development that should be welcomed rather than feared. It is interesting to note nonetheless that the export of job is not only at the lower end of technology spectrum but also in creative industries, such as software development. And, in the absence of adequate social safety nets and adjustment programs, popular resentment in the West is to be expected, forcing political authorities, at least, to demonstrate concern about the loss of employment and, if possible, reverse the trend. Not surprisingly, there are moves in certain US states to stop the export of jobs by denying government contracts to firms that choose to do their work overseas.

These same concerns were prevalent also in Japan in the mid-1980s. A combination of factors, including a sharp appreciation of the Japanese Yen, fuelled worries about a potential "hollowing out" of industrial capacity. That fear of deindustrialization proved vastly exaggerated. Japanese industries certainly ventured out to regional countries and established production facilities in countries that offered cheaper cost structures but that did not result in gloom and doom in Japan. Instead the Japanese economy experienced a speculative boom in the late 1980s.

In the contemporary period, the race to the bottom approach invokes the same irrational fear of hollowing out of industries in the West but that, again, is far from the reality. Firms, for example, do not necessarily want the cheapest labor but rather the most productive work force in the most productive business environment. If there is a hollowing out in advanced industrial countries, it is largely in labor-intensive sectors but that is as it should be, given that developing countries have a comparative advantage in labor-intensive economic activities.

Loss of employment, industrial hollowing out, and structural adjustment problems are not confined to developed countries and the beneficiaries are not all developing countries. Liberalization policies adopted by developing countries or forced upon them have extracted enormous costs. For example, the liberalization of cashew processing industry in Mozambique in the mid-1990s resulted in a steep decline of the processing industry and loss of employment for 8500 out of 10,000 workers in the industry.[22] Imprudent and hasty liberalization under pressure from the US government had similar negative consequences in newly industrialized countries as well. Abandoning the cautionary advise of the Council of Economic Advisors (CEA), the US Treasury Department, for instance, forced Korea to rapidly liberalize its economy in the interest of improving market access but this injudicious process then led to economic vulnerability and susceptibility to the contagion effect of the Asian financial crisis. Reflecting on this episode, Joseph Stiglitz, a member of the CEA at the time, observed that instead of carefully assessing the likely outcome of liberalization, US Treasury, in the mid-1990s, insisted on early and broad ranging reform whereby the US, South Korea and the global economy lost. He writes, "Treasury would probably claim that the liberalization itself was not at fault, the problem was that liberalization was done in the wrong way. But that was precisely one of the points that the CEA raised: It was very likely that a quick liberalization would be done poorly."[23]

Within national economies, there is no doubt that globalization has created losers but this is not a direct flaw in the ongoing economic processes. To a large extent this is a problem of lags in labor market adjustments. Mike Moore, the Director General of the WTO, observed in 2000 that, "Of course, some people do lose in the short run from trade liberalization . . . But the right way to alleviate the hardship of the unlucky few is through social safety nets and job retraining rather than by abandoning reforms that benefit the many."[24]

We may dispute whether hardship is short term or whether only a few are adversely affected but Moore was fundamentally correct in his observation. In the US, the government had recognized that adjustment would be a problem as early as the 1960s, when it was negotiating trade liberalization in the GATT's Kennedy Round. To secure support of organized labor for trade liberalization, the government introduced a new program called the Trade Related Adjustment Assistance (TRAA), to retrain workers in sunset industries and prepare them for employment opportunities in new sectors and sunrise industries. Unfortunately, adjustment programs degenerated into additional unemployment support rather than facilitating the migration of labor from depressed to emerging sectors of the economy. The flaw was in the implementation mechanism and blame for inefficient adjustment can be attributed to political, not market failure.

Non-existent or poorly implemented programs for structural adjustment contributed to the growth of protectionism in the US in the 1970s and 1980s. In a global economy, the same problems persist and are indeed compounded by several additional factors.

1. In earlier periods of limited international integration, governments had greater availability of measures and policy instruments with which to manage national economies than is available to governments in the present period. The ability to manage all aspects of an economy is considerably diminished because globalization has restricted the menu of choice for governments and they have fewer available policy instruments with which to target specific problems.
2. Governments also have a reduced revenue base because globalization has allowed the corporate sectors to move profits around to avoid taxation. Moreover, governments have reduced overall taxation to levels applicable in low taxation territories in order to stay competitive and reduce the risk of capital flight. In recent years, corporate taxation rates, as well as other taxes, have been reduced considerably. At the same time as governments have smaller revenue base, many governments also have compiled large deficits, which also impede their capacity to take on additional roles and responsibilities.
3. Globalization has brought with it a strong ideological commitment to reduce the role of governments in national economies. This dominant intellectual hegemony has limited the capacity of governments to aggressively promote structural adjustment or to protect the most weak and vulnerable groups in society.

Some industries and firms, like for example Harley Davidson and Caterpillar, however have been very adept in coping with increased foreign competition and trade liberalization. To facilitate successful national based trade adjustment, WTO agreements generally involve a transition period and in the worst-case scenario, permit countries to invoke safeguard measures (protection) when a surge of imports threatens a particular domestic industry. WTO's safeguard regime is also much more user-friendly than GATT's Article 19 and does not require the imposing country to recompense foreign suppliers during the first three years of safeguards measures following an increase in imports. Between 1995 and July 2002, the WTO received 94 notifications of initiations of safeguard investigations, with the two main users being India and the US.[25]

Structural adjustment problems remain unresolved and they are, to return to assertions by Mike Moore, neither a short-term inconvenience nor a problem for a small minority in individual societies. In these circumstances, there is a natural tendency among many of the disaffected to reject globalization, both in developed and developing countries. Dissent has been vocal, loud, and at times violent. The protest movement has had a number of successes. For example, in 1998 a well-coordinated and organized global protest against the Multilateral Agreement on Investments (MAI) aborted attempts by advanced OECD countries to remove all regulatory and structural impediments to the flow of foreign investments. Ironically, the protest against globalization was itself a highly globalized event. Bolstered by their success against political authorities and international bureaucrats, a determined group of about 50,000 protestors descended on Seattle in 1999 to prevent the start of a new round of trade liberalization talks. Unlike the MAI protest movement, demonstrations in Seattle involved violent confrontations with security personnel and police. This was a protest movement that brought together many different interests and groups but one common theme that gave them a semblance of coherence was the way globalization had produced outcomes inimical to the interests of a large number of developing countries.

At the international level, globalization has produced many losers among developing countries. Obstacles to development not only persist but may also have increased over time. For many countries developmental prospects seem more remote than before with no resolution to a persisting debt problem. Existing inequities can be largely attributed to regulatory defects, whether by design or default, in the global system. These can be traced to previous international bargains but developed countries have proved reluctant, even now, to remedy the flaws and instate a level playing field. In preliminary trade talks prior to the start of the Seattle meeting of the WTO, developing countries had submitted several position papers decrying the implementation of the earlier Uruguay Round agreements which had imposed onerous obligation without providing any significant benefit to developing countries. They had been led to believe that inclusion of agriculture and intellectual property would expand developmental opportunities but these promises had failed to materialize. Developing countries were, understandably, less than convinced about the merit of launching a new round with many more new inclusions in the agenda. Not for the first time, developed countries brushed their complaints and suggestions aside in the march toward extending liberalization to new issue areas.

The siege of Seattle forced the abandonment of a new trade-negotiating round. This was the second time, following the abandonment of MAI, that a protest movement had derailed attempts to accelerate economic liberalization and globalization. In the euphoria of the moment, Barry Coates, Director of the World Development Movement (WDM) declared the outcome of WTO's Seattle meeting "a spectacular derailment of the free trade juggernaut."[26] At the other extreme, Mike Moore, Director General of the WTO offered the following reflections about the outcome in Seattle:

> Seattle is now recorded as a victory for the anti-globalisation movement. Nonsense. We didn't need their help to fail . . . we did it on our own. The situation wasn't ripe. The differences across the Atlantic and North/South were too large to bridge.[27]

Neither position is an accurate assessment of events and realities. For example, Mike Moore's reflected denial of the effectiveness of the protest movement was at odds with his comments at the time of the Seattle meeting. Addressing the assembled ministers, Moore had confidently declared that "this conference is doomed—doomed to succeed."[28] His reflections on the protest movement in Seattle are a contrived and unconvincing rationalization meant only to downplay and marginalize the protest movement. It is true nonetheless that most WTO members were not enthusiastic about launching another trade liberalization round so soon after the Uruguay Round. Developing countries, for instance, had a number of reasons to be reticent. According to Gary Sampson, "The willingness of a large number of developing countries to stand in the way of a ministerial consensus—a consequence of their perception that they were being excluded from key meetings and that some of their principal negotiating objectives were not being addressed—contributed significantly to the collapse of the Seattle meeting."[29]

It was significant also that the US government had failed to secure Congressional fast-track authority (renamed Trade Promotion Authority or TPA), which would require the Congress to vote on the agreement in its totality rather than on individual aspects. Fast-track authority is essentially a confidence building measure and increases the probability of final ratification without which negotiations will of course have been futile. Fast-track authority is considered essential with the proliferation of agenda items, especially as the final resolution of each item may not be a net positive for each GATT/WTO member countries. As such, it is vital that legislative authorities vote on an agreement as a single package rather than unpack it for a line by line vote.

Earlier trade negotiating rounds had commenced with Congressional fast-track authority but by withholding it before the proposed start of the first WTO round, the US Congress essentially signaled its reservations as to the merits of initiating a new round of negotiations. In the absence of Congressional mandate for American negotiators, other WTO members could not be confident that any final agreement could be shepherded through the various stages prior to implementation and found little merit, therefore, in investing their time and effort in what would be lengthy and difficult negotiations.

In this inauspicious start to the Seattle meeting, protestors, and the violence that ensued, sealed its fate. In the long run, however, it is improbable that dissenters and protestors will significantly impede the progress of global economic integration. Thus, protestors in Seattle managed only to disrupt and delay the launch of a new trade-negotiating round. They failed to derail the process of trade and economic liberalization and the WTO initiated a new trade liberalization round, the Doha Round, a couple of years later. Even so, we cannot underestimate the psychological impact of Seattle on free traders nor the relief when the Doha ministerial meeting in November 2001 launched a new round.

A new administration in the US made a more determined effort toward initiating the new trade round and negotiated fast-track authority with the Congress. The Doha Round was launched in 2001 and the US Congress granted the Administration a five-year Trade Promotion Authority, in 2002. Doha put to rest the fears that the WTO, likened to a bicycle that must either keep moving forward or topple over, had been fatally weakened in Seattle. It helped also that the venue for the third WTO ministerial meeting was Doha where personal liberties are restricted and that the WTO Secretariat had the authority to grant entry visas to Qatar, which it exploited to deny entry to various NGOs and preempt the explosive situation that greeted WTO delegates in Seattle.[30] Since September 11, 2001, meetings of the World Bank, WTO, or the IMF, which might have been expected to prompt large-scale protests, have invited only the isolated incidents of disruptive behavior. The protest movement has become a victim of the September 11 terrorist attacks and protestors are wary of being labeled unpatriotic. It is ironic that while September 11 has unleashed a wave of emotive patriotism and nationalism in the US, it has also played into the hands of globalizers by removing the obstacle of visible and violent dissent. September 11 has also heightened security concerns and police presence at major international events and these have also weakened the voice of the protest movement. In June 2003, protestors of the Group of Eight (G-8) summit meeting could not even make their presence felt in Evian, France, the location of the summit meeting and instead were forced to converge in Geneva for an "alternative summit." Even without September 11, however, dissenters could not hope to permanently block the march of globalization.

By the definition of globalization adopted here, the genie of global forces cannot be easily returned to the bottle. However, Gilpin maintains, ". . . an open and integrated global economy is neither as extensive and inexorable nor as irreversible as any assume."[31] These sentiments are echoed by Alan Deardorff and Robert Stern. They argue that globalization can be reversed just as had happened earlier following the First World War and the Great Depression. Moreover, public policy change in the US and Europe leading to abandonment of the key global institutions, the IMF, World Bank and the WTO, could also see a reversal of economic globalization.[32] Writing in 2004, Faini was convinced this had already happened. According to him, ". . . globalization is retreating. FDI fell markedly by 41 percent in 2001 and again by 20 percent in 2002. International trade virtually stagnated in 2001 and failed to rebound in 2002."[33]

Theoretically, of course the process of globalization can be either reversed or impeded by a return to protectionism but this will not be easily achieved. Liberalization may be rescinded and yet contemporary liberalization is less susceptible to being scaled back, compared to nineteenth and early twentieth centuries, because of the presence of a large number of formal institutional structures and rules, which give the system greater stability and staying power. Of course, within this framework of embedded liberalism, there are periodic surges in protectionist policies, such as American resort to steel protectionism in 2002 despite a ruling by the WTO that the US was in breach of its international commitments. A widespread and drastic retreat from economic liberalism will disrupt the globalization agenda but there are powerful vested interests to ensure that this does not become an easy option for states. Global corporations and multinational corporations (MNCs) are unlikely to remain passively on the sidelines while political leaders dismantle the underpinnings of economic globalization. Already, global corporations are a powerful presence in the international political economy with considerable political influence in shaping agendas and outcomes. Indeed, critics of globalization, such as J. Madeley, have labeled it a corporate-led economic structure, propelled by corporations to promote corporate interests, like liberalization, privatization, and deregulation.

At the same time, globalization is irreversible also because it is much more than simple economic and trade liberalization. It is possible for the momentum behind liberalization to run out of steam, mark time, or even be reversed, but liberalization is only one aspect of contemporary globalization which is a complex network of global production and MNCs, underpinned by breakthroughs in information, communications and transport (ICT) technology that have rendered even remote areas accessible to outsiders. At least in so far as globalization implies a passing of the tyranny of distance, ICT makes a reversal all the more unlikely. Just as these technologies cannot be uninvented, globalization too might be difficult to wind back. And, if we accept that the march of globalization is relatively inexorable and enduring, governments everywhere have a stake in ensuring that global economic rules are not intrinsically antithetical to their particular interests.

Finally, to the extent that globalization is an inexorable force, there remains the important task of somehow resolving the so-called political trilemma. Dani Rodrik highlights the difficulty of simultaneously achieving each of the three desirable political and economic objectives in the contemporary environment, state sovereignty, democracy, and globalization, such that at least one must be sacrificed. Thus, for instance, state sovereignty and globalization requires states to sacrifice some democratic principles as governments focus on maintaining international competitiveness by keeping a lid on inflation even at the risk of higher unemployment outcomes, even though these policy choices may be unpopular domestically. The choices do not have to be made immediately but presumably will be forced upon governments at some point in future as globalization deepens and throws up the inherent contradictions in a more acute form. And as the most recent development, it is possible that globalization will be given up but so far states seem more prepared to compromise on standards of democracy and sovereignty than globalization.

Globalization and development

There have been periods of greater or lesser trade and capital flows but contemporary economic globalization is unprecedented. There are no parallels in history to serve as reference points although some aspects of globalization can also be found in earlier periods. For instance, economic globalization is sometimes compared to nineteenth-century free trade under *Pax Britannica* because of similarities in trade dependence ratios. The comparison is only partially relevant because there are important dissimilarities. It should be noted, for example, that nineteenth-century free trade was instigated by an industrial Britain when it decided to repeal the Corn Laws and facilitate trade expansion in agricultural commodities with Continental Europe and other parts of the world. The British government understood that its industrial growth, even preeminence, could only be maintained by allowing other countries access to British agricultural markets. Without such opportunities for others to earn foreign exchange, Britain could not expect to continue to export industrial products to the rest of the world. Industrialists in Britain, too, wanted access to cheap agricultural products in order to keep costs of living, wages and production costs down. British repeal of the Corn Laws, onset of freer trade led to growing international interdependence as measured in terms of foreign trade and investments, price movements and common economic crises.[34]

Similarly in the postwar period, the US provided hegemonic leadership to re-establish the principles of economic liberalism but all industrialized economies, including the US, retained high agricultural tariffs to deny developing countries, with an agrarian economic base, opportunities to increase their export revenue. Moreover, agricultural subsidies in many developed countries have tended similarly to diminish the earning capacity of developing countries. Yet, these countries were also subject to pressure to lower barriers to developed country exports of industrial goods and services. Mercantilist policies in developed countries would have been unsustainable under ordinary circumstances but for the combination of official foreign aid and loans programs, and private capital flows, policies that have exacerbated developing country indebtedness.[35] Foreign aid and Official Development Assistance (ODA) is significant in maintaining exports to the poorer countries and it is not surprising that ODA is often criticized as aid essentially to manufacturers and exporters in the developed countries rather than for the purpose of promoting development in recipient countries.

The above does not necessarily corroborate dependency arguments about the inverse relationship between development and underdevelopment and, indeed, it should be noted that developed countries do not rely on exports to developing countries for their economic well-being and that the bulk of global trade is among OECD member countries. But policies of developed countries have certainly confounded the aspirations of developing countries. Critics of foreign aid and ODA also present cogent arguments that it is far superior to teach developing countries to "fish" than to provide aid, because the latter only breeds a culture of dependence. We can take the analogy further to argue that in order to promote development, developed countries should provide a ready market for imported fish from developing countries. Trade restrictions on developing country exports are a fundamental defect in existing structural arrangements and their removal will help developing countries escape the trap of poverty and underdevelopment. Liberalization can be an effective tool to promote manufacturing, exports and development in the same way that developing countries have utilized available textile quotas to the limit rather than lose their export entitlements.

The present structure of liberal international economic organization provides fewer opportunities for developing countries to develop their industrial capacity than the nineteenth-century period of free trade. British repeal of the Corn Laws was initially interpreted, in Continental Europe, as a ploy to delay or even abort European industrialization but if that were, indeed, the thinking of British policy makers, they were spectacularly unsuccessful. In the twentieth century, under *Pax Americana* only a few politically sensitive East Asian countries have been able to graduate into the ranks of the OECD countries. In general postwar economic liberalism has presided over widening economic inequities.

It would be inaccurate to suggest that underdevelopment is a result entirely of systemic failures or that developing countries are lacking in agency. Instead, a large source of their economic malaise can be attributed to national policy failures and corruption. Some might even include their relatively authoritarian political structures as part of the bigger problem on the assumptions that democracies are better able to avoid the extremes of corruption found in many developing countries. The political argument might be stretched to demonstrate that one reason why India has avoided the misery of famine and starvation is because of its political openness and democracy, in contrast to the experiences of African countries. Carrying the logic of this argument to its extreme, Herbert Werlin argues that poor, developing countries suffer from a "political illness" that is manifest in policy failures, weak bureaucracies and general problems of governance.[36]

Even acknowledging however that economic development is multidimensional and that governance issues may restrict a country's ability to respond to existing export opportunities, developing countries have by and large rationally exploited structural opportunities. The reality is that many developing countries confront structural impediments to growth and development. Conversely, when systemic economic hurdles have been relaxed for political and or strategic considerations, businesses and governments have exploited opportunities to advance national economic development and industrialization, as happened in some East Asian economies.

There are, as yet, many controversial and unresolved issues relating to economic globalization. One is whether globalization should become a force for the advancement of global regulatory and structural harmonization, where national differences, attributed perhaps to social and cultural attributes, are replaced with a level playing field. The position of the American government has been to support regulatory harmonization so that business everywhere operates with minimal national differences and under a universal code, that is presumably authored by the developed countries led by the US. It was this fundamental belief that led to negotiations on a MAI. Many other countries find national differences an integral attribute of cultural and geographic variations. Indeed, even in the US, there is opposition to an absolute leveling of the playing field because of the potential damage to uncompetitive American industries from more dynamic foreign firms.

As mentioned earlier, globalization is variously associated either with rising national economic prosperity or widening income inequalities. There is statistical evidence that globalizing developing countries have grown at rates that is at least twice as rapid as rich developed countries whereas non-globalizing developing countries experienced negative GDP growth in the 1990s.[37] The trouble is that it is not so easy to demarcate globalizing and non-globalizing developing simply because globalization is a broad phenomenon and many of the so-called non-globalizers are indeed charges of the IMF and the World Bank and subject to liberal structural adjustment programs that underpins the Washington Consensus. It is incorrect to argue that African countries have missed out on the benefits of globalization by defying the tide of globalization. More accurately, they are either the victims of deliberate design and choice or poorly devised and misguided rules of globalization. As with any process, there are winners and losers and the gains of globalization are not equitably distributed. Inequality has been present for several centuries but, these have become more pronounced in the contemporary period of economic globalization. For example, according to the *World Economic and Financial Surveys* (2003) of the IMF, the 29 OECD countries with 15.4 percent of the world's population constitute more than 56 percent of the world's GDP (the G-7 alone makes up nearly 45 percent of global GDP). Even so, there are many critics of globalization within developed countries, troubled by perceived erosion of democratic governance and worker rights, and of the environmental consequences of globalization.[38]

Greater prosperity has produced wider income inequalities between the developed and developing countries. Inequalities have also widened within developed and developing countries. Critics of globalization assail it for not having reduced inequities and poverty but it is wrong to assume that globalization is a "magic bullet" to eliminate existing economic injustices. Yet developing countries have also been promised that by embracing globalization, and through the trickle down effect, all individuals in society will improve their welfare. That this has not happened is not an intrinsic flaw of globalization but a flaw of redistributive policies and of governmental failure. Economic globalization is not a panacea for policy failures or a safeguard against implementation flaws and, as in Fukuyama's liberal democracy,[39] imperfections can be traced not to the essential principles of globalization but rather to implementation failures. Joseph Stiglitz writes:

> Globalization itself is neither good nor bad. It has the *power* to do enormous good, and for the countries of East Asia, who [sic] have embraced globalization *under their own terms*, at their own pace, it has been an enormous benefit, in spite of the setback of the 1997 crisis. But in much of the world it has not brought comparable benefits.[40]

That for much of the developing countries, globalization has been a dismal failure is nothing very remarkable. From the perspective of dependency theory, development and underdevelopment are the opposite sides of the same coin and development in a few countries has always been at the expense of underdevelopment in many other countries. Dependency theorists were convinced that there was no justice, only exploitation, for developing countries that participated in the international capitalist system. Consequently, they maintained that development could be achieved only by severing all economic links to international capitalism, either through voluntary policies of economic autarky or through a revolutionary break from global capitalism. Those that advocated a revolutionary upheaval did so on the assumption that a voluntary break from international capitalism was impossible because ruling classes in developing countries were one of the beneficiaries, indeed the main relative beneficiary on a per capita basis, and hence supporters, of the exploitative mechanism. This is clear from the following mathematical notations, based on Johan Galtung's core propositions. Although the concepts are imprecise and difficult to operationalize, they provide a simple understanding of dependency theory and of the distributive consequences of dependency.

$$\lim_{t \to \infty} \frac{lc\, C}{lc\, P} > 1$$

$$\lim_{t \to \infty} \frac{lc\, cC}{lc\, cP} = 1$$

$$\lim_{t \to \infty} \frac{lc\, cC}{lc\, pC} > 1$$

where,

C = Center P = Periphery
cC = center in Center cP = center in Periphery
pC = periphery in Center
lc = living condition

Dependency theory originated with the Economic Commission for Latin America (ECLA) and appeared to provide a good explanation for Latin American industrialization during the First World War when normal trade and economic relations with European countries were disrupted. The dependency approach and insular developmental strategies were discredited by the Latin American debt crisis of the 1980s. At the same time, East Asian economies were charting a new industrialization strategy based on export led growth. They participated actively in the global economy and the success of export led growth opened up a new pathway for developing countries to emerge out of underdevelopment and poverty. Multilateral agencies, like the IMF and World Bank, have also used their conditionality clauses to force developing countries to accept neoliberal paths to economic development and use access to international markets and capital to advance their national economic priorities. Critics disagree that economic liberalism is necessarily a better policy option for developing countries and, indeed, that liberal policies of openness and privatization impose a heavy cost on the socially disadvantaged groups, as a result of withdrawal of state subsidies and welfare programs. They argue that privatization and downsizing of governments have the practical effect of disenfranchising the poor, to the benefit of the corporate sector. Globalization and participation in the global economy is controversial, as well, in developing countries because of its potential to destabilize the domestic economy, as has happened in a number of East Asian and Latin American countries in the 1990s. Thus, in early October 2002, Luiz Inacio Lula de Silva, leader of the left-wing Workers Party, won the first round of presidential elections in Brazil by appealing to popular sentiments against globalization and liberalization. With nearly twice as many votes as his nearest rival, Jose Serra, in the first round of presidential elections, he easily emerged victorious in the run-off elections on 27 October.

The shift to the left in Brazil was a result of prolonged economic and financial turmoil, with sharp falls in the Real (R$3.99 against the US Dollar in mid-October 2002), poor growth forecasts (in October growth was predicted at 1.1 percent for 2002, half of what had been predicted 3 months earlier), and inflation in excess of official targets (nearly 8 percent, against targets of 5.5 percent). The outcome of the first round of voting was a massive show of opposition to President Cardoso who held the view that dependency did not homogenize the periphery and that development was still possible within a dependency framework. Indeed, as the Asian tigers had demonstrated, success was not beyond reach with the right mix of public policies.[41]

Lula's triumph created uncertainties about Brazil's economic direction in international financial markets but the new President veered away from populist politics to demonstrate responsible engagement with economic globalization, pushing taxation and pension reforms unpopular within his own Workers Party. This was reflected in the lower risk premium on Brazil's foreign debt that, in June 2003, fell below 700 basis points for the first time since early 2001. At the same time, the new government shifted spending away from military to social programs as part of the campaign to provide relief to the poor. The government was aware of the difficulties in steering a middle ground between popular expectations and internationally responsible policies. Unfortunately while Brazil attempted to maintain international credibility, its main trading partners were less than supportive. Brazil, for example, is highly competitive in ethanol, shoes, steel and sugar exports but faced steep protectionist barriers in the US.

The economic achievements of East Asian countries had a profound impact on the key tenets of dependency theory. Unlike dependency theory, which maintained that development in some countries produced underdevelopment in others, the East Asian countries demonstrated powerfully that it was still possible for developing countries to achieve development. Faced with this empirical anomaly, the response of dependency theorists was to try and preserve the core of their beliefs with auxiliary formulations and new categories to explain the possibility of "intermediary" states and development conditioned by dependency. According to Cardoso and Faletto, the "present situation of dependent development goes beyond the traditional dichotomy between the terms 'development' and 'dependence', because it permits an increase in development while maintaining and redefining the links of dependency."[42] But while terms like "semi-periphery," "sub-capitalism" and "dependent development" were innovative additions to the literature; they tended to gloss over the substantial achievements of the East Asian tiger economies. The financial crisis of 1997, notwithstanding, East Asian economies had benefited greatly from economic liberalization and integration. If there are lessons to be derived from the crisis, it is that trade and economic integration is useful but that capital market liberalization should be held in abeyance until domestic structures had matured sufficiently to withstand the vagaries of volatile and irrational capital flows. Indeed, even European countries had withheld capital market integration until well into the 1960s despite a commitment to achieve full financial openness under IMF rules.

In the 1980s, following the Latin American debt crisis, East Asia became a model for reforms in developing countries. Multilateral aid agencies and financial institutions, like the IMF and the World Bank advocated and contractually enforced economic liberalism to enhance long-term economic efficiency and other economic gains, including better job opportunities in the privatized sectors. Their research supported the appropriateness of structural adjustment reforms, that countries with a good record of implementing reforms had outperformed others that had allowed political expediency, for example, to frustrate reformist goals. This message together with the desperate financial situation of indebted countries sustained the march of economic liberalism and of globalization. This spread of liberal economic ideas, spearheaded by the US government and aided by multilateral agencies, became known as the "Washington Consensus." It was set back only slightly by the Asian financial and economic crisis of 1997.

The term "Washington Consensus" was coined by John Williamson to describe a set of desirable policies emphasizing macroeconomic stability and discipline, market orientation and trade liberalization. The term also implied a tacit understanding between senior US policy makers and advisors and the World Bank and the IMF, whereby the two Bretton Woods institutions became agencies for the uniform application of the intellectual content of the Washington Consensus on developing countries.[43] The IMF and the World Bank enforced these ideas on developing countries through their structural adjustment programs, initially in Latin American countries in the early 1980s and later in other regions as well.

Policy recommendations were justified on the basis of their capacity to promote better economic performance, in terms of growth. There was an expectation that growth will also improve the position of those in poverty through a so-called trickle down effect. Mainstream economists have a strong belief in the trickle down effect to improve welfare for individuals in all tiers of society. Joseph Stiglitz, former Chief Economist at the World Bank, however, was skeptical about trickle down economics and pointedly observed that since it had "not worked in the United States, why would it [trickle down] work in developing countries?"[44] He cited the example of the US in the 1980s, when sustained economic growth accompanied income decline for those at the bottom of the economic ladder.

However, as far as economic growth was concerned, there was nothing particularly controversial about the intellectual content from the perspective of prevailing economic theories but the recruitment of IMF and the World Bank represented an arrogant American determination to remake the world in its image, without regard to actual effects in target areas. The application to developing countries also often had a negative effect because of the formulaic approach to development. Structural adjustment programs enforced trade liberalization policies on developing countries but these, for example, require a certain level of institutional robustness in order to take advantage of global opportunities. The emphasis of multilateral agencies was on inculcating the values of economic liberalism and consequently little attention was paid to institutions and regulations, which in any case was anathema to the broader objective of reducing the role of the state and expanding the dominance of unfettered markets. Shrinking the size of state sector and spinning-off public sector activities and services to the private sector, on grounds of efficiency, has been a hallmark of IMF/World Bank policies in developing countries. In Nicaragua, for example, in the first three years of the post-Sandinista regime, the number of public sector employees shrank from 290,000 to 107,000, resulting in a loss of employment for more than 9 percent of total workforce. Elsewhere,

• In Kenya, the government committed itself to reduce the size of public sector by 50,000 employees.
• In Uganda, by early 1997, the size of public sector was cut in half to 150,000 with a target of 58,100 by June 1997.
• In Yemen, in 1999 expectations were that the size of public sector would be cut by 20 percent.
• In Zambia, 20 percent of public sector was laid off in 1998 and 1999. IMF loan documents set a target of reducing government employment from 110,000 to 10,000.[45]

It is true, of course, that developing countries have not always implemented IMF/World Bank requirements faithfully, primarily because of political imperatives rather than economic bad-faith. For example, in 1985, under the watchful eyes of visiting IMF delegates, the Mexican government retrenched 50,000 public sector employees, ". . . but then rehired 35,000 of them in the next few weeks when it thought no one was looking, and by the end of the year had found ways to put the rest—and more patronage persons besides—back on the public payroll."[46] Still, even with widespread back sliding and inconsistent implementation of agreements, there has been a general withdrawal of the state from a range of public service activities in developing countries. The IMF too, has learned the hard political lessons and decided that implementation is easier when policies are not seen as external dictates but nationally "owned."

In the aftermath of the Asian financial crisis, the focus on reducing the shadow of the state on markets has become mixed with messages of good governance. East Asian governments had strong reputation of macroeconomic and fiscal discipline but after lauding these governments in the *World Development Report 1997*, the World Bank noted also that,

State enterprises were inefficient and over-protected. State regulation was excessive and ineffectual. Government policies thwarted competition. Civil service rules were antiquated, and internal systems of checks and balances to ensure governmental accountability were often lacking. The abuse of public office for private gain was widespread, but largely ignored. Such problems did not shake investor confidence, however.[47]

After July 1997, the deficiencies of public sector became incorporated into a renewed focus on good governance. Good governance is defined, by the World Bank, as strong state capacity, first, to define its role in line with economic rationale, and second, to enhance its performance in discharging that role. This may mean not only reducing the size of government but also strengthening state institutions and regulatory structures. This reorientation has accompanied the assessment that the Asian crisis was partly a consequence of government failure, of corruption and poorly performing public institutions. Accountability, therefore, is a key component of the emphasis on good government.

The Washington Consensus built on the successful experiences of East Asian economies and their miraculous growth experience in the 1980s and early 1990s. However, the Asian countries that experienced a crisis of confidence in 1997 arguably had liberalized their economies at a rate faster than sustainable from an institutional perspective. Their banking and financial industries were weak and relatively small, and hence unable to withstand international competition after liberalization, which emerged as one factor in the ensuing financial crisis. The crisis did not sway the conviction of Washington policy makers in the validity of their core ideas but, in response to criticisms, implementation by the multilateral agencies was modified to suit and reflect local conditions and incorporate social considerations in policy formulations. While the World Bank was one of the instruments for the promotion of the Washington Consensus, its Chief Economist, Joseph Stiglitz, became a subsequent critic of the misguided and narrowly economistic focus of the Bank's structural adjustment agenda. He argued instead for a "post-Washington Consensus" that "moves beyond the narrow goal of economic growth to the more expansive goal of sustainable, equitable and democratic development."[48]

John Williamson, too, acknowledged problems with the term and its application to all developing countries, when it was primarily intended to illustrate problems and needs of Latin American countries. Without compromising, however, on the basic strictures of liberalization, Williamson admitted that it had to be tempered with institutional development in order to avoid crises and other dysfunctional outcomes. He also acknowledged that liberalization had to include an anti-poverty component, even including redistributive policies.[49]

The reaction to globalization is, at best, mixed in both developing and developed countries. In developed countries, pessimists fear a quick "race to the bottom," where wages and labor conditions are whittled down to standards prevailing in developing countries without which industries would be unable to compete with low cost production centers and ultimately be forced to emigrate, taking with them jobs and taxation revenue. In developing countries, skeptics see globalization less as an opportunity and more often as either a threat to national independence and sovereignty or as a process of domination. Commenting on the impact of globalization in India, one opposition figure stated that, "for the first time [since 1948] there is a genuine feeling that our independence is at stake."[50] This despite the fact that India appeared to have done well in the 1990s following liberal market-oriented reforms. Others point out that globalization can have a particularly detrimental impact on the poorest population groups, especially in times of economic crises. To a large extent, however, this is largely a result of politically motivated misallocation of resources rather than an inherent flaw in the processes leading to globalization.

Yet, globalization can also unleash forces of economic volatility as a result of sudden and substantial capital flows. In order to expunge the system of dysfunctional capital flows, Tobin, for example, suggested in the 1970s the imposition of a tax on currency transactions to reduce the scale of speculative international capital movement.[51] Since the East Asian financial crisis of 1997 there has been renewed interest in the Tobin tax[52] to contain the more egregious forms of financial globalization. If globalization of production was unanticipated by the architects of the postwar international economic order, financial globalization was regarded by both the American and British negotiators as positively dysfunctional and detrimental to the interests of welfare states and to exchange rate stability. Following the Bretton Woods Agreement, John Maynard Keynes explained that:

> Not merely as a feature of the transition but as a permanent arrangement, the plan accords every member government the explicit right to control all capital movements.[53]

In the early postwar period there was strong antipathy to financial capitalists for instigating the economic crisis of the 1930s and leaders were determined to keep them in check. The later relaxation of financial controls resulted from changes in American interests and the dominance of neoliberal economists, like Milton Friedman and Friedrich Hayek who argued for liberalization in order to produce a more efficient global allocation of capital.

Capital control has resurfaced as an important issue but critics argue, however, that a small transaction tax would be no deterrent to currency speculators and that a large tax would destabilize international financial system. Barry Eichengreen also pointed out the practical difficulties of imposing such a transaction tax because it would only induce transactions to be executed in tax havens, like the Cayman Islands, which would also then become major financial centers, as well as being tax havens.[54] Even if a Tobin tax were to be implemented, it is unlikely to reverse the tide of globalization. Efforts to rein in speculative capital may be desirable from a standpoint of financial stability but globalization, as discussed earlier, is not defined by capital flows alone.

There are different measures of participation in the global economy, including membership in the GATT/WTO. The number of developing countries within the GATT/WTO system has increased from 61 in 1980 to 110 in 1999, about four-fifths of total. The GATT rules applied mainly to the non-Eastern bloc countries but since the collapse of communism, the WTO has become globally representative, with only a small number of exclusions. If we measure participation as a share of global trade, the achievement of developing countries is mixed. Only a handful of developing countries have increased their level of participation in the global economy, as measured by their share of global merchandise exports. This is shown in Table 1.1.

As can be seen in the table only two groups of countries, in East and South Asia, have increased their relative share in global exports, while others in Latin America and Africa have failed to maintain their share of world exports. African countries have been the least open of developing countries and have performed badly in aggregate terms and also in terms of income inequality. East Asian countries, which have maintained a policy of engagement, have experienced relatively high growth rates and have also benefited from increased FDI flows, and evidence suggests that the more open economies have tended to outperform developing countries that are less connected to the global economy. According to one study, 24 developing countries that had

Table 1.1 Changing shares in world merchandise exports, 1983–98 (%)

	1983	1998	Change
East Asia and Pacific	5.5	10.2	+85
Latin America and Caribbean	5.6	5.2	−7
Middle East and North Africa	6.8	1.9	−72
South Asia	0.8	1.0	+25
Sub-Saharan Africa	2.8	1.4	−50

Source: Killick, Tony, "Globalization and the Rural Poor," *Development Policy Review*, vol. 19, no. 2 (2001), p. 160.

integrated well into the global economy had achieved high growth rates of about 5 percent per annum in the 1990s, compared to a growth rate of 1 percent in the 1960s.[55] Certainly, growth correlates well with other policies promoting macroeconomic stability, rule of law and others but Kym Anderson, confident of human rationality asserts that it is natural for people to respond to incentives that accompany liberalization and globalization.[56] Moreover, according to David Dollar and Aart Kraay, if decadal changes in trade volume are used as a proxy for changes in trade policy, there is evidence that growth rates are highly correlated with changes in trade volumes. They find that:

> The recent globalizers have experienced an increase of their growth rates, from 2.9 percent per year in the 1970s to 3.5 percent in the 1980s, and 5 percent in the 1990s, while rich country growth rates slowed down over this period. What about developing countries not in the "globalizing" group? They had a decline in the average growth rates from 3.3 percent per year in the 1970s to 0.8 percent in the 1980s and recovering to only 1.4 percent in the 1990s.[57]

Nonetheless, it is necessary to introduce a couple of caveats. First, while there is strong evidence of a correlation, causation is harder to establish. It is indeed possible that growth outcomes are a result of some other factor. The advocacy of market openness has been questioned by analysts suggesting that while a correlation between trade and growth is real, the flow of causation is from growth to trade liberalization. It is argued, for instance, that liberal reforms in India post-ceded improved growth performance. Our inability in determining absolute causation means that there is no simple solution to this conundrum. We are forced to fall back on economic logic that, other things being equal, liberalization and globalization will have a positive impact on growth performance. The qualification applies to the fairness of rules of economic engagement, which makes it difficult to assert that all developing countries will necessarily do well by removing all obstacles to international trade. Past record does, at least, confirm that a few entrepreneurial countries were able to overcome any systemic impediments to growth leading to development. To the extent that equity of rules is an important condition, it is important for developing countries to remedy flaws and propose modifications so that they may realistically aspire to their developmental goals.

Second, it is possible that growth figures for the globalized developing countries is distorted by the inclusion of a few large countries, like China and India, but even dyadic comparisons, say between Bangladesh and

Pakistan, also confirm that the more globalized economy tends to outperform its insular counterpart. Moreover, even single country case studies, such as India, reveal that economy has performed better in the period following its departure from policies of economic self-sufficiency. Considering that average growth in the advanced industrial countries in the 1990s was well below 5 percent a year (in part a result of Japan's continuing economic crisis) it is clear that the gap between globalizing developing countries and industrial countries has narrowed. The success of globalized developing countries in recent decades is an entirely new development given that over the last couple of hundred years, the gap between developed and developing countries has widened (see Table 1.2).

Thus, from rough parity in 1750, incomes in developing and developed countries have continued to diverge. The disparity was 1 : 6 in 1900 but increased to 1 : 8.5 in 1953 and to 1 : 13 in 1970. If we allow for price differences, the gap at 1 : 8 in 1970 is considerably smaller, but still substantial. Bairoch hazarded a guess that ". . . divergence for 1980 will be larger still, since . . . the next few years will bring a slowing down of growth rate of per capita national product due to the combined effects of population growth and a reduction in industrial expansion."[58] Although the globalized developing countries have improved their economic standing, there remains a considerable and widening gap between the rich and the poorest 20 percent of countries. Moreover, while globalized developing countries may have reduced levels of domestic poverty, they, such as Bangladesh, have also experienced an exacerbation of income inequalities. Income gaps have widened even as growth achievements have been remarkably superior compared to more insular economies. In the 1990s, Bangladesh achieved an

Table 1.2 Long-term changes in per capita national incomes (1970 USD)

Year	Developing countries	Developed countries
1900	110	640
1913	120	775
1929	130	930
1952/54	150	1,360
1960	170	1,780
1970	210	1,780

Note: The estimates for developing countries excludes Latin America, Africa and communist countries (but includes China).

Source: Paul Bairoch, *The Economic Development of the Third World Since 1900* (Berkeley, CA: University of California Press, 1977), p. 191.

average annual growth rate of 5 percent and while overall incidence of poverty declined, income inequality, as measured by the Gini coefficient increased from 0.259 in 1991–92 to 0.306 in 2000.[59] The World Bank observed that had growth been more broad-based, the cumulative decline in poverty would exceed the 9 percentage point drop observed in the decade.[60] In the early years of economic globalization, inequality has increased not only between developed and developing countries but also within the globalizing developing countries. This is not necessarily an indictment of globalization *per se* but rather of policy failures at the international and national levels.

A Widening gap between the developed and developing countries has accompanied a drop in global poverty levels, if we hold the poverty line constant and assume that growth benefits all income levels. The United Nations (UN) has a declared Millennium Development Goal (MDG) of halving poverty from the levels of 1990 by the year 2015, a target that is eminently achievable even with growing income disparities. Most studies indicate declining global poverty since the early 1990s and, indeed, according to one estimate by Bhalla in 2002, the MDG had already been achieved by 2000.[61]

Third, while liberal reforms and participation in the global economy has produced better growth outcomes, it is unclear whether growth is broadly based or has contributed to reduction in overall poverty levels. It is possible that it has only benefited the urban middle and upper classes with little trickle down effect. Measures of poverty are highly unreliable as can be evidenced from two recent World Bank reports; one reporting that the number of people living in poverty had increased by 20 million between 1987 and 1998 while the other reporting a decline of 200 million between 1980 and 1998.[62] The problems are not only that measures are arbitrary and available statistics highly suspect but that methodologies used also lead to different results reducing credibility of poverty analyses.

Acknowledging problems associated with poverty measurement and analysis, Angus Deaton offers suggestions for improvement of analysis and finds that actual world poverty has indeed declined but not to the same extent as reported in the second World Bank report, *Globalization, Growth, and Poverty: Building an Inclusive World Economy*. Even this, however, failed to convince other critics troubled by the arbitrariness of the entire process and slippery statistical data. Srinivasan, for example, argues that "global counts have little meaning and even less policy relevance. Abandoning them and focusing on national and subnational poverty analysis that goes beyond headcounts would be the sensible choice to follow."[63]

2
Governing Globalization

The dynamics of regime creation

In a speech to the Trade and Development Board of the UNCTAD (UN Conference on Trade and Development) in October 1996, Renato Ruggiero Director General of the World Trade Organization (WTO) observed that the postwar trading system had undergone a profound change. He then proceeded to point out that institutions like the WTO were no longer simply writing the rules of interaction between separate national economies but were ". . . writing the constitution of a single global economy . . ."[1] In the case of the WTO, this is easy enough to appreciate now that negotiations deal less with tariffs and border measures, and increasingly with "behind the border" issues, including regulatory structures, labor and environmental standards, intellectual property rights and others, that previously were the exclusive domain of governments of each of the "separate national economies."

The process of rule-making for a global economy invites comparison with processes and the rules that emerged after the Second World War to govern economic exchange between countries. Through the latter half of the twentieth century, rules and multilateral institutions have served primarily the interests of developed countries and discriminated against interests of a majority of developing countries both procedurally and substantively. Procedurally, according to Ngaire Woods, the WTO is only ostensibly democratic. The practice of "green room" meetings among select countries and behind closed doors effectively empowers the Quad countries (US, EU, Japan and Canada) as rule makers and relegates others (the majority of WTO members) to a position of relatively passive rule takers.[2] The majority have limited opportunities to influence decisions within the WTO. In earlier trade negotiating rounds, leaders of the bloc of developed countries were able, effectively, to dictate outcomes to the contracting parties of the General Agreement on Tariffs and Trade (GATT), the predecessor of the WTO.

The other main global institution, the International Monetary Fund (IMF), with quota based voting and decision rules, is even more undemocratic and exclusionary than the WTO. Similarly, the World Bank is effectively dominated and run by the main donor countries, and principally the United States (US). Traditionally a European and an American lead the IMF and the World Bank, respectively. US control of the World Bank was effectively demonstrated, in 2005, when the American nominee to head the institution, Paul Wolfowitz, was approved unanimously despite the misgivings of many of its member countries, both developed and developing.

In its 1999 edition of the Human Development Report, the United Nations Development Program (UNDP) criticized existing structures that had allowed a grotesque polarization of people, where a "fifth of the world's population live in the richest countries and account for 86 percent of the world gross domestic product (GDP), 82 percent of world export markets, 68 percent of foreign direct investment, and 74 percent of telephone lines."[3] These, and other indicators of global inequalities are common enough and the Report exhorted states to construct rules of globalization that prioritize people over profits. However a fair system will not emerge through moral suasion alone and will have to be forged out of struggle and determination. Inequality has a long history but the problem is more urgent in the context of globalization, which has removed the comfort of separation and brought the two worlds into closer contact.[4]

In the context of entrenched inequities, the process of rule-making for new economic circumstances is especially significant. With a hint of optimism, Jay Mandle writes that given the rules of globalization are still in a nascent stage it "is not too late to reform globalization. The institutions associated with it are still under construction, and it is therefore possible to reduce the one-sidedness of the process."[5] In the first seven trade liberalization rounds of GATT, developing countries were sidelined by the focus on industrial products and issues considered important by the developed countries. The first time issues of interest to the South were placed on the negotiating agenda was in the Uruguay Round, which brought under its purview new issues like services, trade related intellectual property (TRIPs), agriculture and textiles. The last two were of particular significance to developing countries. Even so, developing countries remained marginalized and the outcomes proved, on balance, to be detrimental to their interests. Apart from systemic marginalization, developing countries also showed little interest in actual negotiations. In general, developing countries' role in multilateral fora can be characterized in terms of "passive negotiation and active criticism" of outcomes. And they tend to oppose because they had little power, even capacity, to propose.

However, it serves little purpose to complain after the fact. Michalopoulos writes that developing countries, in the period since the conclusion of the Uruguay Round, have complained that benefits from textile and agriculture liberalization had failed to materialize because the liberalization agreements were backloaded but that these complaints were pointless since "it was quite obvious at the time the agreement was signed that the benefits were to be backloaded, and that the developed countries could stay within the letter of the agreement without liberalizing meaningfully in the first few years."[6]

Even though the Uruguay Round broke new ground it perpetuated the legacy of ignoring developmental needs. Throughout the postwar period, developing countries have been subject to systematic discrimination and been forced to compete on inequitable terms by the more dominant players. In 2003, The Center for Global Development prepared a new index of countries with policies that are either beneficial or detrimental to developing countries. The list of 21 rich countries placed Japan and the US at the bottom as least helpful to developmental objectives of the poor countries with only Germany among the Group of Seven (G-7) countries making it to the top half of the list.[7] The purpose of this novel new index was to shame the rich countries into improving their performance by implementing "affirmative action" policies at the international economic level. The orthodoxy however is that rules should be uniform and universally applicable rather than contextualized. This was the case with the TRIPs agreement that was part of the Uruguay Round outcomes and the same pattern was followed also when Organization for Economic Cooperation and Development (OECD) countries began negotiating the Multilateral Agreement on Investment (MAI) in the 1990s.

Perhaps, in light of past experiences and dangers of inaction and marginalization, developing countries have taken care to ensure that the pattern does not repeat itself in the Doha Round of the WTO. They face the same systemic disadvantages but have shown a determination to have their voice heard, if not singly then as a collective. Developing countries cannot afford to be left out of the rule-making process for the new era of globalization but their greater involvement initially produced only a negotiating stalemate in 2003 with developed countries unprepared to remove remaining protectionist policies and subsidy schemes that were harmful to developing countries.

The challenge for the WTO, as successor to the GATT, is to create a more inclusive economic regime in which all member countries participate and benefit equitably and fairly. This will not be easy as vested domestic interest groups in the West, sustained and nurtured by selective protectionist policies, resist attempts at significant liberalization of uncompetitive sectors, such as textiles.

Unfortunately too, multilateral agencies are not impartial and neutral architects of rules but hostage to the interests of the larger member countries. In these circumstances it is more than probable that emergent structure of rules will favor a few, mainly the developed countries, over the majority, the developing countries, just as the postwar rules of international economic engagement had also failed their developmental aspirations. The postwar liberal international economic order was negotiated among a number of key developed countries, particularly UK, and US and developing countries were incorporated into the system as rule-takers. Developmental interests were not given serious consideration until the 1960s and then only in an ad hoc manner. The Generalized System of Preferences (GSP) was approved following lengthy advocacy by the UNCTAD. It was approved by the GATT in 1971 and developed countries then introduced a GSP scheme to give preferential access to developing country exports. The GSP scheme varied for each country but gave many export commodities from developing countries duty free entry to developed markets.[8] This was significant at a time when most favoured nation (MFN) tariffs were still high but over time, the actual benefit, defined as the gap between MFN and GSP tariff, has been progressively eroded with reductions in average global tariffs.

Regime theory and international trade

Rules and structures governing international issue areas are known as regimes. Their purpose is to modify state behavior and to narrow the range of policy options available to national policy makers. The former mitigates an excessively competitive and anarchic policy environment and the latter adds to the certainty and predictability to state behavior. Regimes make an anarchical international reality more manageable and obviate the need for costly calculations (in time and resources) by decision makers to determine the impact and consequences of a particular course of action. Regimes are attractive because they lower transactions costs even if they imply a certain diminution of national sovereignty.

In the international political economy literature, it is assumed that rule-making and therefore regime creation is easier when there is an asymmetric distribution of power in the international system. The economic historian Charles Kindleberger and "realist" scholars of international politics have placed hegemony and power asymmetry at the center of regime creation.[9] The hegemonic stability thesis asserts that the dominant power possesses specific advantages in structuring rules for stability and economic liberalism. Thus the two periods of economic liberalism in the modern period are associated with *Pax Britannica* in the nineteenth century and with *Pax Americana* in the twentieth century. Conversely, "beggar thy neighbor," competitive and destructive policies prevailed in the inter war period when there was no hegemon willing to undertake the task of regime creation. A hegemon has to be willing to exercise its historic role and while the US already qualified as a hegemon in the first half of the twentieth century, it opted to shun international obligations. For this dereliction, Charles Kindleberger accused the US of "global economic irresponsibility" that led initially to the Great Depression and then to the Second World War.

After the Second World War, the US emerged as a more constructive player and set about establishing a liberal international trade regime that would deepen economic linkages and produce enduring peace. The structure that emerged, however, was not unilaterally or coercively imposed but a result of negotiations, largely between the US and UK. This led to the Bretton-Woods Agreement and the General Agreement on Tariffs and Trade. The trade regime paved the way for lower tariff barriers but also legitimated many pockets of protectionism. This mix of liberalism and protectionism resulted from concessions to others in order to entice them join the liberal trade regime. On balance, of course, the deal was more favorable to the US, as the war ravaged European states, dependent on US aid, were in no position to be too assertive. For instance, the British government, expecting sustained trade deficits, proposed a system of extensive international financing for countries in balance of payments deficits but the US, unprepared to write a blank check, would only countenance temporary financing by the IMF. Britain also asked for adjustments obligations to be shared between deficit and surplus countries but the US shifted the burden squarely on deficit countries.

It is conceivable for regime creation to be based on non-hegemonic and liberal principles of cooperative behavior but that is generally more likely in technical and functional areas, such as air traffic control. In most areas of international exchange where rules constitute the basis of privilege, such as in the areas of international trade, access to seas, environment and so on, divergent self-interest can be an obstacle to cooperative behavior. In these areas, political power becomes an important factor in rule-making. If we accept hegemonic stability thesis as a plausible explanation for regime creation, we can also assume that the US, as the only dominant contemporary superpower, will exercise disproportionate influence in formulating rules for the global economy. But apart from regime creation, a hegemonic state also has to secure conditions for long-term regime maintenance, or recreation. Socialization over time is one source of regime recreation but this is easier also when the process and final shape of a regime are not perceived to be too one-sided. Negotiated bargains that involve compromise, however limited, have the advantage of disguising the exercise of hegemonic influence. In turn, that imparts regimes with a degree of legitimacy and makes them more palatable to members. However, regardless of whether regimes are a result of hegemonic domination or negotiations, they will inevitably reflect the interests of dominant and powerful states, or more precisely the interests of dominant societal groups in those states, defined either in terms of economic or political influence. Thus, in the postwar trade regime, the economically dominant groups were able to achieve their fundamental goal of liberalizing international trade and access to foreign markets whereas the economically weak but politically influential groups were able to secure protection from trade-led threats to their survival.

As mentioned earlier, in negotiations leading to the Bretton Woods Agreement, British and American governments had conflicting visions about the future of international monetary order but the final outcome was a compromise, even if it ultimately favored the US. War ravaged Britain, dependent on aid from the US, was in no position to be too assertive but neither were its interests completely ignored by American negotiators. On many issues, there was some give and take but on the important ones, the American views prevailed and were accepted by others. In trade negotiations, the GATT was much more a product of American interests than the proposed International Trade Organization (ITO). The ITO Charter, negotiated in Havana, writes Judith Goldstein, "included compromise, especially to British interests, [but] the GATT did not . . . GATT rules reflected American demands."[10] And since ITO was not entirely consistent with American interests, Congress remained skeptical about an institution that had failed the critical compatibility tests, and the Administration wisely chose not to submit the Havana Agreement for Congressional ratification. Although the US dominated the process and outcomes, according to Goldstein, the US failed to realize what was in its "objective" interests but only because of "domestic institutional, ideational, and social constraints."[11]

All regimes are incomplete structures given the limited base of existing knowledge and inability to predict future directions. They do not, as has been pointed out, " 'spring forth full blown'—they grow."[12] For instance, in the establishment of the global monetary system, negotiators assumed that cross-border capital flows would be determined largely by the flow of goods and services and did not, indeed could not, anticipate the growth of speculative and non-trade related capital flows that have overwhelmed the flow of capital in payment of goods and services. The GATT and Bretton Woods system were also limited in that they excluded trade in services, agricultural commodities and textiles, as well as trade related investments flows. Protection of intellectual property rights was also rudimentary and inconsistent across political boundaries.

As evolutionary structures, regimes may, over time, acquire new and shed some defunct functions but it is important to note that originating conditions largely define the path of evolution. That would be true under normal circumstances but globalization has added to the task of developing new rules to respond to global pressures. The regulatory structures introduced at the end of the Second World War are being overtaken by economic globalization, leading to a search for new rules of global economic engagement not limited to cross-border interactions.

In this, there is much at stake for developing countries because globalization is not a passing or an easily reversible phenomenon. At the same time, there exists a historic opportunity to influence the structure of rules to remove some of the inequities, and inject greater transparency and fairness. Theoretically, of course, it is possible to devise non-prejudicial rules, devoid of power considerations, but under conditions that are near impossible. John Rawls argues that a "veil of ignorance" can contribute to a just and fair order but acknowledges also that it makes demands of negotiators that are unlikely to be met, including complete abandonment of all national, ethnic, and cultural identities that could conceivably inject bias into the negotiating agenda and strategy. At the other extreme of fairness and justice is rule-making based entirely on power considerations with no attempt to disguise vested interests. Somewhere in between these two extremes are normal rule-making procedures where countries try to exercise influence and are successful depending on their power positions or ability to forge negotiating coalitions and so on. This requires, at a minimum, that all interested parties have access to the negotiating process. This is a more realistic rule-making strategy than the veil of ignorance in contemporary international politics but even this does not adequately explain contemporary processes. To a considerable extent, developing countries are excluded from many negotiating forums through strategic decisions that limit negotiations to principal buyers and suppliers; exclude issues of particular interest to developing countries from negotiating agenda (textiles and agriculture); secretive negotiating processes, such as the "green room" option that is employed by the WTO, and the weighted-voting norm of the International Monetary Fund.

Regimes are confining mechanisms that are established to superimpose order on an otherwise anarchic situation. Justice and equity issues have not been central to regime creation. For a regime to be a disciplining influence and at the same time incorporate relatively fairness, it will have to be a compromise settlement between the two extremes. In contemporary international politics, even a Rawlsian negotiating strategy is unlikely to produce universally equitable and just outcomes, given that states are at different levels of development and no one set of rule is likely to meet the interests of all. A test of fairness cannot, therefore, be an assessment of outcomes but must be based on processes and procedural equality. No set of regulatory structure will be universally fair but what we might expect, at best, is some international equivalence of national equal opportunity and affirmative action stipulations.

As mentioned earlier, globalization is an immutable reality. And while developing countries may have suffered from exclusion in earlier negotiations, their interests are best served by working within the system to achieve greater substantive justice and procedural fairness. They cannot protest against the system by withdrawing from it and, instead, that protest must be within the system. Developed country interests, too, must be to preserve the principles of multilateralism. While developed countries, following the collapse of Cancun multilateral talks in September 2003, showed a proclivity for bilateral preferential trade agreements, these are all second-best options given that bilateral deals cannot safeguard the interests of global production networks that have altered the nature of modern industry and production. It is in the rational interest of both developed and developing countries to stay committed to global multilateralism and rule-making even if negotiations periodically become strained and deadlocked. Indeed, it is indicative of this commitment to global multilateralism that the US only negotiated free trade agreement with relatively minor trade partners.

At this point, it is worth reflecting on the role of developing countries. In early regime theory literature, states were classed into four categories;

a hegemon, regime supporters, challengers and free riders. Developing countries are by no means free riders as the costs of compliance are not inconsequential and high relative to benefits. Nor are they large enough to either become system supporters or challengers. Japan, was at one time categorized as a free rider and then predicted to be a potential challenger if it fulfilled expectations that it was destined to be a future hegemonic power. Instead, Japan has emerged as a system supporter. But the two identities of challengers and supporters are too extreme and do not allow for states that seek not to challenge but simply to reform existing regulatory structures. Developing countries today, in the Doha Round, are in that "reformer" category.

As reformers they must be engaged. For developing countries, apathy and disengagement from the rule-making process can only reproduce existing structural inequities and impede their capacity to improve material conditions, especially in relative terms. And inequality matters not only in the domestic context but also in international terms, and not only from the perspective of economic theory but also in so far as system stability is concerned. Widening cross-national inequality within a global economy may heighten frustration levels among disadvantaged groups, delegitimize the system and add to systemic volatility, to the detriment of all countries. Inequality produced systemic problems even when countries were not as well integrated and is likely to be more consequential in the contemporary period of near seamless integration.

The governance structure for the global economy, like regimes defined as an agreed set of rules, norms and principles of behavior, will emerge as a combination of many rules and norms that already exist and those that are being negotiated in the WTO and other international forums. It is a slow process that is unlikely to ever reach a finished state. Finkestein defines global governance as ". . . governing, without sovereign authority, relations that transcend national frontiers. Global governance is doing internationally what governments do at home."[13]

As indicated earlier, developing countries have a unique "window of opportunity" and are reasonably well positioned to influence rule-making with the designation of the Doha Round as the "development round." Developed countries may not have realized the full impact of such an appellation but there is, at present, a heightened sense of expectation that the Doha Round will produce outcomes and processes that will be more conducive to developmental objectives and that developing countries will have a say in formulating rules. Developing countries, excluded from the earlier exercise of rule-making after the Second World War have in turn seized the opportunity and participated actively and with greater vigor in the Doha Round when before their participation, as described by Bernard Hoekman, was "*a la carte.*"[14] Rordan Wilkinson writes,

> the evolving character of global governance brings with it moments of opportunity—moments in which pressure can be brought to bear on the emerging patters of governance. In such moments, alternative possibilities have the potential to emerge, thus altering the way in which global governance is constituted.[15]

However, as events have shown, the task is not easy. Draping the window of opportunity is the iron curtain of western intrests and inertia. As their leader, the US casts a long shadow over global rules and norms and yet is accountable only to its citizens. Developing countries, instead, have to negotiate within structures that, historically, have served to marginalize their voice. Thus, the GATT negotiating rounds dealt primarily with industrial and manufactured goods while agriculture and textiles remained outside framework, not subject to the same liberalizing discipline as most manufactured products.

Perhaps for that reason, when the opportunity arose, developing countries tried to install their preferred candidate as head of the WTO. This immediately led to a bitter leadership struggle that ended with the installation of Supachai Panitchpakdi to only a half-term directorship of the WTO. While some developed countries, such as Australia and Japan, supported this nomination, the US was concerned that control of the WTO would pass to countries that did not share the American vision for the global economy and could either delay or subvert agreement in the Doha Round. The developing countries were partially successful in their nomination bid but only after a long and hard struggle against embedded discrimination and marginalization of their interests within multilateral agencies. These countries not only had to contend with the hostility of the US government but also that of the WTO Secretariat, which is a supposedly neutral and unbiased bureaucratic machinery. The role of the WTO Secretariat in favoring one position over another can be seen in proceedings of the Doha Ministerial meeting. At that meeting, a wide gulf separated the developed and developing countries over the future of the so-called Singapore issues. The West insisted that these be included in the Doha Round negotiating agenda while developing countries were equally adamant that other priority issues deserved to be resolved before new issues were incorporated into the agenda. However, the Chairman of the General Council again mysteriously produced a draft declaration suggesting that negotiations were to begin in the Doha Round. This ignored the majority position against any expansion of the agenda. Only after considerable pressure from developing countries a clarification was issued at the closing ceremony of the Doha Ministerial that negotiations could commence only after explicit consensus of all countries.[16]

Similarly, even during the leadership contest between Supachai and Moore, the Chairman of the General Council of the WTO made no attempt to encourage a consensus around Supachai Panitchpakdi even though he had majority support for much of the time but when the US suggested later that Mike Moore had a few more supporters than Supachai, the Chairman of the General Council promptly urged members to form a consensus around the preferred western candidate. In this leadership tussle, even the WTO Secretariat became involved to confound the campaign of developing countries to install their candidate as head. This blatant exercise of partiality drew protests from many developing countries, which demanded a vote, but rather than allow an unwelcome and damaging democratic precedence, the West reluctantly accepted a compromise of split tenure between Supachai and Moore. These episodes highlight difficulties confronting the weak developing countries in influencing governance structures. Neither side achieved their objectives but, on a positive note, these episodes also give the hope of possible future compromises in the rule making process.

Moreover, while there is a window of opportunity, developing countries also must battle a deficit of negotiating capacity. The negotiating issues and agenda are complex and developing countries have limited expertise and resources to deal with them as effectively as the developed countries. Developing countries also are at a disadvantage because trade negotiations after the Uruguay Round have become far more complicated. Prior to that liberalization meant action on tariff barriers in the main, but the Uruguay Round Agreement extended the agenda to many more complex issues, including intellectual property rights, investments measures and others. As such, even as developing countries prepare to negotiate more actively and intensely, they also find the negotiating agenda very demanding, given their limited resources and capacity. With the Doha Round, they have been thrown into the deep end of the pool. Marathon negotiating sessions, not uncommon at the WTO, take a greater toll on the understaffed negotiating teams from developing countries and fatigue can lead to suboptimal agreements.

There are not many options for enhancing their negotiating strength but one possibility, as always, is the formation of a bargaining coalition.

Indeed, some of the larger developing countries formed just such an alliance in 2003 to press their case for a radical overhaul of existing trade policies and practices. Developing countries are in an inferior bargaining position despite being more numerous but just prior to the start of the Cancun meeting of the WTO, they established the Group of Twenty (G-20) to add weight to their voice and indicate resolve and determination. The formation of this grouping of developing countries was intended mainly to prevent the WTO from adopting another iniquitous agreement, as had happened in the final stages of the GATT's Uruguay Round.

The process of rule-making inevitably advantages the powerful countries but the less powerful countries can establish negotiating alliances and even rely on moral suasion.[17] Moreover, while multilateral agencies inevitably favor interests of the powerful group of countries, they also at least ostensibly subscribe to democratic norms that constrain the exercise of unilateral power by the hegemon. It is this constraining influence of institutions that developing countries could exploit in the ongoing "struggle" and negotiations to develop and design rules, which are more balanced and equitable. Despite the overwhelming negotiating advantage that the US enjoys, it cannot ride rough shod over democratic norms, especially at a time when it has assumed the role of facilitating the spread of democratic norms around the world.

Rule-making for a global economy has exposed serious and significant differences between developed and developing countries. While the struggle between developed and developing countries need not become the equivalent of a "clash of civilizations" there is tendency for it to be interpreted as a zero-sum game in a purely mercantilist understanding of economic exchange. Developing countries must negotiate within parameters established by existing structure of rules and norms and these are not conducive to their campaign to secure fairness and justice. It is true that regimes, at inception are rational constructs, well planned and negotiated, but they also undergo progressive change as circumstances change. Planning and negotiation always take place in the context of bounded rationality and that explains the incompleteness of the regime creation exercise. At the same time, amendments and modifications that creep into a regime over time do not override the parametric bounds of regimes. Fortunately, developing countries are not acting out a revolutionary struggle, in a Kuhnian sense, to replace an existing and flawed paradigm with another that is fairer to their aspirations. The task for developing countries is not to engineer a step-function change in international economic regimes but to make existing liberal regimes more conducive to their developmental interests by removing the many pockets of illiberal practices and securing recognition for special and differential treatment that has wide acceptance in the domestic politics of developed countries.

Developing countries have enlisted the support of non-governmental organizations (NGOs) to bolster their claim for a more spatially equitable deal, in a manner that is equivalent to the inter-temporal call for generational equity. In 1987, the Brundtland Commission report titled *Our Common Future* identified the importance of "sustainable development" to ensure cross-generational equity. Most governments readily accepted, as meritorious, the idea that the current generation has a responsibility to future generations but many of these governments have also found it politically difficult to implement this through their policy processes. In a democracy, political leaders are accountable to current generation of voters and predictably future values have not received full attention. Authoritarian regimes are relatively insulated from immediate popular pressures but again have been ineffective because these regimes are accountable neither to the present generation nor to the future. Equally as important as inter-temporal responsibility and fairness is the task of "spatially balanced development." Unequal distribution of benefits has been a constant feature in the international political economy but at the start of the Doha Round, Western countries committed themselves to redress this when they dubbed the new round as the "development round." This will require rules that are balanced and provide comprehensive coverage to issues of importance to developing countries. But just as inter-temporal responsibility has become confused by superficial platitudes, so is spatially balanced equity undermined by a surfeit of empty rhetoric.

At a rhetorical level all countries agree that it is vital to devise rules that are more equitable. Thus, at the Doha ministerial meeting of the WTO, the new round was dubbed the development round, in anticipation that the resulting agreement would provide significant benefits to the poor countries of the world and redress some of the embedded injustices. In devising flexible rules for the benefit of poor countries, the Doha Declaration was clear about special and differential treatment. But rhetoric aside, little was actually accomplished in negotiations leading to the mid-term review of the Doha Round in 2003. According to Clare Short, the former British Secretary of State for International Development,

There was a commitment to consider both changes to existing provisions as well as the wider question of how to make WTO rules flexible. Developing countries submitted over eighty proposals for suggested amendments; a more modest twenty two were put forward by the chair of the committee on trade and development, of which over half were specifically aimed at assisting least developed countries. Only four were agreed by the December [2002] deadline. This is deeply disappointing.[18]

Most analysts and policymakers agree on the need for equity but it is an extremely vague concept that needs to be properly operationalized so that it has practical meaning and relevance. Alexander Keck and Patrick Low of the WTO suggest that equity can mean two things.[19] First, we can understand it to imply equal outcomes but such a claim would be difficult to reconcile within liberal economic regimes, because equality of condition is more closely identified with Marxism and socialism. Second, equity can mean equality of opportunity, which is indeed one of the central tenets of liberal governments everywhere. Existing trade and economic practices have denied equal opportunity to the poor countries that need it most.

The global economy is composite of international trade, foreign investment, capital flows, technology transfer and others. Each of these issue areas is governed by a set of rules, norms and principles that may vary, however, in terms of scope, detail, and comprehensiveness. These regimes provide stability and order which helps to facilitate economic interaction between countries by lowering transaction costs. The main regimes in trade and finance were established at the end of the Second World War and while there has been progressive refinement of rules and norms, globalization has injected new pressures to align regulatory structures with changes in global circumstances. This has elevated the salience of not only the proposed new content of regulatory structures and regimes, but also the processes for arriving at these decisions in a fair and equitable manner.

As regimes lower transactions costs for member states, all benefit from orderly processes but rules are rarely, if ever, completely free of bias and value neutral. Rules determine the allocation of benefits to regime members. In trade and economic regimes, apart from the two extremes, where benefits accrue exclusively either to the developed or developing countries, rules may be designed to achieve a relatively equitable and fair distribution of costs and benefits. Because so much is at stake, multilateral forums have become a contested battleground for developed and developing countries to construct rules of globalization that will advance their particular interests. The postwar liberal regimes were western in design and construct and did not reflect developmental aspirations of states. Any later concession to developing countries, such as the GSP, was haphazard and partial at best. As such, it is understandable that developing countries, coerced, compelled and cajoled, as they are to embrace globalization, should want to influence the rule-making process and remove some of the existing inequities. For developing countries there is much at stake in ongoing multilateral negotiations. With limited resources and bargaining leverage, their goals are to ensure that emergent regimes will be sympathetic to their needs. Their quest is not for perfect equality, justice and fairness which is possible only in an idealized world but for outcomes that, for instance, provide easier access to developed country markets for their exports and regulatory burdens that are not too onerous or demanding. Even this limited pursuit of relative fairness however will not be easy given that the dominant ideology favors uniform rules over differential schemes. No universally applicable set of rules can meet the disparate needs of countries located at different levels of development.

There are disagreements on most issues and a final resolution that fulfils the implied objectives of the development round must entail a compromise between US demands for uniform and high standards and the developing countries' insistence on special and differential treatment. Such a compromise may have to include guidelines and markers for how uniformity might be progressively phased in after an extended transitory period during which countries build up their capacity to implement and enforce stricter regulations.

Formulating and revising existing rules is complicated by the larger number of countries that participate in the negotiating process. Mancur Olson observed that in larger groups the fraction of benefit received by each individual member is reduced, which in turn lowers the probability of collective action. That may be true for many types of collective action problems but Kahler adds that there may be issue areas where benefits actually increase with size of the group as, for instance, in the case of the Law of the Seas.[20] Even so, the Law of the Seas negotiations was protracted and difficult to conclude and the same is likely to hold for laws governing globalization. Hegemony is supposedly an advantage in multilateral rule-making but the US, despite being the sole superpower is constrained from a capricious exercise of power by the force of international public opinion and norms of fairness. Here, the role of international non-governmental organizations in mobilizing public opinion is particularly noteworthy. The rule-making process of the MAI, for example, which would have entrenched developed country interests over those of developing countries was thwarted primarily by NGO activities. Similarly, the Seattle meeting to start a new round of trade negotiations was undermined by protests led by NGOs against systemic inequities and a range of other concerns. They utilized the basic enabling technology of globalization, the internet, to undermine an important piece of regulation for the globalized economy.

The gulf separating developed and developing countries is indicative of difficulties in reconciling norms that militate against rational objective interests. Prolonged membership in multilateral agencies with prescribed and proscribed rules of conduct may help to socialize members but do not harmonize interests that are a product of objective socio-economic circumstances, despite common expectations that membership in liberal regimes helps socialize behavior. In this context, it is important to understand that the principle of special and differential treatment (SDT), presumably to address different interests of a group of WTO members, is not applicable only to developing countries but this same principle of SDT has also been introduced into developed country trade practices. In trade, developed countries have a long history of providing SDT to their farm sector as well as to textiles and other selected industries. It is incorrect to assume therefore that SDT applies only to developing countries.

There is some hypocrisy in western advocacy of harmonization around universally applicable rules and in using multilateral agencies as agents of change for this purpose. Agencies, like the IMF, have become institutions not of gradual norm socialization but of hard compulsion, based all too frequently on ideological considerations. The Washington Consensus, embodying a set of ideas congruent with the ideological preferences of the US Treasury and government has not served the particular needs of developing countries. Critics, like Stiglitz, fault the Washington Consensus both for its alleged universally applicable content and the sequencing of implementation. First, he suggests that the liberal economic norms that are being propagated cannot be demonstrated to be in the interest of all states regardless of specific economic circumstances and stage of development. Second, that the Washington Consensus inappropriately recommends that countries adopt liberal policies in one fell swoop rather than time it according to national capacity to compete effectively in the global marketplace. These shortcomings of the Washington Consensus then are evidence of the difficulties in norm diffusion where rational material interests are incongruous. The ideational constructivist approach may be consistent with liberal principles of change driven by the force of ideas but the rationalist approach provides a better fit to the realities of North–South debate.

One of the guiding principles of the GATT system was non-differential treatment, codified as the most favored nation (MFN) treatment. Developing countries however, have always insisted on SDT that takes into account their developing country status and interest in being given preferential treatment. From the inception of the GATT in 1947 till the completion of the Uruguay Round in 1993, developing countries had secured SDT in five areas.

• The right to infant industry and balance of payments protection as per Article 18 of the GATT.
• Exemption from making reciprocal tariff concession as per Part 4 of the GATT (1964).
• The right not to sign the Tokyo Round codes.
• Exemption from Article 24 of the GATT.
• The right to preferential market access through a nationally implemented GSP.[21]

Although a granting country could withdraw the GSP at any time, it was still the most significant of the five areas and was secured through the UNCTAD,[22] after prolonged debate and discussion. The GSP granted preferential entry to developing country products into Western markets, at tariff rates that were well below MFN tariffs. Over time, however, the margin of GSP preferences was whittled away by the progressive lowering of average industrial product tariffs. The Uruguay Round completed the departure from SDT in favor of common and uniform disciplinary codes and any remaining preferential scheme was reduced to a mere extension of the phase-in period for commitments. This was known as the "single undertaking" in which all countries committed themselves to the same outcomes. The only concession to developing countries was let them phase in the single undertaking over an extended period. As Oyejide writes, the Uruguay Round agreement whittled away the principle of SDT to "extended transition periods over which the same levels and scope of obligations as those demanded of developed countries would be assumed [by developing countries]."[23] In the Doha Round of the WTO, developing countries resumed a push to regain lost ground and secured a commitment to enhanced SDT provisions but which will grant them only longer implementation periods for the removal of export subsidies on agricultural products. Developing countries need more than time to commit to uniform standards. Their developmental objectives require instead preferential standards, given that they are starting from a very low base. This is an important issue and is discussed further in Chapter 8.

The Doha Round of the WTO has brought into sharp relief the conflict of interest and of priorities between the developed and developing countries. The term "the West and the rest" was coined to depict a particular aspect of civilizational and political disagreement but is equally appropriate in defining the struggle between developed and developing countries in the field of global economic management. Of course, outcomes in the Doha Round will be evaluated and judged for their success in protecting and advancing the interests of developing countries in a forum dominated by the developed countries.

Globalization itself is neither inherently iniquitous nor the great leveler of economic conditions. Its practical consequences depend largely on the ways globalization is institutionalized and governed. The search for a governance structure does not imply a search for global government but for simply a set of rules and norms of behavior for participants in the global economy, including states and private actors. The global political economy is a juxtaposition of economic globalization with national political arrangements. Even as artificial economic demarcations are being whittled away, state-based political authority and legitimacy remains the dominant mode of political interactions. In this structure, proposals for world government, whether federal or confederal, remains a project for the distant future. With the march of economic globalization, other actors have also gained prominence, such as NGOs and transnational business but the reality of state dominance is unlikely to erode markedly in the near future.

With states retaining substantive sovereignty and independence, no governance structure can ensure complete compliance but to the extent that regulatory rules are not excessively biased or coercive, it may be possible to limit the incidence of defection. The level of institutionalization may be informal or highly developed in organizations and multilateral agencies like the WTO, the IMF and, which derogate to themselves aspects of state sovereignty and authority. The purpose of any governance structure is to impart order upon an otherwise anarchic situation that is prone to crises. No system of governance is ever comprehensive in regulating all the intricacies but globalization, as a relatively recent development has exposed some of the deficiencies in the present structure devised largely after the Second World War.

Under globalization, with systemic threat levels considerably dissipated in the absence of ideological rupture, there is theoretically a greater potential for factoring in questions of justice in the pursuit of order and stability through regime formation and rule-making processes. Indeed, good governance might be conceptualized as striking a balance between order and justice, which empowers rather than disenfranchises weaker members of the global order. As far as justice is concerned, the objective need not be strict equality of condition, in the Marxist sense, but at least procedural justice and equal opportunity that have become the hallmark of western liberal democracies through such episodes of reform liberalism like the New Deal and the Great Society Programs.

Absolute procedural justice is impossible in the absence of a "veil of ignorance"[24] to shield negotiators from knowing their interests and prevent them from acting on those same interests but some modicum of justice is still possible if negotiators act not on the premises of a zero-sum game but rather in the knowledge that developmental opportunities for all will enlarge the existing economic pie so that none needs to be any worse off, at least in an absolute sense. Even this may require a level of enlightenment that has been missing in the past. For instance the Bretton Woods Agreement allocated the responsibility for balance of payment adjustments to deficit countries because US negotiators were well aware that their trade balance was likely to remain in surplus for quite some time after the War. Without the equalizing force of a veil of ignorance, it is inevitable that international negotiators will seek to draw upon all available resources to even out the existing disparities. Developing countries, in particular, confront a steep learning curve but displayed a new found capacity to maximize their prospects in international negotiations not only by forging a semblance of unity among themselves but also by securing the specialized skills and advice of various NGOs.

To the extent that globalization is an irreversible trend,[25] developing countries naturally have a stake in influencing the rules that will ultimately pattern global economic interactions. This interest also follows from western intervention, mediated often by the IMF and the World Bank, to force developing countries to engage with the global economy through liberalization and privatization of their economies. This is the thrust of the Washington Consensus, designed to bring about neoliberal economic reforms in developing countries and open them up to international economic exchange. Indeed, it could be argued that apart from a charm offensive to encourage developing countries to embrace globalization as beneficial to growth and development, there are punitive measures alongside it to ensure that the reluctant globalizers are forced to embrace globalization through, for example, structural adjustment programs of the IMF. Finally, we can also trace the interest of developing countries in emerging governance structures to the Asian financial crisis of 1997, which demonstrated powerfully that globalization has serious downside for countries that seek to profit in the global economy without possessing the necessary capacity to withstand global market forces.

Just as the end of the Second World War witnessed a burst of rule-making activities and new regimes were established to discipline international interactions, the emergence of globalization has engendered renewed focus to modify regimes to suit the changed circumstances and to develop rules for many other issue areas, such as government procurement, investments, labor and environmental standards, and intellectual property rights. The first WTO ministerial meeting in Singapore in 1996 identified four areas where new rules had to be devised: foreign investment, competition policy, rules on government procurement, and trade facilitation. These were areas of particular concern to developed countries while developing countries adopted a lukewarm attitude, insisting that existing anomalies, such as agricultural subsidies and protection, be rectified before new items were placed on the negotiating agenda. In the end, trade ministers agreed to establish working parties to study and analyze the four so-called Singapore issues.

1. *Investments*: At the time of the Singapore ministerial meeting, OECD had been negotiating the multilateral agreement on investments to create a regime of uniform rules. The OECD negotiations however excluded developing countries at the insistence of the US, which felt that their inclusion would only lead to watered down provisions rather than an agreement of high standards. In 1998 MAI negotiations collapsed in the face of public pressure and attention refocused on the WTO as the negotiating forum. The European Union (EU) and Japan were keen to take this option whereas the US was now even more reluctant to do so having already achieved a high standards investments rules in the North American Free Trade Agreement (NAFTA) and could be expected to achieve those same rules, such as prohibitions on performance standards on incoming foreign investments and dispute resolution mechanisms between investors and national governments, in bilateral or regional agreements.

2. *Competition*: The main purpose of competition policies is to prohibit trade restrictive business practices through global anti-trust regulations. Proponents argued that there should be international

regulations to prevent firms from collusive and anti-competitive behavior. Such regulations are well established in the EU and other developed countries but many developing countries questioned its urgency and argued that benefits would be incommensurate with the potentially high implementation costs.

3. *Government Procurement*: In many countries government procurement is not open to foreign firms, which others with a more open and liberal regime, find to be discriminatory and inconsistent with WTO provisions. Japanese government procurements, until the 1980s for example, were closed to foreign companies.

4. *Trade Facilitation*: Many countries have complex and time-consuming import procedures that hinder rather than facilitate imports. Whereas, most developed countries process imports swiftly and efficiently, imported products into India may take up to 11 days to clear customs, as a result of excessive and onerous documentation requirements. Developed countries argue that trade rules should be harmonized to reduce transaction costs, which ultimately would benefit both consumers and producers. The extent of the gain however is estimated to be marginal. An UNCTAD study estimated that transaction costs add about 2–3 percent to the landed cost of a product.[26] Again, as far as developing countries were concerned, new international obligations would only strain government capacity and make it harder for them to collect customs revenue, a major component of tax revenue for a large number of developing countries.[27] Moreover, as noted by Barry Desker, developing countries resisted trade facilitation talks because of their limited capacity to implement and police any resulting agreement, that would only lead to disputes over non-compliance.[28]

At a subsequent WTO ministerial meeting in Doha, trade ministers launched the Doha Round of trade negotiations and agreed also that negotiations on the Singapore issues should start following the fifth ministerial meeting (Cancun 2003), on the basis of a decision on modalities of negotiations to be taken by consensus. This inclusion in the Doha Declaration was not supported by developing countries. They argued that the next round should focus on resolving their concerns with some of the provisions and implementation of the Uruguay Round Agreement. The Declaration however contained only perfunctory references to their grievances.

On the Singapore issues, developing countries felt reassured that negotiations would begin only after the 5th ministerial meeting on the basis of explicit consensus of all countries on the parameters of the negotiating agenda. However, correctly or otherwise, even in the interim period developed countries interpreted the provisions of Doha Declaration to signal the practical initiation of formal negotiations. This prompted some developing countries (Uruguay, Pakistan, Malaysia, Indonesia and Cuba) to formally remind members "that the exercise consist[ed] merely of a review and not negotiations."[29] Stiglitz and Charlton observe that since these issues "are not priorities for developing countries, their [the Singapore issues] emerging centrality in the agenda is an incongruous feature of the 'development' round."[30] There is a history of trade rounds imposing onerous obligations on developing countries without much benefit in return. At the end of the Uruguay Round, developing countries accepted obligations on protecting intellectual property rights despite limited capacity to fulfill these obligations while the US reneged on its commitment to liberalize farm trade, when it passed the Farm Bill in 2002 and increased support to farmers. Also, at the end of the Uruguay Round, developing countries were forced to accept liberalization of trade in services, such as financial services, without there being any developed country commitment to liberalize trade in labor-intensive services, such as construction, that would be of interest to developing countries. It is true that developing countries have not been able to implement all their undertakings but that is primarily a result of inadequate capacity whereas developed countries that have reneged on commitments have no excuse other than political expediency.

The Singapore issues are not the only ones that developed countries have tried to place on the negotiating agenda. They made repeated suggestions that uniform labor and environmental standards are essential to smooth development of globalization but again there was total reluctance on the part of developing countries to open a new negotiating front. At the Singapore meeting, the US tried to force negotiations on uniform labor standards but this was rejected on grounds that the proper forum for labor standards was the International Labor Organization (ILO) not the WTO. Developing countries do not necessarily object to uniformity of standards but fear that developed countries will impose "high standards," that is regulations already in place in developed countries, on developing countries, which either do not possess state capacity to implement or enforce such high standards, or which may make it harder to achieve other priority goals. Uniform standards may be appropriate and in line with principles of national treatment and MFN clause that are part of the WTO and apply to all countries but developing countries also have advocated SDT such that the uniform standards do not become an obstacle to development. The principle of SDT had been a hard won victory for the developing countries which secured the GSP in the 1960s but that principle has been lost in the march to liberalization and in danger of being completely overwhelmed by demands that rules had to be uniform and consistently applied to all countries, regardless of level of development. The basic difference is that while the US proposes uniformity as the guiding principle for rule-making, developing countries want to ensure somewhat greater flexibility, rather than a straightjacket approach to global governance. Flexibility, that would be sensitive to the particular needs of individual developing countries and enable them to partake of the benefits of globalization without being asked to pay too high a price for that, in terms of development. Developing countries also are apprehensive of being manipulated and overwhelmed by the West and as such tend to view western demands of uniformity as an attempt to remake the rest of the world in their image.

Globalization may be potentially beneficial to all countries but the processes and substantive rules for the orderly development of economic globalization has exposed divisions between developed and developing countries. This is evident, for example, in ways developed countries of the OECD tried to monopolize negotiations for an investments regime by excluding developing countries. The motivations again were to formulate a regime of high standards, which would, in time, be forced upon all WTO member countries. Some of the rules that were proposed as part of the MAI privileged multinational corporations (MNCs) over sovereign states and their right to defend the national interest. Conversely, the forceful bid by developing countries to capture the office of the Director General of the WTO was based on belief that it would bring with it an ability to control the agenda for the next round of trade negotiations and influence the final outcomes.

Identifying as the primary divide the disagreement between developed and developing countries is not to suggest complete harmony within each group of countries. The developing countries are a diverse group and speak rarely with a single voice. They are at different levels of development and have divergent needs and interests. Unity is difficult also because of their numbers and because of coordination problems associated with large groups. But when they do speak with a common voice, developing countries can be an influential force within the global system. In the Doha Round negotiations, they displayed a high level of unity in demanding agricultural liberalization at the WTO ministerial meeting in September 2003. The formation of the G-20[31] just prior to the meeting in Cancun was a significant development that translated numbers into bargaining advantage and conveyed the main message that developing countries, led by a handful of key states like India and Brazil, were not prepared to have a flawed and iniquitous agreement go through. Contrary to expectations that a diverse group could not maintain unity, the developing countries refused to be confined to a position of rule-takers and stood firm in their conviction that no agreement was better than a one-sided agreement. Unlike earlier trade rounds, Cancun was the first time that developed countries failed to have a minority agreement ratified by the membership of WTO.

In this unprecedented situation, the meeting ended in a stalemate. The developed countries of course rejected demands of the G-20 but it was significant that developing countries did not buckle to pressure to accept modest liberalization in exchange for negotiations on issues of interest to the developed countries. Apart from this example of resolve and determination, developing countries, in general, have been susceptible to divide and rule tactics. For instance, developed countries have, or have tried to exploit divisions among the ranks of developing countries to secure advantages for themselves, as we shall see in the context of intellectual property rights, pharmaceutical trade, and the global AIDS crisis. According to one source, Lamy and Fischler in June 2003 had circulated a letter in the WTO suggesting that only the least developed countries should be exempt from liberalizing obligations. This proposal to limit special and differential treatment to a subset of developing countries was apparently not well received by middle-income developing countries and dismissed as a ploy to create dissension.

When it comes to rule-making for a global economy the primary divide is between the North and the South, but developed countries too have internal disagreements about rules and institutional structures to govern global economic relations. At the time of the Asian financial crisis, for instance, the Japanese government proposed establishing an Asian Monetary Fund (AMF) to fill an institutional void in the Asia Pacific region but this idea was quickly quashed by the US which perhaps felt a threat to its ability to dominate the rule-making process and a threat also to US led institutions, such as the IMF.[32] The US has used IMF conditionality and structural adjustment programs to promote globalization but an AMF, with more liberal lending conditions, as proposed by Japan, would have weakened the capacity of IMF to achieve these goals in the Asia Pacific region. Nonetheless, the developed countries have a much greater sense of unity and purpose.

Even if deep fissures have emerged between developed and developing countries over rules, and their relative costs and benefits, in principle, rules and regulations are beneficial to all countries participating in a global economy. The advantage of operating within a rule based structure is that it lowers transactions costs and lengthens the shadow of the future such that states do not have to engage in constant and costly determination as to whether others will abide by certain expectations. Rules free states from such exercise by making the behavior of others more predictable. It was this advantage of regimes based international relations, that is, lower transactions costs that also contributed to China's desire to rejoin the WTO. Prior to its membership, China had to go through the costly exercise of negotiating MFN trade privileges with the US, for example, on a bilateral basis annually. This was fraught with difficulties as the US tried to link MFN with human rights conditions within China.

The WTO is an important actor in the process of devising rules for a global economy but the IMF perhaps has the more central role through its consistent advocacy of the basic principles of the Washington Consensus when applied to developing and transitional economies. Structural adjustment programs of the IMF have been at the forefront of liberal market oriented principles that have also seen a progressive diminution of state involvement in economic activities. The IMF is usually headed by a European national but its presence in Washington has led to close links with US government agencies and a willingness to submit to American intellectual leadership. Over the years, the IMF has come under intense criticism for its lack of openness and transparency in dealing with client countries. The IMF also has considerably more impact on actual and future prospects of developing countries but developing countries have little direct access to its policy making processes, given that voting rights in the IMF are allocated to countries in proportion to their assessed quota. Developing countries are in a weak position also because of their position as loan recipients. However, within the IMF, there have been changes, such as the formation of the International Monetary and Financial Committee (IMFC) in which all countries can raise issues of international governance and the role of the IMF in global finance.[33] This innovation cannot override the stumbling bloc of weighted voting. From the perspective of developing countries, the WTO is potentially a more democratic institution as its decision-making is based on the principle of "one country, one vote" rather than weighted voting.

NGOs and global rule-making

States retain primary negotiating authority for any global governance structure but they are not the only international actors and share the stage with global civil society groups, such as NGOs. The nature of world politics has evolved considerably since the golden age of state dominance, epitomized, for example, in the Concert of Europe and the Congress of Vienna in the nineteenth century. In that system, five European powers, after the destabilization of the Napoleonic Wars, reached an understanding to protect the established order through balance of power politics and periodic inter-state congresses. They were able to do this without having to factor in public opinion or other external pressures.

In the contemporary period, interaction between states is buffeted by a range of non-state actors on the world stage, such as NGOs, MNCs, and media organizations, as well as by domestic public opinion which may, alongside NGOs and IGOs (inter-governmental organizations), exert moral pressure on states. As constituent elements of a global civil society, defined as "a parallel arrangement of political interaction, one that does not take anarchy or self-help as central organizing principles but is focused on the self-conscious constructions of networks of knowledge and action, by decentered, local actors, that cross the reified boundaries of space as though they were not there,"[34] NGOs, in particular, have been important not only as lobby groups but also as policy partners. Not all NGOs however can be co-opted as partners in rule-making. Participation of each type of actor is influenced by their evaluation of the existing system and their ultimate objective.

As noted, developing countries, protest the inequities in the system but their protest is delimited by their commitment to the system. They accept the system as potentially beneficial to their developmental objectives provided the rules and norms can be modified to reduce inequities and unfairness. As such, developing country protest activity can be classified as protest within the system since they are not necessarily advocating systemic change. Most NGO activities can also be classified as protest within the system but some are clearly designed to subvert the existing system. Their protest can be classified as protest about the system. While they purport to champion the cause of developing countries, they may actually be causing harm, not necessarily by design but by default. NGOs have launched protest campaigns against development projects, such as hydroelectric projects, even when such projects can be demonstrated to be beneficial to developing countries and the affected population. Thus NGO activism forced the World Bank to pull out of a dam project in Qinghai, China on grounds that it would be an environmental disaster and adversely affect Tibetan culture through the influx of Chinese in the region. The withdrawal of the Bank did not deter the Chinese government which pressed ahead, with even less regard for either the environment or Tibetan culture. Examples such as this have prompted some to question the role of NGOs in the global economy. Sebastian Mallaby writes:

> They [NGOs] claim to protect the environment, but by forcing the World Bank to pull out of sensitive projects, they cause these schemes to go ahead without the environmental safeguards that the bank would have imposed on them. Likewise, NGOs purport to hold the World Bank accountable, yet the bank is answerable to the governments who are its shareholders; it is the NGOs' accountability that is murky.[35]

Other examples of protest about the system include the Seattle protest movement that prevented the start of a new WTO negotiating session. It was in this context that the Director of the World Development Movement (WDM), Barry Coates, declared that Seattle had derailed the free trade juggernaut. Similarly, in the months leading to the establishment of the WTO, Ralph Nader, a leading consumer activist, traveled to a number of countries to lobby against the WTO, because it would be an un-elected supranational bureaucracy antithetical to principles of state sovereignty. NGO activity against the MAI can also be classified in this category, with the ultimate objective that of halting the progress of globalization, rather than improving on its shape and form, if we assume that the proposed MAI was a flawed document. More recently, developed countries were wont to blame NGOs for the collapse of the Cancun ministerial meeting for advising developing countries against any compromise on the so-called Singapore issues. The MAI might have become a reality if NGOs and activists had not questioned its impact on developing countries or on the principle of sovereignty. Equally important, they saw the MAI as another step toward the eventual realization of economic globalization and were determined to halt its sweep across the world and to wind it back. Protestors in Seattle were inclined similarly to reject globalization.

Protest within the system is likely when actors see the system as potentially beneficial, when the system itself is amenable to reform and improvement, and when actors positively evaluate their capacity to act as agents of change. Without agency, protest within the system is meaningless. By contrast, protest about the system is more likely when the system is evaluated as beyond repair and discriminatory and when actors, with agency, consider the system as potentially reversible or replaceable. The two forms of protest are not always mutually exclusive and there may be areas of overlap. What begins as protest within the system may eventually lead to a step function change in the system. Protest about the system by some NGOs may be a reason why WTO and other multilateral agencies have tried to screen NGO presence during important meetings, as happened at the Doha WTO talks. These are issues that will be discussed in subsequent chapters.

Civil society groups, like NGOs have a long history of involvement in international relations, whether in direct negotiations or in influencing outcomes through working in partnership with sympathetic countries. Unlike states, which are essentially similar and perform similar functions but differ mainly in terms of their power potential, civil society groups are very diverse in their objectives and orientations. Civil society groups and NGOs include Oxfam, Medicins Sans Frontieres, Greenpeace, Sierra Club, Third World Network, Amnesty International and so on.

They enter the policy process with specific interests and their activities may be either sporadic or sustained. In international policy process, NGOs frequently work close with state actors and poor developing countries tend to rely more on NGOs to supplement their inferior negotiating and bargaining position. A good example of NGOs acting in concert with developing countries was the 5th WTO ministerial meeting at Cancun in 2003 and they were consequently blamed, rightly or otherwise, for the hard line and unwavering position of developing countries on agricultural liberalization and the developmental objectives of trade negotiations. Alternatively, NGOs exercise influence by raising and mobilizing public opinion, as happened in the final stages of the MAI when NGOs and interested individuals used the world wide web (www) to mobilize opposition to the draft agreement. NGOs were also actively involved in lobbying the US to withdraw threats of trade and economic sanctions against South Africa, which wanted to bypass TRIPs to address its AIDS crisis. The US was acting to protect the interests of pharmaceutical industries even though the actions would be catastrophic to AIDS patients. And, according to Abbott, it was not until NGOs "threatened to disrupt the political campaign of Vice President Gore that the US backed away from its threats."[36]

NGO participation is consistent with democratic policy making processes and has a long history in international negotiations. There were, for instance, 1200 such organizations at the founding conference of the United Nations (UN) in San Francisco in 1945. Moreover, as observed by the UN Secretary General Kofi Annan, their role was significant also in the Geneva Conventions of 1864, the multilateral labor conventions adopted in 1906 and the International Slavery Convention of 1926.[37] In the post-Cold War period, as democratic transition has gained momentum, civil society groups have strengthened their role and influence and in recognition of this important shift in global politics, the WTO too, adopted a guideline in July 1996 that duly acknowledged the role of NGOs in increasing public awareness of WTO activities. At the first WTO ministerial meeting in Singapore in 1996, 159 NGOs (235 individuals) were registered participants. At the Geneva ministerial meeting, 152 NGOs (362 individuals) were registered as participants. This was a marked departure from the GATT, which made little attempt to connect with civil society groups, unlike all other UN agencies.

The WTO having made a start is still a laggard behind its sister organizations, like the World Bank and the IMF. This might partly be because the WTO is a relatively small organization (500 staff and an annual operating budget of US$100 million compared to 5000 staff of the World Bank and a budget of US$1375 million) and has limited resources to devote to NGO liaison but even with the beginning it has made, WTO accreditation processes favor business linked NGOs over grass roots civil society groups, trade unions, or environmental NGOs that tend to be more critical of the WTO. For example, at the second ministerial conference, 65 percent of participating NGOs represented business organizations and again primarily from the northern countries. Moreover, unlike other UN agencies, accreditation to the WTO is on an ad hoc basis rather than permanent.[38] In response to standing criticisms of the WTO as unwelcoming of NGO participation, the WTO established guidelines for the development of relations with NGOs in 1996, which ironically, committed the WTO to develop linkages primarily with like-minded civil society groups. As a result, the more critical NGOs are marginalized and excluded from consultative processes.[39] This gives the WTO greater capacity to control participation of NGOs and to exclude groups deemed disruptive and undesirable.

NGOs are not always welcome and quick to be blamed for resulting difficulties. The collapse of the Cancun talks following acrimonious debate and disagreement between developed and developing countries was attributed by some governments and analysts to spoiling tactics of NGOs, which had, allegedly, encouraged developing countries not to be conciliatory and remain steadfast. Earlier, NGO mobilization of public opinion had been blamed for the collapse of the Seattle meeting of the WTO and for the failure of the OECD to conclude a high standards investments regime. At Doha, the WTO did not have to contend with homegrown protest movements nor with disruptions from foreign-based NGOs. It was able to ensure smooth deliberations by regulating entry visas to Qatar, which enabled it to better control NGO participation and prevent the angry display of civil discontent.

NGOs participating in WTO meetings have consistently criticized the absence of clear rules and procedures for rule-making, even for drafting of declaration, in which text often appears "mysteriously" with the purpose of precluding debate and dissent. The WTO Secretariat is itself unable to put in place a more transparent policy making process in the absence of consensus on rules. The murky policy making process, including the infamous "green rooms" works to the advantage of developed countries and they seem unprepared to surrender their undemocratic privileges.

Apart from critical civil society groups, businesses and MNCs corporations have also sought to influence the rule-making process. Big business and MNCs are legitimate players given their central role in economic globalization through the establishment of global production networks. MNCs were the main force behind the push for uniform investment regulations that protected and privileged their global investments and business groups initially were adamant also about not weakening the TRIPs agreement reached in the Uruguay Round, even in the face of pressure from developing countries that existing rules had made it harder for them to combat AIDS and other public health challenges. The involvement of MNCs is not surprising since they are the primary engines of globalization, through their foreign investment activities and establishment of regional and global production networks. In the MAI negotiations discussed in Chapter 3, American MNCs were in the forefront of demands for a high-standards agreement.[40] Like NGOs, MNCs too operate through country representatives in the WTO and in the Doha Round, the big pharmaceutical companies were major players in discussions on TRIPs reforms and for initially blocking agreement that would have made it easier for developing countries to access cheap generic medicines to combat public health issues.

Conclusion

The clash of interests that exists between developed and developing countries about the nature of global governance and regime structures means that there is no common contract zone to allow for regime formation based only on common interests or bargaining. As the ensuing case studies reveal, the role of political power, influence and coercion has become a prominent feature of the rule-making process. Developing countries are at a distinct disadvantage but have an ally in INGOs which can either provide specialized knowledge and negotiating know-how, or mobilize public opinion in order to exploit democratic national policy making structures.

The task of regulating economic globalization has resulted in a struggle between developed and developing countries to protect and advance their respective and, in many ways, inconsistent interests. Rule-making may be the preserve of state actors but the role and influence of civil society actors cannot be played down. These NGOs have a long history of protecting the public good and, in the contemporary period, various factors, including the prominence of democratization and transparency, have worked to increase their influence and strength. They are not always welcome participants but the rule-making exercise of globalization cannot proceed without the inclusion of civil society groups.

States and multilateral agencies liaise and interact with NGOs at various points but rarely are NGOs allowed direct participatory rights in international negotiations. Even so, NGOs can still be a powerful force in the regime making process by developing and promoting alternative conceptions of regime structure, in the constructivist tradition of international relations. This denies that regimes are necessarily always formed by agents with a well defined preference structure, an assumption common to political realism, and that institutions themselves are able to "play a constitutive role in shaping the identities of their members and, to be more specific, influencing the way in which these actors define their interests."[41]

3
Foreign Investments and the Multilateral Agreement on Investments

The Multilateral Agreement on Investments (MAI) was an ambitious undertaking by members of the Organization of Economic Cooperation and Development (OECD) to remove domestic controls over foreign direct investment (FDI). This significant initiative in rule-making for foreign investments did not include developing countries on grounds that open multilateral negotiations would produce only a compromise agreement and undermine the goal of achieving a "high standards" agreement. While it is true that a majority of FDI flows is between developed countries, in refusing representation to developing countries, negotiators were dismissive of the important role that FDI plays in developing countries, as a source of acquiring technology, managerial expertise, and export revenue through mandatory export requirements. It was, of course clear that developing countries would not initially be subject to the MAI discipline but expectations were that the MAI would be adopted also by the World Trade Organization (WTO) and become part of the multilateral trade regime. And countries that refused to submit to it could then be "punished" and denied FDI. In the final analysis, therefore, it would have had a major impact on developing countries and to their developmental aspirations.

The fight against the MAI, however, was not led by developing countries but by a coalition of protestors and non-governmental organizations (NGOs) based in developed countries that saw the MAI as according far too many privileges to multinational corporations (MNCs), for not protecting consumer interests, and for the secrecy surrounding the negotiating process. The episode is illustrative of the lack of transparency in the global economic system and of systemic inequities and it is ironic that one of the justifications for a MAI was that it would enhance the transparency of international rules governing the flow of investment capital. This chapter will focus on the negotiating process, the role and importance of FDI in developing economies, the protest movement against MAI, and the road ahead.

Apart from levels of trade, economic globalization is defined and driven by substantially increased capital flows. Capital flows may be in settlement of trade accounts but increasingly take the form of speculative transfers, portfolio investments and direct investments. When the Bretton Woods system was established after the Second World War, it was assumed that capital flows between countries would be primarily in settlement of trade accounts. Today that is dwarfed by non-trade related capital flows. Speculative investment can be characterized as money chasing money profits and its expansion can be attributed largely to improved technology that has made it possible to transfer large funds quickly and without excessive costs. However, speculative capital is fickle and foot-loose. That makes it potentially destabilizing especially as speculative investors tend to move in herds and a sudden departure from one economy can have major adverse consequences, as some Asian economies discovered in 1997.

FDI involves ownership of productive capacity and confers on the investor ownership rights. While the original General Agreement on Tariffs and Trade (GATT) mechanism did not include investment flows as being relevant to the trade agenda, investments have become increasingly linked to international trade, especially in the period following the establishment of global production networks. Global production networks are prominent features of contemporary globalization and it is also true that a bulk of total international trade is intra-firm trade. Impediments to investment flows influence the pace and dispersal of production networks and consequently, as well, the direction and levels of trade.

It is understandable therefore that attention should increasingly focus on liberalizing investment flows as a complement to trade liberalization. It is not controversial to assert therefore that investments and trade are interlinked but the MAI negotiations were controversial partly because the forum was not a multilateral agency but rather the OECD. Indeed, the Multilateral Agreement on Investments was a misnomer and it should, more appropriately, have been termed the Plurilateral Agreement on Investments. Perhaps, the MAI was so named in the expectation that it would become quickly multilateralized through the WTO. Indeed the WTO participated in the OECD negotiations as an observer and was on record as sympathetic to the endeavor, having agreed that "based on the available evidence, the case for a multilateral agreement on investment is strong."[1]

Developed countries had reasons for not utilizing the WTO mechanism for MAI negotiations. They wanted a high standards agreement with no controls and impediments to FDI flows whereas most developing countries still favored regulating foreign investment to ensure consistency with developmental goals and aspirations. Using the WTO as the negotiating forum would have led, necessarily, to compromises to appease the less enthusiastic members whereas limiting initial participation and implementing a process of sequential expansion would have allowed for a more liberal regime on investments. In general, Downs *et al.* observe that

> the sequential construction process provides the more regulation-oriented or liberal states that usually play an important role in creating multilaterals with an ability to expand an institution's size while maintaining more control over the evolution of its policies than would otherwise be possible. The result is a multilateral that is far more liberal than if the desires of the "median states" of the potential population of members carried the day.[2]

FDI is not always easy to differentiate from portfolio investments but it is generally assumed that equity investments that confer on the investor an ownership stake greater than 10 percent constitutes FDI rather than portfolio investment. The primary flow of investment capital has been between developed economies, as both providers and recipients of direct investment. The OECD countries are major players in FDI, accounting for 85 percent of FDI outflows and 60 percent of FDI inflows, or $243 billion and $191 billion respectively, in 1995.[3] Apart from a few large developing countries, FDI flows to developing countries in general are modest but may still make up a significant portion of domestic investment capital. Foreign investment levels peaked in 1997, the year of the Asian financial crisis, and have since returned to more sustainable levels. In 2000, roughly 80 percent of global FDI was generated by Britain, France and Germany and in that same year the United States (US) and European Union (EU) accounted for more than three quarter of stocks of inward and outward investments. Japan was a large contributor to the outward flow of global FDI in the 1980s but has not been as receptive to inward foreign investments. Since the economic crisis of the early 1990s, Japanese foreign investment has been scaled back significantly.

The inward flow of FDI adds to domestic capital base and to the pool of capital available for investments. Where foreign investment does not overwhelm domestic industry, the introduction of foreign producers can inject competitive efficiencies in the economic system. Many countries have specific incentive schemes to attract foreign investment, such as tax holidays, but there is little empirical evidence that incentives alone are sufficient to alter the investment calculus of MNCs, which are based primarily on assessment of economic merit. On the margins however, firms may vary their investment decisions depending on the specific incentives provided by governments to secure an investment. As such, countries often compete with each other to attract foreign investment. This competition for FDI is also visible at the sub-national level and there is some evidence that national location of FDI is influenced by incentives schemes of local governments. In Australia, for example, the state government in Queensland was successful, through taxation and other incentive schemes, to entice Virgin Blue, a low-cost domestic airline, to locate its national headquarters in Brisbane, Queensland. Similarly, in the US, a number of state governments have provided generous subsidies to foreign car manufacturers to locate production facilities in their state. Such competitive behavior often is part of a general business strategy to attract all business, foreign and domestic, to locate manufacturing facilities or corporate headquarters in one state. States may gain through employment generation potential of new investment but incentive schemes to influence investment decisions usually benefit corporations at the expense of taxpayers and consumers who have to defray the costs of inducement packages.

While most FDI flow is between developed countries, a select group of developing countries have also received significant foreign capital inflows. Capital flows to developing countries first showed a marked increase in the decade of the 1970s, following the oil crisis, which generated sizeable surplus international liquidity.

The Latin American and East Asian countries were prime beneficiaries of foreign investment but while this produced a debt crisis in the 1980s in the former group as a result of mismanagement and poor investment decisions, foreign investment made it possible for East Asian countries to grow at a faster pace than would otherwise have been possible.

In the 1960s and early 1970s, many analysts and policy makers were skeptical about foreign investment, preferring to view it as a tool of exploitative foreign domination. MNCs, the main vehicles of FDI, also stood accused of being poor corporate citizens, for engaging in transfer pricing,[4] introducing inappropriate technologies and for crowding out domestic competitors. At the extreme, MNCs were also seen as agents of home country governments, interfering in domestic politics of host countries. These negative impressions of FDI were replaced by a more positive outlook following the rapid growth and transformation of East Asian countries with the assistance of substantial capital inflows. Net FDI flows to the "tiger" economies of East Asia increased rapidly in the 1980s and to other East Asian countries in the 1990s. In the late 1980s, net FDI flows to Cambodia, the Lao Peoples Democratic Republic and Vietnam were close to zero but increased to 9.4 percent, 6.4 percent and 5.6 percent of gross domestic product (GDP) in 1996.[5] Vietnam, in particular, has used high tariffs to encourage foreign firms to invest as a way of getting around trade restrictions but this strategy usually is appropriate in cases where national decision makers have established policies to enhance confidence in their economies. The Indo-Chinese countries, for instance, became attractive to foreign investors following the introduction of structural reforms and privatization in the mid-1980s. In East Asia, the Peoples Republic of China perhaps has benefited the most from foreign investment. In 2003, total FDI into China was about US$50 billion.

Apart from being more positively valued, the nature of FDI has also changed in the period of globalization. Linked to global production networks, FDI is now more a complement than a substitute for foreign trade, as it used to be, when foreign investment and production substituted for exports from the home market.[6] Consequently, the two tend to co-vary rather than move in an inverse relationship.

FDI flows are a relatively small fraction of total global capital flows and speculative and portfolio investments also had a significant economic impact in East Asia before the financial crisis of 1997. The crisis was a result of a number of domestic and international factors that triggered capital flight from several East Asian countries and was a sobering signal that capital inflow had to be carefully managed for it to be beneficial to growth and development. Nonetheless, the negative perceptions of the 1960s did not resurface and, on balance, developing countries have maintained conditions conducive to inflow of FDI. For instance, in 1998, UN Conference on Trade and Development (UNCTAD) identified 145 changes to FDI regulatory policies in 60 countries, of which 94 percent was intended to create a more welcoming environment.[7] But to maximize the benefit of foreign investments, developing countries also rely on regulatory structures to encourage industrial deepening, technology transfer, and introduction of labor and managerial skills into the country.

From a supply side perspective, however, it is inevitable that as the significance of foreign investment grows, investors will seek to harmonize and, indeed, to lower regulatory standards to create a more simplified FDI environment. In this, it is to the interest of developing countries that they engage in negotiations to ensure that any new and emerging global compact allows for special treatment for developing countries. The push for regulatory standardization however, was led by developed countries as part of an attempt to ease the burden on the corporate sector, which must deal with a fragmented global regulatory structure. And the choice of venue was rationalized by arguments that the WTO, the likely alternative forum for such negotiations, should deal only with trade, not investment issues.

However, the dichotomy between trade and investments is unconvincing since globalization can be understood, to a large extent, as the establishment of global production networks, based on FDI flows to appropriate production destinations with significant trade consequences. For example, the Ford Capri is produced in the United Kingdom (UK) with parts procured from more than a dozen countries where Ford, for example, has invested in production activities. This trade is related directly to a dispersed investment strategy by the Ford motor company. It is therefore disingenuous to suggest that trade issues and investment issues should be kept separate. Globalization has blurred any distinction that may have existed in earlier periods of trade interdependence. A position of denial is unlikely to serve the interests of developing countries and ultimately they will have to cede to pressures from the West and the corporate sector. Instead of denial, it may be worthwhile to prepare for such an eventuality.

At the same time, it was a tactical and strategic mistake, as we shall see next, for advanced countries to confine negotiations on an investments treaty to OECD countries, in the expectation that developing countries will then accede to the terms of the agreement. Any treaty should include participation and input from developing countries and the appropriate venue is the WTO rather than the OECD. By confining negotiations to the OECD, developed countries alienated developing countries and NGOs with interest in developmental issues. What was ultimately fatal to the MAI was the alienation of sections of their own society but, in future, success will require both developed and developing countries to agree on the merits of a standardized agreement that does not sacrifice the developmental interests of poor countries.

As mentioned, while capital flows have increased exponentially, there are no clear rules governing such flows. In the absence of uniform standards, bilateral investment treaties have proliferated and there were, in 2003, more than 2000 bilateral and regional investment treaties. Most of these treaties were concluded during the 1990s at a time when FDI was increasing rapidly. This proliferation of agreements has complicated the task of foreign investors, funds managers and currency traders, who must deal with a very complex and complicated legal environment that also provided no certainty about the long-term investment climate.

The Uruguay Round made a tentative start to global investments treaty. The agreement on trade related investments measures (TRIMs) proscribed local content requirements as well as subsidies to industries to encourage the use of local over imported inputs. All countries, except the least developed, committed themselves to gradually phase out these trade-distorting measures. The TRIMs agreement forced developing countries to give up some of the entry conditions imposed on foreign investors but stopped short of requiring, as the developed countries wanted, non-discrimination and national treatment of FDI.

To continue the process of liberalization and to bring order and consistency to the haphazard development of global investment regulations, developed countries initiated negotiations for a comprehensive MAI. The object was to standardize rules governing capital flows related to direct investment. As investors, it was understandable that developed countries wanted an investments regime that protected their interests but it was clear also that any agreement which excluded the input of developing countries would impede their capacity to use and exploit foreign investments to promote their developmental objectives by forcing them to compete with industrial countries on a level playing.

Initially, the European Commission proposed that simplification and harmonization of investments standards be negotiated under the auspices of the WTO. The US argued instead that the appropriate vehicle for negotiations was the OECD, composed of leading industrial countries. The American proposal for limiting negotiations to a small group of countries was not inconsistent with WTO procedures of conducting negotiations on specific products and commodities to the principal suppliers, producers, and consumers. This rule has been followed by the WTO for the sake of simplicity but has the obvious implication that others may choose only to accept or reject it, not to renegotiate the terms to suit their specific interests.

In any case, developing countries were opposed to a universal code on investments and their rejection precluded the WTO as the venue for negotiations. Developed and developing countries have very obvious and divergent interests in terms of foreign investments and capital flows and any WTO based negotiation would have no more than a slim chance of success. While the developed countries have an interest in unencumbered FDI flows, developing countries, in the past, have imposed various performance criteria on foreign investments to develop local managerial skills, enhance export revenue, transfer technology, and strengthen backward or forward linkages to the domestic economy. By excluding developing countries from the negotiations, the OECD seemingly played down the significance of foreign investment to total investments in many developing countries and their legitimate interests in ensuring a balanced agreement.

While negotiation was confined to the OECD, there was an implicit expectation that, in time, the developing countries would either willingly or under pressure agree to be bound by the resultant agreement. In a sense, limiting negotiations to OECD members was not too unlike policy making process within the WTO, where key decisions are formulated by the so-called green room groups, comprised mainly of the developed countries but forced upon all WTO members. LDC acceptance of the MAI was more likely to be the case once participation in the MAI had reached a critical mass, which would endow investors the power "simply to choose between MAI participants in their locational decisions" and starve others of foreign investment funds.[8] According to Woodward, the proposed terms of the MAI would intensify competition among potential host countries to attract FDI with offers of concessions and inducements that will in the end limit the developmental and welfare benefits per dollar of investment.

As major players in global capital flows, the developed countries expected to be key beneficiaries of a liberal code on investments. A Canadian study, for example, found that an increase of US$1 billion in incoming FDI produced, over a 5-year period, an additional 45,000 jobs and added $4.5 billion to GDP. It is understandable, therefore, why the OECD should be interested in a liberal and transparent code that is comprehensive and uniform. The argument for liberalization was extended also to developing countries on the assumption that existing barriers to foreign investors had choked off the supply of foreign investments.

The US government also reasoned that negotiations within a smaller group of countries with similar interests was most conducive to the conclusion of a treaty of very "high standards," meaning a virtually unfettered regime for foreign investments. US-based MNCs wanted the right to engage in direct dispute resolution with host countries as well as freedom from performance requirements. The US government felt that divergent interests of developed and developing countries would complicate negotiations under the auspices of the WTO and produce a considerably watered-down agreement catering to the lowest common denominator. For instance, it was well recognized that developing countries would not agree to withdraw performance requirements imposed on foreign corporations. The US was also arguably driven by a desire to multilateralize the tough provisions of North American Free Trade Agreement's (NAFTA) chapter 11 and the privileges granted to corporations. This, in turn added to the concerns of Canadian NGOs and environmentalists that the MAI was "NAFTA on steroids" and, therefore, had to be resisted. They ultimately played a critical role in mobilizing popular hostility to the provisions of MAI.

Although developing countries were excluded from formal negotiations, there was an expectation that these countries would eventually accept the terms of the final agreement. Indeed, once negotiations were underway, the concern for developing countries was that a refusal to accept the terms and conditions of the MAI would adversely affect their capacity to attract foreign investment. If successful, the proposed MAI was to be a freestanding treaty among the 29 OECD member countries but accession was to be available to non-OECD countries that met its obligations. The ultimate stated objective was that the MAI would, at some stage, be adopted by the WTO. The WTO Secretariat, along with a few non-OECD members, like Brazil, participated in the MAI negotiations as observers.[9]

Negotiations on the MAI began in 1995 and agreement took a year longer than originally scheduled. When the draft text of the treaty became public, consumer and citizens' groups within OECD countries denounced it as undermining state sovereignty and for favoring MNCs. While developing countries had legitimate grounds for rejecting an investments regime in the first place, critics in developed countries worried being swamped by foreign corporations. In the US, critics raised the specter of European and Japanese multinationals becoming dominant players in the American economy. Public criticism was fueled also by a perception that negotiations were carried out in secrecy to benefit MNCs and without adequate safeguards of national interests. The main provisions of the MAI were:

1. National treatment: treat foreign investors at least like domestic investors but for all practical purposes, more favorably.
2. Most favored nation (MFN) status: All foreign investors to be treated alike.
3. Elimination of performance criteria: No regulatory requirement on foreign investors to employ local managers, meet export conditions, or transfer technology.

4. Ban uncompensated nationalization: foreign investors had a right to full and fair compensation for any expropriation of assets.
5. Investor-to-state dispute resolution: private investors could directly challenge the legality of states policies.[10]

The draft of the MAI read like a bill of rights for the corporate sector. It appeared to enfranchise large MNCs while disenfranchising the ordinary people. Indeed, MNCs were the main advocates of a regime of high standards that would protect and promote their global interests. By 1993, for example, annual sales of foreign affiliates of parent MNCs were estimated at US$6 trillion, greater than total world trade in goods and services. MNCs also account for two-thirds of all global trade.[11]

The draft made it clear that national governments could not enact policies to favor domestic corporations over foreign corporations but went on to propose that "there would be nothing to stop governments from treating foreign corporations more favorably than domestic ones."[12] Of course the underlying assumption was that any concession granted by governments to a foreign MNC would automatically be extended also to domestic firms to ensure they were not unfairly disadvantaged. Still, according to Barlow and Clarke,

Under the MAI, virtually all the rights are accorded to foreign-based corporations, while governments are saddled with virtually all the obligations . . . They [MNCs] are supercitizens in a new world order where ordinary people, disenfranchised and unprotected, have had their political rights stripped away.[13]

The draft MAI agreement replicated the GATT principles of MFN and national treatment. States agreed not to differentiate and discriminate against foreign investment and they will also be obligated not to discriminate against the source of foreign investment. This meant that states could not be permitted to apply discriminatory performance standards (export quota; local content etc) on foreign investment. The only concession was that members could prepare a list of exemptions, such as for cultural industries, upon joining or acceding to the MAI.

The MAI was hostile also to the interests of developing countries. It privileged MNCs but most developing countries, of course, did not have MNCs, which might benefit from provisions contained in the MAI. As such, any LDC that submitted to the agreement would, in effect, be granting market access on a unilateral basis. It is true that developing countries could negotiate an initial set of exemptions but in reality many developing countries do not have in place and also do not know which policies are critical to promoting development of any particular industry or sector. In effect, the MAI provisions prevented developing countries from pursuing the same sort of policies that the East Asian economies had successfully employed in the early stages of development, when FDI was regulated and subject to performance criteria. The argument that a global investment regime would facilitate access to foreign capital for developing countries also was of dubious merit. A World Bank report in late 2002 suggested that a global investment regime was unlikely to lead to capital flows to developing countries. The report observed that existing bilateral treaties had not led to any increased capital flows to developing countries and treaties, like the MAI, were unlikely to be of any significant benefit.[14]

If, however, we assume that removal of restrictions and conditions on foreign investment did lead to additional investments in developing countries, there might still be only marginal benefits to developing countries. Precisely because governments would be barred from imposing performance targets, any additional investment, according to Elissa Braunstein and Gerald Epstein, would be a hollow victory. They argued that:

> To the extent that the MAI increases or enhances foreign investment in developing countries, we argue constraints imposed on developing country governments make it extremely difficult to capture the benefits of increased FDI and portfolio investment, and are likely to result in merely a redistribution of what benefits are created away from host countries to multinational investors.[15]

Yet, even if the MAI was understood to be of dubious benefit, developing countries, on their own, could do little to prevent its passage. That task was taken up by a range of disparate groups and NGOs in developed countries, which objected to the rights and privileges granted to business and to global businesses over local firms and consumers. They objected to the erosion on national sovereignty and democratic governance as a result of privileges accorded to the corporate sector. Fundamentally, it seemed arrogant that democratic governments were negotiating an important economic agreement without, first, having its merits debated in national parliaments. Activists in Canada and the US orchestrated the opposition to MAI and their primary tool for mobilizing global resistance was the internet. Globalization spawned the MAI agreement and protestors used a key prop of globalization, internet and rapid global communications, to mobilize resistance to the agreement. They used the tools of globalization to defend the national interest and for nationalistic purposes. The main criticisms of the MAI were:

1. that it was negotiated in secret and in an undemocratic manner (by international bureaucrats without too much input of elected officials), and
2. that the terms and conditions of the MAI diminished national sovereignty and privileged MNCs over nation-states.

Critics raised concerns that the agreement privileged MNCs at the expense of states because MNCs were granted the right to sue individual states for damages resulting from non-compliance, a right that is not available to either MNCs or to local companies. The defenders of national sovereignty worried, in particular how foreign interests might override domestic political authority. This was a powerful nationalistic argument, and a prominent convert was Ralph Nader. As a recognized consumer advocate might have focused on how globalization might benefit the American consumer but he, instead, was more preoccupied with defending American sovereignty. It was odd also that he was active in opposing the Uruguay Round and the establishment of the WTO because these would erode American sovereignty over trade policy making. Not only in the US, but he traveled also to other countries in the hope of awakening the same xenophobia. It is instructive that the defense of national prerogative had underpinned the refusal of international community to sanction the establishment of the International Trade Organization at the end of the Second World War.

Also, if the idea was to establish an open and transparent system for global capital flows, critics argued that the MAI was itself drafted in secrecy without information being given to people to evaluate and comment. International aid agencies, like Community Aid Abroad, argued that MAI was a crude exhibition of rule-making by the rich and the powerful to the detriment of developing countries. It is not a mystery why developed countries refused to accept a more inclusive negotiating strategy, especially as GATT itself had established a principle that negotiations on trade liberalization should be conducted by, in main, the principal supplier and principal buyer of a particular commodity. By this logic, the exclusion of developing countries was unwarranted as some developing countries, like China, are large recipients of FDI.

The quiet diplomacy of OECD negotiators was disrupted by the loud protests of NGOs and ordinary citizens against the perceived undemocratic negotiations process. Protestors condemned it as a blatant attempt by large corporations to usurp national sovereignty. Under pressure, the French government backed out of MAI negotiations in 1998 and this ended the ambitious attempt of the OECD to create a regime of "high standards" that was, for all purposes, skewed to the interests of MNCs and countries that were primary sources of foreign investments, the developed countries. It is quite likely, as has been suggested, that even had the OECD agreed to a text of the MAI, it would have failed the ratification process through national legislatures, with opposition to it coming from both the conservatives and the progressives, for instance, for failing either the sovereignty or the developmental test.[16]

The EU tried to reintroduce an agreement on investments as an agenda item in the WTO round in the late 1990s. The new EU trade commissioner, Pascal Lamy, proposed this saying that that was what corporations wanted. It is understandable that corporations want a universal set of codes to simplify their investment decisions but the reality is that economic conditions vary and no one set of codes is likely to find favor with countries spread out on the economic spectrum. A universal code would attract the same sorts of criticisms that have been leveled against IMF's structural adjustment programs, that they are formulaic and in conflict with specific economic conditions of the target countries. As such, despite EU push for inclusion of investments code, there was not enough support to reopen debate, especially so soon after the MAI fiasco. The issue however has not died down and is likely to be revived under a different guise at some point in the future. How the issue is finally resolved will depend, to a large extent, on whether developing countries can rise to the challenge and insist on a rules structure that is not overwhelmingly disadvantageous.

Conclusion

Negotiations for a MAI were premised on the erroneous assumption that a functioning global economy required elimination of regulatory controls across political boundaries. It envisaged eliminating political influence and interference from financial markets and if successful would have been a major step forward for the proponents of the Washington Consensus. The purpose went beyond regulatory harmonization or the elimination of egregious contradictions. The flaw was in ignoring the reality of national political sovereignty, diminished but not made obsolescent by globalization, and that independent political authorities have their own agenda for national and community development.

Under the terms of the MAI, governments would have been constrained even from offering community development grants without running foul of treaty provisions and inviting corporate demands for recompense. It was this fundamental weakness behind the OECD drive for sameness that triggered popular protest and disdain.

In the final analysis, the MAI did not pass public scrutiny when its contents became better understood. It deserved to be rejected and was, but for a mixture of right and wrong reasons. Some of the reasons given for its rejection were spurious, such as that an agreement that was drafted by unelected officials and bureaucrats was inconsistent with the spirit of democratic governance. The reality is that most national legislation and bills have considerable bureaucratic influence but the democratic process is preserved when such bills are approved in national parliaments and ratified by elected representatives. The MAI may have been drafted by bureaucrats but ultimately would have to be ratified by elected politicians in the signatory countries before gaining legislative status. Thus, in the end the democratic process would have prevailed when legislatures debated the merits of ratification.

Critics in the US and Canada also assailed the agreement for degrading US and Canadian national sovereignty and for giving undue privilege to foreign investors and corporations over American and Canadian companies, respectively. This was national chauvinism at work, dressed up in anti-globalization garb much like the earlier American rejection of an ITO immediately after the Second World War. There were no legitimate reasons for assuming that the presence of foreign corporations in the US or Canada was any worse than the presence of American and Canadian firms in other countries. Indeed, in most cases where developmental issues are not at stake, the difference between foreign and domestic industries is largely academic, as long as employment opportunities are not diminished, nor state revenue through transfer pricing. Until the early 1980s, the Japanese government maintained strict restrictions on inward FDI but critics argued that it did not matter whether owners or managers had blue or black eyes as long as employment and taxation base were maintained. Even so, the dispute resolution provisions of the MAI, as well a number of other features, were completely at odds with what would have secured popular support.

Jay Mandle argues that the MAI agreement may have been flawed in its design and likely consequences but that in "opposing the proposed treaty the [protest] movement revealed a willingness to employ a language of xenophobia inconsistent with its claim to represent a new internationalism."[17] Indeed the protestors used the tools of globalization to defend antiquated notions of nationalism. The MAI was a proposed agreement among developed countries and the protest movement was largely confined to these same countries. These protestors may have had interests in promoting a fairer system of economic globalization but their protest against the MAI was largely framed in terms of a loss of state sovereignty and the excessive privileging of private actors over the state. This protest movement was clearly a "protest against the system" and they were motivated by a determination to block the MAI rather than suggest improvements to the draft agreement. Protestors were successful in their objective but in the longer term, given the close nexus between trade and investments, it is inevitable that the MAI or something similar to it will rear its head and that just as the success of Seattle was short-lived, so will the anti-MAI coalition.

The MAI had proposed non-discriminatory, national treatment for foreign investment. The agreement deserved to be rejected for wrong-headed assumptions that national governments had no legitimate reasons for regulating MNC activity that might impinge on the economic welfare for their own citizens, and for placing corporations above host governments. If implemented, the MAI would have had particularly damaging consequences for developing countries and even though it was initially only going to be implemented by the OECD countries, once in place there would inevitably be strong pressure on developing countries to accept and to comply with its terms.

One controversial feature of the MAI draft was that it allowed for direct dispute resolution between states and private investors. The GATT and WTO by contrast only sanctioned government-to-government dispute resolution and by broadening the scope of dispute resolution, MAI left open the possibility of private investors commencing legal action against states in order to secure compensation on any number of grounds, expropriation, failure to remove discriminatory practices and so on. This provision irked critics unprepared to accept any diminution in the sovereign status of national governments.

Finally, Elisa Braunstein and Gerald Epstein argue that an MAI might only trigger, on a global scale, the sort of unhealthy competition that exists between states in the US to attract and retain investments within state borders. Individual States in the US offer incentive schemes and tax breaks to attract investments but these have become so widespread as to offset each other. They write that for many states, "the end result has probably been a 'race to the bottom', with little gain in jobs, less corporate tax revenues for the states, and fewer public services and higher taxes for the public."[18] Braunstein and Epstein concluded that the MAI, on balance, would have a negative effect on both developed and developing countries.

However, developed countries have not abandoned the pursuit of an agreement on investments. They managed to incorporate it as a new issue at the first Ministerial Conference of the WTO in Singapore. Admittedly this inclusion was accepted only as part of an "educative process" but Martin Khorr expressed concern that it is sometimes a small step from educative process to formal treaty given "pressures within the WTO towards rule-making . . . within an atmosphere of tension, fear, and suspicion."[19] He added a cautionary note that any MAI-like agreement will constitute a loss of sovereignty over national resources, prevent developing countries from nurturing local businesses and infant industries, and make it harder for countries to manage structural problems in balance of payments by resorting to controls on profit repatriation and so on.

In 2003, the educative process did turn into negotiations between the developed and developing countries on whether to authorize ministerial negotiations at Cancun, Mexico in September on an investment agreement. At the Doha ministerial meeting in 2001, WTO members had agreed to begin negotiations, provided there was "explicit consensus" on guidelines at Cancun. The demand for consensus was insisted upon by India and it has so far resisted the Western push to commence negotiations on grounds that the trade agenda[20] is already full and especially as there has been no agreement on any of the other important issues in the Doha Round.

Beyond Doha, however, it is likely that the issue of an investments treaty will resurface. It may be prudential to prepare for that eventuality rather than assume that the issue can be staved off for an indefinite period. But to ensure that the core interests of developed and developing countries are reflected in a final agreement, Braunstein and Epstein suggest a simplified negotiations format, with two countries from each group entrusted for drafting a text. The precedent for this might be the NAFTA which included both developed (Canada and the US) and developing (Mexico) countries. As far as NAFTA is concerned, however, its investment provisions are "high standard" along the lines of the proposed MAI and that may make it harder for the US to accept lower standards in a different forum, knowing that it could use the precedence of NAFTA to demand equal treatment to foreign investors in any future bilateral or regional negotiations on trade liberalization, outside the WTO should the WTO be incapable of delivering a high standards investments agreement.

But while "high standards" may be attractive Mandle correctly points out that the focus of international negotiations has to move beyond the originally conceived MAI to an appreciation of a compromise investment agreement that protected the interests of foreign investors without undermining development in poor countries. He argued that:

> The MAI failure identified the probable limits of contemporary global integration. It demanded a ceding of autonomy in policy making that was politically unrealistic. Clearly a scaling down from the requirement of the MAI is called for. Nevertheless, the case for a codification of global investment rules remains strong. What is needed is a rethinking of the MAI approach with a view to moving in the direction of its goals of non-discrimination and national treatment of foreign investment but, in so doing, respecting the limits of what is possible.[21]

It is clear also that if the forum of negotiations shifts to the WTO, it will be unable to deliver a high standards agreement and so, for an agreement to become possible, the industrialized countries may have to abandon attempts to draft a high standards agreement and aim for something that is politically viable and not too unfair to certain groups of countries. So far, "high standards" has become co-terminus with the interests of developed countries but any viable agreement will have to be a compromise between developed and developing countries. Moreover, given the incomplete nature of all regimes, it is safer perhaps to avoid the temptation to introduce high standard norms from the outset and aim for something practical and use the regime as a learning tool to devise more comprehensive and detailed norms over a period of time. The skeptics however will not be easily convinced. UNCTAD, for example, suggested that no such treaty was necessary because transnational corporations were flexible enough and experienced enough to operate in diverse conditions and adapt to regulatory differences among countries, without that becoming a deterrent to investments.[22]

4
Developing Countries and the World Trade Organization

Among multilateral agencies, the World Trade Organization (WTO) stands out in allowing equal voting rights to its members regardless of their economic size or trade weight. Thus, the value of a vote cast by a small member, say the Republic of Palau, is the same as that of its largest member, the United States (US). However, although a majority of WTO members are developing countries, power and control of the WTO has always been with the developed western countries because the WTO also enshrines the principle of decision making based on consensus. This gives any one country a potential veto, but for all practical purpose small developing countries encounter a great deal of pressure not to stand in the way of decisions reached among a small group of key states, primarily developed countries.

The one occasion when developing countries exercised their virtual veto was at the Cancun ministerial meeting of the WTO in 2003 but in the months that followed developed countries, in particular the US, exhorted them to be flexible or risk a collapse of the Doha Round. In the end, developed countries too recognized the importance of conciliation and an European Union (EU) willingness to phase out export subsidies on agricultural products, for example, made it possible for the Doha Round negotiations to recommence with the signing of the so-called July Framework Agreement in 2004.

Within the WTO, developing countries enjoy numerical superiority but without any commensurate level of influence. This is a hangover from the General Agreement on Tariffs and Trade (GATT). Indeed, if decision-making processes of GATT were equitable, developing countries might have participated more actively in its proceedings, instead of in the UN Conference on Trade and Development (UNCTAD), as was the case until recently. For example, even though 88 of the 117 countries that participated in the Uruguay Round of GATT negotiations were developing countries, their participation was perfunctory and sporadic rather than active and sustained. And as noted earlier, outcomes of the Uruguay Round were highly unbalanced. This led Michael Finger and Julio Nogues to declare that in "mercantilist economics the North was a big winner over the South at the Uruguay Round—in real economics an even bigger winner."[1] The developing South was compelled even to agree to a new regime on trade related intellectual property (TRIPs) without fully comprehending its long-term consequences.

The Uruguay Round Agreement was unbalanced in a range of issue areas. In textiles, for instance, liberalization of trade was required in four stages on the first day of 1995, 1998, 2002, and 2005 encompassing 16 percent, 17 percent, 18 percent, and 49 percent of imports by volume against the base year of 1990. Liberalization was back ended and in the first two stages only 33 percent of textile and clothing were to be liberalized but in reality the US liberalized only 1 percent, the EU 7 percent, and Canada 14 percent. Another casualty of the Uruguay Round, for developing countries, was the principle of special and differential treatment (SDT), a concession they had struggled hard to achieve in the 1960s. All that they managed to retain was an extended transition period to implement the same universally applicable outcomes. For instance, the TRIPs agreement provided uniform protection to patent holders with flexibility only in the phase-in period. Developed countries had to implement the new requirements by 1996, developing countries by 2000, and least developed countries by 2006 (extended later to 2016).

Leaving aside implementation of the Uruguay Round agreements, it is remarkable that developing countries agreed to the lop-sided agreement of the Uruguay Round in the first place. Finger and Nogues explain this in terms of lack of knowledge and information about actual realities and consequences and to clever strategies used by developed countries. In the Tokyo Round Codes, for example, developing countries could decline the obligations without losing protection of existing GATT rules but:

> The proposal to create a new organization to contain and administer the Uruguay Round agreements changed the rules of the game. The GATT/WTO heavyweights announced that as soon as the new organization existed they would withdraw from GATT. A country that voted "No" on joining the new organization would leave itself out in the cold—with neither GATT disciplines nor those of the new agreement to protect it.[2]

With a history of being manipulated and deceived, developing countries had much at stake in the Doha Round, not only to prevent a repeat of the unfair Uruguay Round agreements but also to try and rebalance the uneven playing field. The importance of rebalancing is highlighted by the double standards embedded into the global trading regime. While not all developing countries were in favor of launching a new round so soon after completing the Uruguay Round and before the Uruguay Round agreements had been fully implemented, South Africa was one of the countries in favor of a new round, if only to level the playing field and remove the inequities. According to Faizel Ismail, Head of the South African delegation to the WTO, developed countries have:

called for developing countries to open their markets [in agriculture], while maintaining huge subsidies and high tariffs that depressed global prices, undermining the development potential of developing countries (e.g. cotton). In the area of industrial products, developed countries retained high tariffs, tariff escalation and tariff peaks, for labour intensive products—precisely in the areas in which most developing countries had a comparative advantage.[3]

The Doha Round is the first time developing countries have negotiated in earnest, perhaps encouraged by promises that this will be the "development round," providing real benefits to the previously neglected majority. Developing countries were also more cognizant that institutions, including rules and norms, do matter in the allocation of costs and benefits.

As indicated earlier, the consensus rule has not necessarily worked in favor of developing countries[4] because they often find themselves excluded from decision-making processes but forced to assent to decisions under pressure from developed countries. They are disadvantaged also because they have little say in agenda setting. Nonetheless, developing countries took an active interest in the Doha Round, partly because it was designated as a "development round." Also, because it marked a new beginning in codifying rules and norms that would have a significant influence in shaping the global economy, and because the UNCTAD, to which they had hitched their economic fortunes, had produced little concrete benefits. As indicated earlier, the high point of developing country activism was the Cancun ministerial meeting in 2003 when they opted, practically the first time, to abandon negotiations rather than include the Singapore issues in the bargaining agenda. This effective exercise of veto was spearheaded by the Group of Twenty

(G-20), a grouping of developing countries formed shortly prior to the Cancun meeting. This critical stance transpired during the watch of Supachai Panitchpakdi, the first Director General of the WTO from a developing country and it is interesting also that developing countries had earlier used their numbers to secure the appointment of an individual who was likely to be sympathetic to their interests in multilateral trade negotiations.

Cancun stands out as an anomaly because developing countries have a history of being browbeaten into submission. Anticipating the start of a new trade round and with a legacy of disappointing results from earlier rounds, developing countries made a determined push to have their own representative installed at the head of the WTO. That decision is not without some justification. If a European and an American head the International Monetary Fund (IMF) and the World Bank, respectively, then there are no reason why a developing country representative should not oversee the third pillar of global multilateralism. Instead, a European national has, traditionally led the WTO and the GATT before it. For developing countries, gaining control of the WTO might not seem to be asking for too much but the reality is that WTO has progressively become a critically important institution, for developed countries and for the US, as it prepares to draft the ground rules for trade in a global economy. The stakes are high for both the developed and developing countries and control of the organization will be a contentious issue.

The Doha Round of the WTO[5] was launched in 2001 and promised to be significant not only for further liberalization in the traditional areas of international trade but also in the many new issues. More importantly, the Doha Round was significant also because, as the first negotiating round both under the auspices of the WTO and in the period of economic globalization, it was likely to set parameters for the evolving structure of globalization. Developing countries, cognizant of this, consequently took a more active interest in agenda setting and in negotiating outcomes, compared to earlier rounds of the GATT. They were keen also to revisit some of the agreements reached in the Uruguay Round and which had proved detrimental to developmental goals. In all this, they were encouraged by developed country promises and assurances that this round, unlike past GATT negotiating rounds, would provide positive pro-development outcomes.

Previous trade negotiating rounds had failed to safeguard the interest of developing countries. The main movers of the GATT were the developed countries and the trade negotiating rounds dealt with issues of concern to them. Developing country priorities were ignored or dealt with separately outside of the GATT system, in order to preserve developed country privileges and restrict export penetration of low cost producers in developing countries.

The Multi Fibers Agreement (MFA) is a good example of this systemic failure. Free of GATT discipline, the MFA became progressively more restrictive in scope and application. MFA restrictions were particularly harmful to developing countries because it denied them opportunities to consolidate their nascent textile industries through export growth. The Agreement protected inefficient but labor intensive, and hence politically sensitive, textile manufacturing in developed countries from foreign competition.

The GATT's major concession to developing countries was the Generalized System of Preferences (GSP). This was a mechanism introduced in the 1960s to grant developing country exports preferential access to markets in developed countries. The introduction of GSP was a belated acknowledgment that developing countries had a legitimate claim to SDT in order to achieve better growth outcomes. This was the international equivalent of "equal opportunity" legislation. The substantive impact of GSP has diminished with the progressive liberalization of international trade through the Tokyo and Uruguay Round trade negotiations but more recently even the principle of SDT has come under western criticism and is rapidly being eroded in favor of uniformity and non-discrimination. The recent attempts to enact a standard MAI or a set of uniform labor conditions are reflective of this fundamental shift in attitudes among policy makers in developed countries.

The final trade liberalization round of the GATT generally applied the principle of uniform rules for all members. This resulted in greater burdens for developing countries in implementing agreements. The Uruguay Round, the final GATT Round, made very little concession to the developing countries, apart from a slightly extended time frame for the implementation of trade accords. The final agreement had particularly substantial asymmetric impact on developing countries because these countries were subject to uniform rules on customs valuation, antidumping subsidies, and product standards and so on. This application of uniform standards ignored the special developmental needs of member groups and disadvantaged developing countries because of the additional compliance costs and greater relative concessions compared to developed countries. The United Nations Development Program (UNDP), in the early 1990s, calculated that the Uruguay Round agreements "would lead to an increase of $212–510 billion in global income . . . But the least developing countries, it argued, as a group would lose up to $60 million a year. Sub-Saharan Africa, containing a group of countries that could least afford losses and their associated social costs, would lose $1.2 billion a year."[6]

In other areas as well, the Uruguay Round demanded much from developing countries but provided only limited benefits to them. For instance, the TRIPs agreement provided copyright and patent protection for at least 20 years, which ignored the needs of some developing countries' for cheaper alternatives to patented products but generously compensated large multinational corporations (MNCs) for their research undertakings. On a positive note, the Uruguay Round was an important step toward broadening the global trade regime by bringing in trade in agriculture, textiles and services, two key issue areas quarantined from earlier negotiating rounds. Developing countries did not actively participate in negotiations on agricultural liberalization but they have invested considerable faith in the promised liberalization of textile trade. Textiles is an important export industry in developing countries but trade has been regulated by the MFA, under which developed countries have allocated quotas to exporting developing countries. An assessment of the importance of tariff and quota protection in developed countries can be gauged from the fact that while tariffs are not significant revenue raisers for developed countries, roughly 40 percent of all import duties raised in the US come from levies on textile and apparel imports.[7]

In return for liberalization of the textile trade, developing countries, as a *quid pro quo*, agreed to negotiate liberalization of services trade. In the end however, the agreement on textiles was a dismal disappointment, providing little significant benefit to exporters. More than half of the MFA liberalization was back-loaded to the end of the ten-year transition period, an outcome that really "dudded" the developing countries. According to one source:

> In their projections of the global economy in 2005, Hertel *et al.* (1995) find that the MFA will be even more restrictive in 2005, absent liberalization, than it is today. Even though products that remain restricted during the transition period benefit from progressively increasing quota, the increase in growth rates still may not be enough to keep up with projected changes in the global economy. The remaining quotas will therefore become more restrictive over time.[8]

The Uruguay Round provided for all textile quotas to be phased out at the end of 2005. However, as the deadline for quota removal approached, industries in developed countries began lobbying against import liberalization. In September 2002 the American Textile Manufacturers Institute, for example, filed a petition with the government for new quotas to be put in place after 2005. By the end of 2004, a dozen petitions had been filed with the US government to limit Chinese textile imports purely on the basis of perceived threat. The concerns of the US textile industry were well grounded. In the late 1990s, when quota restrictions on baby clothes and brassieres were removed, Chinese exports had surged 826 percent and 232 percent, respectively.[9] A repeat of that across a range of product categories will devastate American industry. Still, textiles is a labor-intensive industry and the there is no logical basis for its continued protection in the US and the West, except that as labor-intensive, it generates substantial employment and is therefore politically difficult to abandon to free market forces.

In response to rising protectionist sentiment in the US, the Chinese government announced, in December 2004, that it would impose an export tax on its textiles to prevent a flood of exports to the US. However, a less than prohibitive tax on exports could not appease the US where there is clear understanding that without quotas, US textiles is unlikely to survive Chinese competition. In 2004, total Chinese textiles exports to the US were US$625 million whereas in the first month of 2005 alone, once MFA quotas were removed, exports had reached US$160 million. Not surprisingly, in early April 2005, the US government moved a step closer to reinstating quotas on textiles when the Commerce Department announced an investigation to determine whether Chinese sales were disrupting domestic markets. Later in the year, the US imposed "safeguard restrictions" on Chinese textile imports, as permitted under the terms of China's admission to the WTO in 2001. Such restrictions are permitted through 2008 to protect American textile and clothing industry from any surge in Chinese exports.[10]

The removal of quotas eliminated a systemic obstacle to trade for developing countries but it promises also to be a mixed blessing. The quota system produced a geographic dispersion of manufacturing across a large number of developing countries and its removal could lead to a concentration of manufacturing in a few of the most competitive countries, most significantly China. China is not necessarily the least costly producer in terms of wages but it enjoys other advantages, such as better infrastructure and port facilities than competitors in South Asia. Under the regime of quota restrictions, large retailing giants, such as Wal-Mart in the US, had to source their imports from a large number of countries because of restrictive quotas but will, from 2005, be able to streamline their imports to a select few countries, such as China and some of the Caribbean and Central American countries.[11] The competitiveness of the last group of countries depends largely on American ratification of the Central American Free Trade Agreement (CAFTA) which will remove tariff restrictions. Many more developing countries with growing textiles industry will be hurt by the removal of quotas and the likely dominance of the Chinese in global textile markets. In 2003, China had a 17 percent share of global textile markets but WTO estimates are that its market share will exceed 50 percent in three years.[12]

Apart from safeguard restrictions on Chinese textile exports, Chinese industry, in general, also confronts likely protectionist action as a result of growing trade imbalance with the US. If Japan was the target of US protectionists in the 1980s and early 1990s, China could emerge as the new target country in the new millennium.

As Table 4.1 shows, US deficits in trade with China have grown considerably in recent years. They now exceed its deficits with Japan. Partly as a result of this, all the arguments of unfair trade that used to be leveled against Japan are now being marshaled against China. Former US Trade Representative Mickey Kantor proclaimed China to be in breach of its WTO obligations and suggested that a "shot across China's bow right now could prove helpful in addressing many of the problems we have now with China."[13]

In late November 2003, the US government announced new quotas on selected textiles imports from China. The action was justified under the safeguard conditions negotiated with China when it joined the WTO and meant to protect manufacturers against a surge in Chinese exports to the US. This action against Chinese exporters was popular domestic politics especially at a time of sluggish jobs growth. Overall,

Table 4.1   US trade deficit against China and Japan (US$ billion)

Year	China	Japan
1999	68.7	73.4
2000	83.8	81.5
2001	83.1	69.0
2002	103.0	69.9
2003	124.0	66.0
2004	161.9	75.5

Source: Foreign Trade Statistics, US Census Bureau.

since 2001 and late 2003 the US had lost 2.6 million jobs in the manufacturing sector, not necessarily because of foreign competition but perceived as such by many. Under these conditions, the prospect of losing more jobs in the labor-intensive textile sector as a result of trade liberalization could be politically damaging to the administration in an election year. Reimposition of quotas affected only a small portion of Chinese exports to the US but the Chinese government immediately canceled a scheduled trade mission, raising fears that China would cut expected imports from the US.[14] A trade war between these two large economies will be disastrous to the world economy and so, hopefully, after the electioneering is complete, the US government will step back from these protectionist measures, just as it did in the case of steel tariffs.

Global trade policymaking has been dominated by developed countries to advance their interests. Developing countries, with fewer resources and limited capacity, have found it difficult to structure trade rules to suit their developmental goals. Trade liberalization agreements have failed to deliver any significant gains to developing countries while demanding onerous policy changes and reforms. Developing countries have also been adversely affected by antidumping regulations of the WTO and their natural trade advantage in labor-intensive manufacturing has been subject to a number of unfair antidumping retaliation by developed countries. These weaknesses in existing trade arrangements were acknowledged in an August 1999 Trade and Development Report published by the UNCTAD.

Developing country push for control of the WTO

Given the potential gain from better access to foreign markets and the relative paucity of benefits from previous trade liberalization rounds, developing countries, with the support of Japan and Australia, nominated Supachai Panitchpakdi of Thailand, as the next WTO Director General in 1999. Within the WTO the members, of course, are the main players. It is essentially a member-driven, not a policy-driven organization and in that sense there are limits on the powers of the Director General. Indeed, a commonly heard argument is that the provenance of the Director General is immaterial to policy outcomes. But the Secretariat and the Director General do have some influence in shaping the agenda and developing modalities for negotiations. The Director General chairs the Trade Negotiating Committee and in that capacity can influence the direction or broker deals. Much depends on the style and ability of the Director General but they have considerable leeway in constructing negotiating parameters and influencing outcomes. This requires a willingness to take calculated risks to move negotiations forward and to breakthrough deadlocked situations. Among the more recent Directors General, Peter Sutherland was crucial to the completion of the Uruguay Round of the GATT as was Mike Moore in launching the Doha Round of the WTO.

In nominating a developing country candidate, the assumption was that such a representative would allow developing countries a greater say in finalizing the negotiating agenda as well as ensure a more balanced outcome in the Doha Round.[15] This was a legitimate strategy given that developing countries had failed to have their concerns addressed in previous rounds. Developing countries, for example, have special interest in liberalization of agricultural markets, textiles and other labor-intensive manufactured products. These are also among the most protected markets in developed OECD countries. For example, OECD protection of agriculture is highest in products in which developing countries have a comparative advantage, such as rice and sugar. Average developed country tariff on the agricultural exports of developing countries is about 16 percent, far higher than average industrial tariffs. Manufactured exports of developing countries, nearly 80 percent of total exports, are concentrated in textile and apparel and these are, as noted earlier, also the most heavily protected markets in industrial economies.

Three quarters of WTO members are developing countries, but the nomination of Supachai was not well received by many developed countries. The opposition to Supachai was led by the US, which instead proposed Mike Moore of New Zealand to be the next WTO chief. Although neither candidate had much experience in multilateral organizations, each was well-qualified to lead the WTO, having played prominent roles in national politics. Moore was a former trade union activist and served briefly as prime minister of New Zealand while Supachai was a former deputy prime minister of Thailand.

The split over leadership was largely about influencing the agenda for the next round of trade talks, Supachai having publicly declared that his first priority would be to ensure that benefits of free trade were evenly distributed, and not concentrated in advanced countries. According to Jean Francois Boittin, minister counselor for economic and commercial affairs at the French Embassy in Washington, "The US prefers Moore because Supachai is more likely to listen to lesser developed countries' concern on revising the WTO statutes on antidumping."[16] By the same token, Moore was perhaps the preferred candidate because he was more likely to protect Western interests especially as the WTO had been shown to have the powers to intrude into national sovereignty, for instance, when it struck down an American law that restricted the import of shrimp from countries that permitted shrimp catch without the use of "turtle exclusion devices."[17] The US law had been termed discriminatory because WTO provisions proscribe against exclusion of imports based on production processes. Moreover the necessity of exercising control over the WTO was felt more keenly as the next round of trade talks would include agriculture and textiles, issue areas of concern not only to developing countries but also to developed countries.

Developing countries hope for better access for their exports, especially agricultural goods and textiles, while steering away from a broadbased agenda that would only add more to their plate when they were already struggling to implement the measures from the last round. They also want existing inequities redressed before being burdened with additional obligations. For instance, developing countries see antidumping provisions as unfair and subject to misuse by developed countries to protect their markets from cheaper developing country exports. There are numerous examples of successful developing country exports that have been denied market access by developed countries, with the help of antidumping charges. Developing countries also are not keen to negotiate labor and environmental standards in the context of trade negotiations, preferring to deal with such issues elsewhere, such as the International Labor Organization (ILO).

By contrast, the EU and the US are committed primarily to market liberalization and access, investment and competition rules, labor and environmental standards, and agricultural and services trade. With different agenda, each side was simply trying to protect its interest by controlling the office of the Director General of WTO. The dispute was acrimonious and it was the first time small and weak countries had stood up to resist American–European hegemony. Supachai was subject also to a dirty tricks campaign to oust him from the leadership contest. For example, the Chairman of the WTO General Council announced prematurely that a consensus should be formed around Mike Moore as the next Director General. Supachai was even enticed with offers of interesting but essentially "non-existing" jobs, such as that of policy liaison between WTO, IMF and International Bank for Reconstruction and Development (IBRD).

The leadership contention had no easy solution given WTO's consensus rule; the decision, in the end, was to split an extended term of six years between the two candidates. The compromise, and subsequent appointment of Supachai as WTO Chief in 2002 strengthened the position of developing countries in the ongoing Doha Development Round but whether it would translate to superior outcomes was uncertain. The Doha Round launched under the leadership of Mike Moore was less than favorable to developing countries, which wanted the new round to focus also on problems and inequities created by the Uruguay Round. However, the Doha Declaration contained no firm guidelines to resolve the issues raised by the developing countries. Instead, there was considerable pressure on them not to delay a consensus agreement on the pretext that in the aftermath of September 11, failure to commence trade liberalization talks would endanger the health of the global economy and exacerbate a global economic downturn.

The following WTO ministerial meeting, at Cancun, was convened under the leadership of Supachai Panitchpakdi and there was again pressure on developing countries to cede on their opposition to the Singapore issues, including liberalization of government procurement policies. For example, at Doha, the US and EU pushed an "unbalanced draft declaration" on which there was allegedly consensus, restricted the arena of substantive discussion and made it difficult for developing countries to raise objections without seeming obstructionist.[18] Developing countries, in a rare display of unity, remained unmoved and demanded firm commitments of agricultural liberalization, an issue of considerable importance to developing countries. They chose to be obstructionist rather than have an unfair agreement thrust upon them. In the end, the outcome at Doha was unhelpful to developing countries but the collapse of Cancun, again, does not represent a triumph for developing countries, since it is in their interest to preserve global multilateralism rather than see a proliferation of bilateral and regional trade deals from which they are likely to be excluded.

Developing countries may be a majority in the trade organization but that fact brings no intrinsic voting advantage because of the consensus rule of the WTO. Decision making in the WTO is based on consensus and this undermines the theoretical "one country; one vote" principle. Negotiations are also usually conducted among a small group of countries, known as the "green room group," without regard to transparency, and the outcomes are usually placed before the WTO membership for ratification without changes. The green room group comprises a small number of countries, essentially the large industrialized countries, that meet in the so-called green rooms to decide on policy issues that are subsequently placed before the WTO members for approval. This practice has robbed developing countries of opportunities to influence policy-making inside the WTO. Moreover, if there is any strength in numbers, the developing countries are weakened by dissension and divergent interests. This is a perennial problem in large groups, compounded by countries at different stages of development, different interests, and varying level of connectedness to the global economy.

For these reasons, developing countries, despite their interests in helping shape the rules of engagement are in danger of marginalization, as a result of external environmental constraints and internal group dynamics. One year after the launch of the development round, talks on several issues of interest to the developing countries, such as agricultural liberalization and access to generic drugs, had already reached a difficult impasse with resistance from some European countries and the US to removing existing protectionist measures. Developing countries, too, for a change managed to avoid succumbing to pressure and formed a small group to push for their demands in agricultural liberalization. The G-20 has avoided the weaknesses of large groups in taking collective action but its longer term prospects are uncertain.

The reality is that the WTO, and the GATT before it, has not served developing countries very well. In 2003 a number of developing countries met in Dhaka, Bangladesh for a trade summit and to coordinate their actions at the WTO's ministerial conference in Cancun in September 2003. The summit produced the Dhaka Declaration, a list of demands that was to be presented to the WTO in September. On that occasion, the Bangladesh Minister of Commerce noted the cruel irony that cows in Japan, for example, received daily subsidies of US$7.50 when more than a billion people in developing countries were forced to survive on less than a dollar a day. He asked rhetorically whether the WTO was there in order to protect cows or the underprivileged people in poor countries.[19]

From the perspective of developing countries, neither the WTO, nor its predecessor—the GATT, have delivered any substantial economic benefit to promote their development. The question still was unfair as the mandate of the WTO is not specifically to protect the poor but rather to promote liberal trade practices and provide a firewall against any resurgence of protectionism. If the WTO is to be faulted, it is that it has failed to apply the principles of free trade uniformly and across the board. Yet again, the fault is not entirely that of the WTO, which has so far only been a handmaiden of the large member countries that dominate policy making. The developing countries are a majority and they will have to continue to press hard for a more democratic representation that extends beyond the sham of consensual decision-making.

Déjà vu in 2004–05?

Developing countries may have had high expectations from a Director General representing the global South but, in retrospect, it should be noted that Supachai's tenure as Director General was not a resounding success for the WTO, which witnessed the sidelining of its Secretariat while the EU and US assumed the initiative in pushing trade negotiations forward. Insiders also portray Supachai as unprepared to take risks by being more active and assertive and if developing countries had expected his tenure to help their cause, they will have been somewhat disappointed.

In late 2004, as the term of Pantichpakdi Supachai neared completion in August 2005, several developing country candidates nominated for the position of Director General, including Jayakrishna Cuttaree, the Mauritian Foreign Minister, Carlos Perez del Castillo, Uruguay's Permanent Representative to WTO, and Seixas Correa, Brazilian Ambassador to the WTO. It is interesting to note that Uruguayan candidate Carlos Perez del Castillo had, in 1999, represented a group of ten countries which included the US and read out a statement on their behalf calling on Dr Supachai to bow out voluntarily from the contest.[20] In early December 2004 the EU nominated Pascal Lamy, the former EU Trade Commissioner for the position of Director General.

The US endorsed Lamy as a "strong candidate" even though in WTO negotiations he had, expectedly, been a partisan advocate of the EU position on agricultural issues. Reflecting western sentiments, the *Financial Times* declared Lamy the front runner and the position of Director General for him to lose, a belief strengthened by the split in the Latin American bloc.[21] In a bid to avoid a repeat of the earlier leadership contest, western observers were quick to argue against political considerations (the numerical superiority of developing countries) in selecting a successor to Supachai in favor of competence and merit, qualities that Lamy would presumably bring to the position. Peter Mandelson, Lamy's replacement as EU Trade Commissioner, added his support for Lamy saying that "Our starting point should be to get the best person to do that job for a full mandate."[22] Lamy certainly is an experienced trade negotiator and presumably will position himself as a neutral arbiter if appointed as Director General but developing countries can be forgiven for being wary because Lamy had played a leading role in hammering out the July [2004] Framework Agreement on Agriculture along with his American counterpart Zoellick.

The July Framework Agreement has become the basis for continuing agricultural negotiations in the WTO and in one of his last acts, Lamy cleverly put the EU's export subsidies up for discussion in the Doha Round. This may attract the support of poorer developing countries but the Framework Agreement also provided for countries to include certain commodities as so-called sensitive goods and exempt from liberalization. A recent World Bank study by Will Martin and Kym Anderson found that only a limited number of inclusions in the sensitive category, such as rice, beef, milk, fruits and vegetables, would be enough to negate much of the potential benefit for developing countries from any future agreement.

Developing countries may worry that Lamy will be partisan but western media portrayed him as the front-runner in the contest. Lamy's candidacy was respected as strong but he had also created unnecessary opposition. In particular, a proposal to declare the Amazon region and other rain forests as "global public assets" because of their critical role in maintaining environmental balance and worthy therefore of global management angered Brazilian nationalists who dismissed the proposal as an attack on their national sovereignty. This could prompt the Brazilian government to mobilize consensus against Lamy among the seven countries that share the Amazon region.[23] Lamy was also reported to have remarked after Cancun that WTO decision making is medieval. He has made numerous strong statements that could potentially come back to haunt his candidacy.

At the same time, Brazil's nomination of Luiz Felipe de Seixas Correa was widely interpreted more as a spoiling tactic rather than a genuine bid for the top WTO position. The Brazilian government did not hide its antipathy toward the Uruguayan candidate and the entry of Seixas Correa was essentially to prevent consensus around del Castillo, who was known to be friendly toward the US. Del Castillo also had the support of a key Cairns Group member, Australia, because he was educated in Australia. Of the two Latin American candidates, del Castillo had less strong developing country credentials because of his support for initiating negotiations on two of the four Singapore issues. On the other hand, Brazil was a prominent member of the G-20 and while Brazil and US seemingly had stepped back from angry finger-pointing, the US was still unlikely to support Seixas Correa in his bid. Seixas Correa was well liked by many WTO members because of his advocacy of developing country interests and interestingly, even the newly elected leftist government of Uruguay was rumored to switch its support to Seixas Correa rather than its own WTO representative.[24] With three candidates, developing countries were well placed to have their preferred candidate selected to the top position but there was a strong possibility that Latin American rivalry would play into Lamy's hand as del Castillo and Seixas Correa spoiled each others chances.

Each candidate represented a particular geographic region and success required, as an essential condition, the capacity to win overwhelming regional support. The choice of a Director General is based not solely on considerations of merit but to a large extent on bloc politics. The Latin American countries had complicated their chances by fielding two candidates. Cuttaree, on the other hand claimed he had the support of the 79-country ACP (African, Caribbean, and Pacific) group, including the 53 nation African Union.[25] If correct this would have given him majority support within the WTO but his candidacy was weakened by doubts about his experience. Mauritius is a small country with a population of around one million and it is questionable that a ministerial post will have adequately prepared him to lead a major multilateral institution. These factors enhanced the prospects of Lamy succeeding Supachai. By mid-May 2005, following a series of elimination rounds, the three developing country candidates had withdrawn and Lamy's nomination as the next Director General was a mere formality, pending endorsement by the General Council. The General Council reached a consensus decision on the next Director General in mid-2005, and Lamy began his tenure on September 1, 2005.[26]

Conclusion

Developing countries had pushed hard for their own nominee to head the WTO and expected much from him. Supachai however, was hobbled by an abbreviated tenure and his personality as a mild-mannered individual has led him to shy away from exercising forceful leadership and take risks in forging consensus. The fact that the position of Director General has no clearly laid out job description can be either a source of strength or weakness. In this instance, it proved to be the latter but in similar situations, individuals have been able to carve out a significant role for themselves. Thus analysts have identified the "Estrada Factor," the role of the Chairman of COP3 (Conference of the Parties) in completing a consensus based agreement on reducing greenhouse gasses at Kyoto in 1997.[27] Unlike his predecessor, Estrada the Argentinian Ambassador to China, played an "outstanding leadership role" and was crucial in moving the negotiations toward differential targets for individual countries. He also resisted the push by the US governments to include developing countries on grounds that such a move would be in violation of the Berlin Mandate reached at COP1 in 1995.

Supachai was content with a low-key, honest broker role at the WTO and his truncated term, too, did not help him become a more assertive player. In his absence, it was sometimes left to the Chair of the General Council to step in with creative solutions to break negotiating deadlocks. According to one interviewee, Supachai was sidelined when the US and the EU hammered out the July Framework Agreement in 2004, about which he was completely unaware. While Supachai has been less than an effective advocate of developing country interests within the WTO, the position is not inconsequential, as some have observed. Some of his predecessors have, indeed, been more assertive and while the WTO is ostensibly a member-driven organization, the Director General can use his office to put forward creative proposals to bridge disagreements among members or to move then in a particular direction. There have been influential director generals in the past but any developing country nominee will be compromised if the larger countries chose to do so.

5

The Doha Round and Pharmaceutical Trade

The Doha Round was initiated in 2001 with an expectation that negotiations will be completed by end of 2005. By September 2003, it had become obvious that the deadline was unrealistic, as negotiations had come to a grinding halt. If negotiators hoped for an early re-start after Cancun that too, proved impossible. For nearly a year the fate of the Doha Round hung in the balance. Finally the July 2004 Framework Agreement restarted negotiations with an expectation that, if not by the original deadline, the Doha Round will ultimately be brought to a close at some later date. Cancun, at this stage, marks not a tragic watershed for multilateral trade policy but a temporary setback that may, indeed, produce a more balanced and equitable outcome for all members of the World Trade Organization (WTO). A key test of members' commitments to find common ground will be the sixth ministerial meeting of the WTO in Hong Kong in December 2005. To appreciate the pitfalls and potential, we need to examine and explore the issues and negotiating agenda of the Doha Round as well as domestic political difficulties confronting negotiators.

The agenda for the Round is vast and, as the officially designated development round, a test of its success will be outcomes that deliver real benefits to developing countries. Apart from expectations that agriculture will be liberalized, developing countries to expect to negotiate a fair deal on access to drugs, complicated by the earlier Uruguay Round agreement on trade related intellectual property (TRIPs).[1] In this chapter, I will look at issues surrounding trade in pharmaceuticals and, in Chapter 6, discuss the many complications that have plagued negotiations to liberalize agricultural trade.

The Doha ministerial meeting that initiated negotiations also produced a declaration on TRIPs and Public Health that recognized the gravity of public health issues in developing countries and the obstacles to treatment posed by the TRIPs regime. The agreement on intellectual property was part of the Uruguay Round Agreement and has become the third pillar of the WTO, alongside trade in goods and services. When it was negotiated, some governments, like India, opposed its restrictive implications but few recognized its full potential import. According to Arvind Subramanian TRIPs has "turned out to be among the more significant elements of international cooperation and treaty making in the past decade."[2] Under TRIPs, member countries are obliged to protect technological innovations for a period of 20 years. The agreement has made it difficult for developing countries to access cheap generic medicines produced under license by other countries, even though the TRIPs agreement includes formal provisions for compulsory licensing especially where matters of public health are concerned. Recognizing the health consequences of trade restrictions, the Doha Declaration stated in paragraph 4 that:

> We agree that TRIPS agreement does not and should not prevent Members from taking measures to protect public health. Accordingly, while reiterating our commitment to the TRIPS Agreement, we affirm that the Agreement can and should be interpreted and implemented in a manner supportive of WTO Members' right to protect public health and, in particular, to promote access to medicines for all.

This was significant because the TRIPs Agreement had become, as developing countries feared, an instrument of the West to "prevent them from addressing their public health needs."[3] The United States (US) threatened sanctions against South Africa and took Brazil to WTO dispute settlement mechanism to prevent them from using generic antiretroviral medicines (ARV) to treat human immunodeficiency virus (HIV) infections. The US was forced to withdraw under intense international pressure and to avert a public relations disaster but these actions were indicative of dangers inherent to the TRIPs regime.

TRIPs and access to affordable pharmaceuticals

In order to be able to provide adequate health treatment, developing countries have argued for access to cheaper generic drugs but stiff American opposition has stymied their demands. The Doha Declaration on TRIPs Agreement and Public Health, adopted on November 14, 2001, recognized the public health problems of developing and countries, especially those resulting from HIV acquired immune deficiency syndrome (AIDS), tuberculosis, malaria and other epidemics and highlighted the importance of appropriate mechanism to enable developing countries to treat these health concerns with generic drugs without falling foul of existing patent protection. Of the many health issues confronting developing countries, AIDS is of particular concern to the sub-Saharan African countries where there are approximately 30 million people infected with the AIDS virus, out of a global total of 42 million. AIDS is spreading rapidly and figures released by UNAIDS and the World Health Organization (WHO) in late 2003 estimated total AIDS related deaths in 2002 at 2.8. Sub-Saharan Africa alone accounted for 2.3 million AIDS related deaths in 2002. AIDS has become the primary cause of death in Africa and the fourth leading cause of deaths worldwide. UNAIDS and WHO also warned that the epidemic was likely to worsen further before its spread was contained and the trend line reversed.[4] Infection rates in Africa, too, are high and a survey in the late 1980s reported, for example, that in the town of Gisenyi, on the borders of Rwanda and Congo, the virus had infected about 31 percent of the adult population and that more than half of all people aged between 26 and 40 were infected by the AIDS virus. In 2002, South Africa had the highest numbers of AIDS sufferers, 5.3 million, while Botswana had the highest infection rate, about 39 percent.[5]

The economic consequences of the AIDS epidemic will continue to haunt local economies for many years to come. Apart from rising health care costs, AIDS deaths will halt market expansion and lower life expectancy in these countries. The resulting productivity losses will make development even more of an illusory goal. The least developed economies of sub-Saharan Africa face not a decade, as the 1980s was for Latin American countries, but decades lost to development unless there is concerted global response to the health challenge.

Not only has the global community been slow to respond to the AIDS epidemic, existing multilateral agreements, such as the TRIPs, have also stood in the way of effective national response to the crisis. Agreement on TRIPs was negotiated during the Uruguay Round of the General Agreement on Tariffs and Trade (GATT). In May 1990, developing countries (Argentina, Chile, Cuba, Egypt, India, Nigeria and few others) proposed a regime that would not be much different from the position obtaining in the prevalent laws on patents in developing countries. Developed countries proposed a strict regime that would universalize the patent protections available to firms in developed countries. Under pressure, most developing countries, barring India, accepted the western position on patent protection. India remained steadfast against the inclusion of pharmaceutical in patent protection and also argued for patent protection not exceeding 5 years, which was considerably less than the 20 years that developed countries had proposed.[6]

The TRIPs regime provides much more extensive trade protection than is permitted for trade in goods and services. Patent protection delays the market introduction of, and trade in generic pharmaceuticals and allows manufacturers to market their products to developing countries at excessively high prices. Another implication of the TRIPs regime is that it limits competition in developing country markets, resulting in higher economic costs for both consumers and producers. The magnitude of costs are indeterminable but assumed to be substantial and unlikely to be offset by gains in technology transfers from developed countries, or from development of new technologies and drugs specifically for application in developing countries. But Michalopoulos writes that there is little evidence of the supposed positive effects in the years since the new mechanisms were agreed upon.[7] By contrast, there is no evidence that weak protection of property rights has hampered the flow of foreign investments and technology to developing countries, such as China. As a result of TRIPs, developing countries are left with severely limited access to cheap medicines to combat epidemics and other health concerns. In sub-Saharan Africa, members of PhRMA (Pharmaceutical Research and Manufacturers of America) initially marketed ARVs at prices comparable to Organization for Economic Cooperation and Development (OECD) levels before being forced, by international pressure, to reduce its prices to levels offered by the makers of generics in India and Brazil.

Since the introduction of the TRIPs mechanism, the paucity of benefits accruing to developing countries has prompted them to press for revisions that would require demonstrable transfer of technology, extension of the transition period for full implementation of TRIPs, exclusion of biological resources from patent protection,[8] and compulsory licensing. Under the TRIPs regime, several western multinationals and governments in developed countries have resorted to egregious behavior at the expense of developing countries. This is clearly evident in the patents granted to agricultural companies for traditional knowledge and plant derived products that manifest no inventive process. For example, agricultural companies have secured about 70 patents for products derived from the Neem plant. In the United States, the US Department of Agriculture and W.R. Grace, an agricultural company, obtained a patent on fungicide derived from the Neem plant, based largely on traditional knowledge of Indian farmers. The patent was also registered in the European Union (EU) but following strong protests from Green politicians, the European Patent Office revoked the patent in 2000.

That the TRIPs mechanism might lead to such odious behavior was not anticipated and developing countries have advocated revising the agreement to prevent future abuse of provisions. Specifically, developing countries proposed the following amendments to the TRIPs agreement:

- Formal legal protection of traditional knowledge and innovations introduced by farmers and indigenous communities in developing countries.
- Recognition of protection for traditional farming practices, including farmer's rights to save and exchange seeds.
- Restriction of patents on items that are already available in the public domain by virtue of use, written description and so on.
- Assurances that a patent holder on products derived from resources of a developing country will share the economic benefits of the patent with that developing country.[9]

As well, compulsory licensing has emerged as a major issue in the Doha Round given the implications for managing epidemics and other diseases in developing countries. At the Doha meeting of the WTO, ministers adopted the Declaration on TRIPs and Public Health, which recognized that

> WTO members with insufficient or no manufacturing capacities in the pharmaceutical sector could face difficulties in making effective use of compulsory licensing under the TRIPS Agreement. We instruct the Council for TRIPS to find an expeditious solution to this problem and to report to the General Council before the end of 2002 [Paragraph 6].

Countries have recourse to "compulsory licensing" under Article 31 of TRIPs when confronted with national emergencies, such as in dealing with epidemics even without the permission of the patent holder. A licensee usually is obliged to make some reasonable royalty payment to the patent holder but which, in all cases, is considerably below the rate of profit for the original manufacturer. In 2001, the Canadian government granted a compulsory license to a local generics producer for the manufacture of ciprofloxacin (patented by Bayer) in order to access cheap treatment to a potential terrorist assault using anthrax. However, compulsory licensing involves onerous administrative, technical and financial requirements that act as a serious deterrent to many developing countries. They also fear a backlash from the developed countries. For example, when Mexico contemplated the enactment of compulsory license legislation, Eli Lilly's Mexican subsidiary warned that the company would freeze investments in Mexico. Earlier, when Brazil enacted compulsory licensing legislation, Eli Lilly withdrew some drugs from the Brazilian market, in retaliation.[10] More to the point, most developing countries simply do not have the domestic manufacturing capacity to benefit from potential compulsory licensing provisions. For these countries the primary issue is whether they have the legal recourse to import generic drugs from another developing country, like India or Brazil. Article 31.f of the TRIPs Agreement contains injunctions on the export of drugs produced under compulsory license:

> Any such use shall be authorized predominantly for the supply of the domestic market of the Member authorizing such use.

There have been proposals to remove the restriction on exports but that is vigorously rejected by patent holders and the Doha Declaration (Paragraph 6) simply recommended that members should seek out alternatives to help out countries with no manufacturing capacity of their own. But in WTO negotiations over Paragraph 6, developed countries fiercely resisted all proposals to facilitate developing country access to generic medicines through parallel imports.

There has not been a flood of compulsory licensing applications by developing countries and developed countries and drug manufacturers have also tended to oppose compulsory licensing applications.[11] Manufacturers insist that erosion of property rights will undermine their research and development activities. This position has been strongly supported by the US government which points out that 50 percent of all new medicines are invented in the US and that any systemic weakening of patent protection will erode the capacity of drug manufacturers to address the health problems of today and the future. Yet, estimations by Frederick Abbott suggest that the potential decline in R&D funding of US$1 billion will hardly deal a deathblow to large pharmaceutical manufacturers, which in 1995 had R&D expenditures of ECU 22 billion. Moreover, developing countries have not benefited from existing patent protection regimes to any great extent. For example, of the 1393 new drugs approved between 1975 and 1999, only 16 (about 1 percent) were specifically developed for diseases common in developing countries, such as tuberculosis.[12] This despite the fact that about 90 percent of the 14 million deaths a year due to infectious diseases are in developing countries.[13] There is no assurance that strengthening patent protection will improve existing situation but that was precisely the case made by the US to the WHO in May 2003. A resolution to that effect was drafted but was judiciously withdrawn when it became apparent that there was no support for the American position and if put to vote would be roundly rejected.

According to pharmaceuticals manufacturers, consumers in developed countries are likely to revolt if there was substantial discounting in developing countries but this again is disingenuous. Airlines have always priced their tickets based on local market conditions without any serious consumer backlash and there is no reason to assume that medicines will evoke a radically different response. A more legitimate concern is that cheap generic drugs meant for developing countries will somehow find its way through the black market back into developed countries, where prices are much higher. For example, the daily price of Combivir, an AIDS drug marketed by GlaxoSmithKline (GSK), in the US is US$18, compared to $0.90 in 63 developing countries, including all of sub-Saharan Africa. The lower price in developing countries is the result of intense pressure on GSK to lower the cost of AIDS treatment in poor countries, although the annual cost to patients will still be US$63 more than the equivalent generic drug produced by Ranbaxy of India.[14]

Buttressing the above concern is the increasing flow of cheap prescription drugs from Canada to the US, as US consumers take advantage of online pharmacies. The domestic controversy over re-importation of medicines was addressed in a US government report in late December 2004. Rather than recommend a legalization of the practice or the politically incorrect option of market intervention to negotiate lower prices with drug companies, the report boldly defended higher prices and profits for manufacturers as essential to continuing R&D outlays and, ultimately, beneficial to consumers. Steven Pearlstein, writing in the *Washington Post* was sufficiently provoked to ask: "Does this mean that the Bush administration now believes that high drug prices are good and higher prices would be even better?"[15]

On access to AIDS medication, the US government insists that any exceptions be made available only and exclusively to the least developed countries which have no domestic manufacturing capacity, and hence unable to avail of compulsory licensing opportunities, and to drugs to combat only epidemics like TB and HIV/AIDS, as specifically mentioned in Paragraph 1 of the Doha Declaration on the TRIPs and Public Health, for example, HIV/AIDS, and malaria. Developing countries on the other hand rejected a restrictive interpretation of Paragraph 1 of the Doha Declaration, insisting that diseases specifically mentioned in that paragraph were for illustrative purposes only and not to be understood as delimiting the scope of exceptions. They argued that health issues in their countries are many and varied and not limited to recognized epidemics. WHO figures show that most of the 4 million deaths each year due to acute respiratory infections occur in developing countries. As well, diarrhoea claims 2 million children annually, tuberculosis about 1.7 million in Africa and Southeast Asia, malaria about 1 million, and measles results in approximately 900,000 deaths in developing countries. The scourge of malaria in developing countries might be attributed, in part at least, to their decision to abandon the use of DDT to control mosquito. Where DDT is still being used, South Africa and Zambia, malaria has not been the huge concern that it is in other African countries.[16] The high mortality levels from other diseases do not diminish the significance of combating AIDS, however.

Developing countries, with a broad interpretation of the Doha Declaration, have insisted upon an agreement that will confer on them the right to import generic medicines from a third country, say, India or Brazil on grounds of public health considerations. Since the start of the Doha Round, the US and developed countries have insisted upon a restricted interpretation of the Doha Declaration to include only the listed health diseases whereas developing countries have argued for a more general interpretation on the assumption that listed diseases were for illustrative purposes only and not intended to limit the availability of generic drugs. US negotiators mocked the position of developing countries as a demand for access to cheap Viagra. This ridiculed the serious health issues in developing countries that are unlikely to be properly addressed under existing patent protection regimes. Yet, crude as the US attempt was to defend commercial interest of pharmaceutical manufacturers, this was perhaps a result of ambiguities in the Doha Declaration on the TRIPs and Public Health. Where Paragraph 4 seemingly prioritized all public health issues over commercial interests, Paragraph 1 restricted the right of developing countries to override TRIPs only for epidemics.

For its part, the US government and PhRMA cited approvingly research by Amir Attaran and Lee Gillespie-White that the real problem confronting developing countries was not restrictive patent regimes but rather poverty, inadequate infrastructure, flawed health systems, cultural barriers and lack of political will. The research found that across Africa there were a total of only 172 patents, less than a quarter of the 759 patents that could exist, given the number of drugs (15) and countries involved (53).[17] Interestingly however, while industry sources were happy to use this study to buttress the position that weak patent protection was neither a help nor a bar to treatment of AIDS in Africa, Abbott asks if "patents in developing countries are not important . . . why so much concern about obtaining and enforcing them" as the US had tried to do, unsuccessfully, in the case of South Africa.[18]

The American government also attempted, without much success, to divide developing countries and drive a wedge between those countries that were most at risk from HIV/AIDS epidemic (the African countries) and countries that stood to benefit from any weakening of patent protection on pharmaceutical products (India, Brazil and China). It suggested that the interests of the richer developing countries, the latter group, were at odds with the interests of the poorest countries in Africa, which had to deal with the AIDS epidemic on an immediate and urgent basis.

In this grim picture, the US projected itself as the best hope for African countries. In the 1990s very little was done to combat AIDS and government inaction resulted in a worsening of the AIDS situation, with serious deleterious consequences for development and growth. Government in developed countries, understandably, prioritized problems at home while African governments had their heads in the sand.[19] In the new millennium, the African crisis had become acute and the US now insisted that these countries should not hold out for a favorable deal but rather expedite resolution of the pharmaceuticals package so that the immediate crisis could be dealt with without undue delay. To underscore American sincerity, President Bush, in his State of the Union address in January 2003, announced a large package to combat the AIDS epidemic in Africa.

The President announced that he would seek budgetary approval for a five year US$15 billion package to fund treatment and prevention programs in 14 African countries.[20] The was announced with much fanfare but most of the expenditure was back-ended and the *Washington Post* also termed it an exercise in "robbing Peter to pay Paul" because much of the additional funding for AIDS was simply being generated by cuts to worthy programs in child and maternal health.[21] Moreover, in keeping with the conservative and deeply held religious convictions of President

Bush and his key staff, the program emphasized the importance of abstinence and sexual fidelity in preventing the spread of the AIDS epidemic, rather than encourage wider use of prophylactics, which has had demonstrated effectiveness in both developed and developing countries. Abstinence is also not always possible, especially for married women in developing countries because of their low social, political and economic status.

The evidence shows, for example, that in Uganda, up to half of all new infections happens within steady relationships where one partner is HIV positive. In addition, new infections are frequently the result of sexual violence on women or when women are forced to engage in sex work in order to provide for themselves and their families. For such women, abstinence is not a message that is likely to bring much hope. Certainly, there is a role for improving the position and status of women and changing men's perception of women but the AIDS epidemic requires more active intervention. There are lessons to be learned from a successful anti-AIDS strategy in Uganda, which reduced the prevalence of AIDS from as high as 30 percent among sexually active adults to 5 percent by emphasizing the use of condoms and active intervention, such as HIV counseling, testing, treatment, and blood screening rather than simple abstinence measures and behavior modification. According to David Serwadda, Director of the Institute of Public Health at Makarere University in Uganda,

If policymakers want to learn from Uganda's experience, they will act quickly to step up access to a combination of all these proven HIV-prevention interventions. Today access to these interventions is strikingly low, even in the hardest hit countries.[22]

Funding for the AIDS initiative was approved by the US Congress in May 2003 although no monies were actually set aside for that purpose. Actual disbursement of funds was to depend on separate appropriations bills. The President's original plan had by-passed the United Nations Global Fund to Fight Aids, Tuberculosis and Malaria but the Bill approved by the Congress provided for the US to contribute a third of other nations' contributions, to a maximum of US$1 billion a year. The Bill also mandated that a third of total funding should be allocated to programs that advocate abstinence as a core strategy.

The willingness of the American administration, in 2003, to be seen as doing something to combat the AIDS epidemic in the context of Doha Round negotiations, might be seen also as a political move to drive a wedge between developing countries. It is possible to interpret the AIDS initiative as part of a strategy to split developing country resolve and create divisions between developing countries that stood to benefit from a relaxation of the TRIPs regime and others that were enveloped in the epidemic and stood to benefit from the promised additional funds to combat the virus. It may even help the US deflect attention away from its unwillingness to compromise on patent protection. This may be an excessively cynical interpretation of the American initiative but Paul Zeitz of the Global Aids Alliance, called it a "cruel joke" and Sharonann Lynch termed the gesture a "great PR ploy on behalf of the White House."[23]

In July 2003, the US President embarked on a tour of several African countries to demonstrate American goodwill and commitment to fighting AIDS. But the gap between reality and rhetoric was already looming large, as the only new monies from the trumpeted AIDS initiative had been set aside for more bureaucratic enhancement in Washington. Linda Bilmes pointed out that the 2003 budget proposed an increase of only $450 million in the anti-AIDS campaign, not the promised $3 billion. Moreover, most of the new money was to be spent on a "new programme at the State Department to co-ordinate all US assistance on HIV/ AIDs . . . In other words, the only genuinely new money is being spent not on drugs nor health clinics but on bureaucratic reshuffling back in Washington."[24] She was certain that nothing like the US$15 billion would ever be spent on fighting AIDS in Africa despite lofty administration rhetoric.

Negotiations on access to generic pharmaceuticals were scheduled for completion at the end of 2002 but American rejection of a draft agreed to by all other members stalled any meaningful progress. American obstructionism did not bathe the US government in any glory but it was confident perhaps that its separate AIDS initiative for Africa would deflect attention from its dysfunctional role within the WTO framework.

In August 2003, shortly before the Cancun meeting of the WTO, the US finally relented on its objections to trade in generics and gave its assent to an agreement it had chosen to reject in December 2002. This late concession on parallel imports paved the way for poor African countries without manufacturing capacity and the option of compulsory licensing to procure generic anti-AIDS medicines from other developing countries without running foul of patent laws and protections.

The puzzling question is what prompted the US government to relent on its long standing objection to flexibility in compulsory licensing and that too, just before the Cancun meeting. While it is clear that earlier

US policy was costly in terms of loss of prestige and moral authority, Jagdish Bhagwati expressed surprise about the timing. He put forward a view that the timing of US concession was flawed and contributed, inadvertently to the collapse of negotiations at Cancun in September. A better strategy would have been to try and use American concessions on TRIPs and pharmaceuticals to obtain quid pro quo concessions from developing countries at the Cancun meeting. But having offered an unconditional concession, US negotiators were left without a key bargaining tool and dismayed also that developing countries remained uncompromising on agriculture.[25] Bhagwati may be correct but Cancun was clear demonstration also that developing countries were sophisticated in their approach and able to comprehend the inequities in a trade-off between pharmaceuticals and agriculture. The original American position was indefensible on all counts and a poor bargaining chip, if at all.

For the developing countries, agreement on TRIPs was a big step forward, in principle, but in all probability most AIDS patients are unlikely to be able to afford even cheap generic drugs. The crisis is sub-Saharan Africa will not be resolved because of the TRIPs agreement and requires some realistic mechanism to make treatment available to all. In 2005, a US-based Institute of Medicine committee chaired by Kenneth Arrow produced a report, *Saving Lives, Buying Time*, on the malaria epidemic in developing countries and suggested that an international agency become a centralized agency for the purchase and distribution, at deep discount, of malaria drugs to poor countries. The committee estimated that the cost of such a program might run to approximately US$500 million a year, a modest amount given the enormity of the crisis and the substantial payoffs in lives saved and productivity gains. A similar program for HIV/AIDS epidemic in Africa (30 million infections) will cost in excess of US$8 billion a year using only generic medication, an amount that will substantially erode the lending capacity of even the larger developmental agencies. Cost recovery at around US$0.10 per daily dosage will return some capital back to the central agency but net annual expenditures will still run at around US$7 billion. This will be a substantial investment in public health and even if daunting for any single international agency, not beyond pooled global capacity. What is lacking is the political will to sustain such a program over the long term.

Conclusion

In negotiations on pharmaceuticals trade, developing countries demanded a right to access cheap generic medicines in order to combat public health crises including, but not limited to HIV/AIDS. The deadline for completing negotiations on modalities lapsed with the US and developing countries in disagreement about the scope of the Doha Declaration's provisions for exempting developing countries from the strict restrictions of the TRIPs agreements. The US government worried that a broad interpretation of Doha Declaration to include all health crises of developing countries would be detrimental to the commercial interests of pharmaceutical manufacturers. In contrast, developing countries insisted, on compassionate grounds, that health needs of countries overrode profit motives of firms. There was no easy way to reconcile compassion and profits but, as noted earlier, demands of developing countries did not threaten the bottom line profitability of drug companies to any significant extent. Drug manufacturers derive only a small portion of their profits from sales in developing countries. If drug companies opposed change, it was perhaps because they did not wish to trade away their privileged existence under international law. And they found a strong ally in US negotiators. Ultimately, moral pressure on the US government was sufficient to produce agreement shortly before the Cancun meeting of the WTO in September 2003, whereby the US signaled its readiness to accept the public health argument of developing countries and to a broad interpretation of the Doha Declaration that had placed this issue on the negotiating agenda.

6
The Doha Round and Agricultural Liberalization

In many developed countries agricultural protection is a core feature of public policy either for domestic political considerations or reasons of food security. The latter concept was initially popularized by the Japanese government as part of its quest for comprehensive security and Japan currently has an established target of 45 percent self-sufficiency in agricultural products.[1] Political considerations also weigh heavily. Farmers are well organized and influential enough to obstruct liberalization even though their total numbers are relatively insignificant compared to total workforce. With decades of government handouts and protection behind them, the farming sector is not internationally competitive to survive liberalization and farmers are unprepared to abandon the farms to move into competitive industries.

In contrast, developing economies are primarily agriculture based and the farm sector supports a large portion of their working population. They are cheap producers of many agricultural products but export success has been limited because of barriers to trade in developed countries, such as high and escalating tariff walls; quota restrictions; and state subsidies. General Agreement on Tariffs and Trade (GATT) failed to discipline any of these anti-competitive policies as agriculture was deliberately quarantined from multilateral negotiating agenda by the dominant countries. The exclusion of agriculture, until very recently, meant that developing countries were denied opportunities to enhance their growth potential.

Protectionism in developed countries

Average developed country tariffs are low by international standards but on agricultural commodities the tariff peaks can be very high. Moreover, tariff structures also contain an inherent bias against the export of processed grain where developing countries might be expected to significantly boost their manufacturing and developmental opportunities. Table 6.1 provides a summary of the escalating tariff rates in the main developed country markets.

The sliding-scale structure of agricultural protectionism in developed countries has been a disaster for developing countries. It has forced them to specialize in exports with little processing and added value, and made it harder to move up the technology ladder. Protection levels in developed countries also tend to be low for commodities produced only in developing countries, such as coffee. This has encouraged expansion of coffee production in many more countries than in the past resulting in oversupply and depressed prices in recent years. Export revenue and farm income has plummeted and farmers are discouraged from shifting to alternative crops because of protection structure in developed countries that will deprive them of export markets.

Quantitative restrictions have also been extensively employed by developed countries to exclude developing country exports. When agriculture first became part of multilateral negotiations in the Uruguay Round, the main emphasis was on tariffication of quantitative restrictions. Negotiations, however, produced only modest reforms and if tariffication was meant to boost trade, the result was quite perverse. Tarriffication resulted in a dual structure of in-quota tariffs and out-of-quota tariffs and high out-of-quota tariffs proved more restrictive than the quotas it replaced, such that there was no increase in trade in agricultural commodities. In many instances, the level of protection accorded to specific agricultural commodities in developed countries also increased as a result of the Uruguay Round agreements. This happened because the bound tariff rates agreed to in the Uruguay Round afforded

Table 6.1   Tariff escalation rate in agriculture (%)

	Raw	Intermediate	Final	Average	Percentage of lines covered
Canada	6.3	9.6	15.2	11.2	85.5
Japan	1.6	4.0	7.5	4.7	71.8
US	4.6	10.2	16.0	10.9	84.8
EU	13.2	16.6	24.3	19.0	99.5

Source: John Nash, "Issues and Prospects for Agricultural Trade Liberalization in Doha Development Agenda," paper presented at the World Bank (April 2003).

higher protection than what had existed in the base period of 1986–88. The obvious implication is that tariff rates will have to be cut substantially before there is any real improvement in market access for agriculture exporting developed and developing countries.

Subsidies are yet another nefarious feature of global agriculture trade. In absolute amounts, the bulk of Organization for Economic Cooperation and Development (OECD) subsidies are provided by European and American governments and about a third of total farm income is derived from various government programs in these countries. Globally, the rich countries spend nearly US$1 billion each day in subsidies for their farmers. In 2002, total OECD farm subsidies amounted to US$318 billion. This is about twice the total agricultural exports of developing countries. Between 2000–02 average support to farmers as a percentage of gross farm receipts was less than 5 percent for Australia and New Zealand, less than 25 percent for the United States (US), Poland, Canada and Mexico, 35 percent for the European Union (EU), and 60 percent for Switzerland, Norway, South Korea and Japan.[2] For most OECD countries, subsidies, production and export, are concentrated in a few product lines, meat, dairy products, cereals and sugar.

Subsidies have had a particularly damaging effect on developing countries. In 2002, the US provided its 25,000 cotton producers US$3 billion in subsidies, an amount greater than the national income of Mali, one of the main African cotton exporting countries. The effect of subsidies provided to farmers and of subsidized exports has been to depress commodities prices globally and it is estimated that the result has been a net income loss of US$60 billion annually for the developing countries.[3] Cotton subsidies in the US alone are reported to have resulted in lost revenues of US$200 million for west African countries.[4]

Theoretically, subsidies are provided to assist struggling farmers but many of the recipients are only part-time farmers and not in dire need of federal assistance. For, instance, in 2001, David Rockefeller received US$134,556 in subsidies and Ted Turner received a more modest sum of US$12,925.[5] Overall, the growth in subsidy payments to farmers has been pronounced since the 1980s, when the US and the EU became caught up in a subsidy war to protect traditional overseas markets and maintain exports. The subsidy war has of course damaged commercial interests of the developing countries and Cairns Group, which do not have the financial resources to provide countervailing support to their farmers, but also to the government coffers in the US and EU. Budget constraint has forced the US and EU to try and curb runaway expenditures on farm subsidies but in-principle agreement has not translated into agreement on specifics.

Subsidies are an impost on consumers in developed countries. The Common Agricultural Policy (CAP) of the EU, for example, adds Euro 600 a year to the food bill of the average European family. Yet consumers have not protested at their welfare losses. Removal of subsidies will release their purchasing power potential but there are, admittedly, some costs as well, such as higher short-term unemployment and social dislocations. Removal of protectionism will also benefit developing countries, which struggle, under existing protectionist regimes, to break into developed country markets. Overall cost–benefit analyses firmly point to a heavy tilt in favor of benefits. One estimate is that a 50 percent across the board liberalization will lead to static benefits of US$219 billion (of which $64 billion would be the benefit to developing countries) a year during 2006–10, with adjustment costs amounting to about 30 percent of the benefits.[6]

Doha Round negotiations on agriculture

When the Doha Round negotiations started developing countries were particularly keen to redress the inequity in global agricultural trade. Tariff liberalization and withdrawal of subsidies can be expected to provide a major developmental boost through trade growth. A World Bank report issued in September 2003 reported that elimination of agricultural subsidies and other protectionist measures could lift 144 million people out of poverty by 2015 and boost the income of developing countries by US$350 billion.[7] While removal of all forms of protection is not realistically possible, the Doha Declaration included a commitment by World Trade Organization (WTO) members to significantly reduce trade distorting subsidies and barriers.[8]

The importance of agriculture in the Doha negotiating agenda is underscored by the fact that it was a key catalyst for the formation of the Group of Twenty (G-20), a group of developing countries established just prior to the 2003 Cancun ministerial meeting of the WTO, and which boldly signaled a preparedness to walk away from rather than accept yet another inequitable conclusion to the negotiations. They did, indeed, walk away but largely because of a late push by developed countries to include the so-called Singapore issues in the negotiating agenda.

The Doha Round began with much promise but quickly bogged down over disagreements between the US and the Cairns Group on the one hand, and the EU and Japan on the other. As a result, the March 2003 deadline for agreement on negotiating parameters lapsed without any settlement. During the course of negotiations, the US demanded a complete elimination of all trade distorting agricultural subsidies globally while, at the same time, piled on massive additional subsidies for its farmers in 2002. On tariffs and import restrictions, the US and the 17 members of the Cairns Group of Free Traders argued for a maximum upper limit of 25 percent for all agricultural products, compared to existing average agriculture tariffs of about 60 percent. The US proposed elimination of all export subsidies in five years, whereas the Cairns Group argued for a more aggressive phase-out in three years. On subsidies, of all the EU member countries, France has been most reticent about radical changes to existing program in view of the substantial clout of a relatively large farming sector.

The French government restated its opposition to elimination of subsidies provided to European farmers under the CAP.[9] The CAP operates on the basis of common internal prices that are established annually at levels higher than external prices. The target prices are maintained through the provision of support to farmers and other interventionary means to prop up prices artificially. Over time subsidies and support payments have increased and, in 2003, support measures cost the EU approximately US$51.0 billion (Euro 43 billion). Costs have escalated also as a result of a subsidies war with the US and while each realizes that the current system is not economically viable, politically however, farmers constitute a strong lobby group that governments, on either side of the Atlantic, have found difficult to ignore.

The existing structure of the CAP encourages farmers to overproduce in order to maximize their subsidy revenue. Government, in order to maintain target prices have been forced to purchase the surplus production and increase food stockpiles, with mounting storage costs. In turn, this had the odious consequences of foreign dumping and subsidized exports in an attempt to recover costs. This is the primary objection of the WTO, the Cairns Group and US that subsidized European exports have robbed other countries of their foreign market shares and distorted "normal" trade patterns. US Trade Representative (USTR) Block explained in December 1981, "We really are not quarrelling with the internal policies of the European Community. It is only when those policies are exported onto the shoulders of other trading countries of the world that we become concerned."[10] American concern has led to countervailing farm subsidies but the Cairns Group, made up of small agriculture exporting countries led by Australia and Canada, lacks the financial resources to match European and American farm subsidies and has lobbied for the complete elimination of subsidies.

In January 2003, Franz Fischler, EU Farm Commissioner proposed sweeping reforms which prompted intense negotiations between the

15 member states of EU. Rising costs and prospects of a "budgetary Armageddon" had prompted reform initiatives as early as the mid-1980s but differences among EU members proved difficult to reconcile and there have been, as a result, only minimal changes to the CAP structure in the period between the mid-1980s and 2003. Both Germany and France, for example, have relatively large farm-based voters and governments find it politically expedient not to accept reforms that might reduce farm income and alienate the farming population.

A key component of Fischler's reform proposal was to sever links between subsidies and agricultural production, leaving farmers free to tailor production to actual demand. In addition Fischler's proposal called for redirecting a large proportion of existing aid from farmers to rural development schemes, which the WTO might accept as non- trade distorting. In 2002, nearly 75 percent of total OECD farm support went directly to farmers and 17 percent to general services such as research, education, inspection and others. The French government immediately rejected the reform proposals. The French Agricultural Minister Herve Gaymard, in early January 2003, said that France ". . . does not subscribe to the view that the CAP and agricultural policies constitute obstacles to the development of poor countries and for this reason should be eliminated or, at the very least, greatly modified."[11] Leaving aside French objections, other EU members have a more realistic appreciation of the costs of the CAP and of the steps necessary to constructively engage others in the WTO talks. A sign of optimism that members were generally prepared to explore the issue of CAP reforms was the establishment of a high level working group to explore the reform agenda with a view to reaching agreement before the mid-term review of the Doha Round in Cancun in September 2003. Final agreement would depend on whether France remained obdurate in its defense of the status quo,[12] but Fischler expressed confidence that the establishment of a working party meant that there was political readiness to reach settlement before the Cancun meeting, perhaps as early as June 2003.[13]

Prospects of significant reforming European subsidies hinged on German interests in containing escalating costs. Where France has been the main beneficiary of subsidies, much of the financial burden has been on Germany, which presumably gave it a vested interest in pursuing reforms. The successful adoption of the reforms proposed by Fischler depended considerably on German support. By mid-June 2003, however, hopes of meaningful reforms were beginning to come off the rail amid concern that France and Germany had reached a separate understanding whereby Germany would support France in retaining the existing

CAP scheme largely intact. In exchange, the French government had reportedly agreed to support Germany in rejecting a common European company takeover code if it included certain provisions on multiple shareholding rights that other European member states were insisting upon. Where Fischler had proposed a severance of all production linked subsidies France and Germany appeared united in insisting that there had to be some production linked subsidies. Continuing this trade distorting practice has, in the past, led to dumping of oversupply in foreign markets, and could scuttle the badly damaged Doha Round. The *Financial Times* editorialized that the Franco-German understanding had endangered "the best chance for than a decade to curb wasteful, trade-distorting common agricultural policy."[14] The story of European CAP is instructive of how protectionism begets powerful vested interests that make it harder to dismantle such structures. Fischler's ambitious reform agenda collapsed in the final stages over French threats to veto significant change to existing subsidies and protectionism. Rules of the EU allow for agricultural policy making based on a simple majority vote but the French government exploited an unwritten principle that member states will not overrule a country that sees its "vital interests" at stake. The French determination to obstruct reform was bolstered by a reciprocal deal with Germany to support each other's interests. It was not the first time that politics had intruded to undermine sound policy choices.

Only a few weeks prior to the Franco-German *entente* to block the major components of the reform proposals, France had hosted the annual Group of Eight (G-8) summit meetings and taken the unprecedented step of inviting a number of developing countries for parallel talks. This was intended to boost French credentials as supportive of developing country interests but by sabotaging agricultural reforms, France had dashed the hopes of many poor developing countries, for whom agricultural subsidies in Europe and the US are major obstacles to development and poverty alleviation. Without significant European reforms, there is little likelihood that the US government will unilaterally decide to roll back subsidies to its farmers.

Negotiations on salvaging CAP reforms resumed for the third time in two weeks on June 25, 2003 and Fischler expressed confidence that France would make the necessary concessions to allow a consensus agreement. And after a 16-hour negotiating session, agreement was reached on a much-diluted plan than proposed by Fischler. The reform plan did not envisage any significant spending cuts but did break the link between subsidies and production that had been a major source of contention in WTO as trade distortionary and damaging to developing countries. Fischler declared the agreement as the beginning of a "new era", Supachai, the WTO Director General welcomed it as an important breakthrough but the refusal to scale back spending or to agree to lower support prices for agricultural commodities was a disappointment. The agreement ruled out any cut to spending until at least 2013. In a sense, the EU had done precisely what reform efforts over the last 30 years had achieved. In a review of CAP reform activities in the past, Secondo Tarditi concluded that the rationale seemed to have been ". . . not to eliminate, but rather to disguise, the huge economic and financial costs generated by the CAP supply management policies . . . ."[15] An Oxfam representative criticized it as "hugely disappointing."[16]

But rather than guarantee farmers an assured market at a fixed price for their production, farmers will, in future receive a fixed amount based on past subsidies. The reform provided no relief for European consumers and taxpayers but it is possible that by delinking subsidies from production, there might be less of an incentive to overproduce, lessening future prospects of dumping and subsidized exports. There was also no agreement to reduce protection levels and Fischler specifically warned that the reform plan should not be interpreted as "unilateral disarmament."[17] This was a note of caution not to expect significant concessions in WTO negotiations but the agreement nonetheless gave the EU reasons to be less defensive about its agricultural policies. It should be emphasized that the reform was only partially motivated by a sense of responsibility for WTO negotiations and more by the immanent addition of ten new members that were inefficient agricultural producers and likely to be a significant drain on EU resources. With European agreement on reforms, attention shifted to the US and whether the government in Washington will resist pressure from farm lobbies and muster the political will to rein in subsidies.

Internal EU reforms of the CAP cannot be separated from multilateral trade negotiations. As its starting position, the EU opened Doha Round negotiations with a proposed 55 percent reduction in Aggregate Measure of Support (AMS) to domestic farmers through such vehicles as output subsidies and price regulation. The existing approved AMS limit for EU is ECU69 billion whereas actual total AMS in 1999 were ECU48 billion. A 55 percent reduction would reduce actual AMS from ECU48 billion to only ECU31 billion, not a significant reduction. Using this formula, countries like Australia, Japan and Canada would also not be required to reduce their AMS at all, with only Norway required to make a significant reduction.[18] The EU proposal for a 45 percent reduction in export subsidies was similarly very modest and would not have required a radically reduced subsidies program.

On tariffs, the EU, Japan and South Korea proposed a 36 percent average tariff reduction, with a minimum tariff reduction of 15 percent across each line item. The separation between the two sides precluded agreement on negotiating parameters by the March 31, 2003 deadline. The US defended its inflexibility by asserting that EU, Japan and the US had an obligation to provide the same liberal trade opportunities to developing countries that the US had provided after the Second World War and which had enabled Europe and Japan to achieve speedy recovery and reconstruction.[19] There is no doubt that substantial tariff reductions and elimination of subsidies will boost the developmental objectives of the Doha Round but whether the US position was simply moral posturing or a genuine commitment to reform is uncertain. Even assuming that it is a genuine pledge, it is hard to see how the government will wean domestic farmers off government handouts and subsidies.

A possible justification for the European position might be that the Doha Declaration only contained an in-principle agreement to significantly reduce trade distorting and other subsidies without requiring outright abolition and elimination. At the same time, EU negotiators also latched onto the Declaration's reference to food security and protection of the rural way of life,[20] but these were mentioned only in reference to developing countries, which are largely rural in their demographics, and not applicable to the European context. The disagreement between EU and the US was reminiscent of the Uruguay Round and it was possible that an agreement would be reached when the WTO met in Cancun in September 2003 for a mid-term review of the Doha Round.

Like in the Uruguay Round, all indications were that the Cairns Group will be marginalized and inconsequential to the final resolution. As a third group in the agricultural debate, it could probably achieve more by brokering a compromise deal between EU and the US, even though the US had placed itself in a position not amenable to compromise solutions. However it threw its lot in completely with the US, a strategy that was more likely to sideline it during the final negotiations between the two main protagonists. A more charitable assessment of the Cairns Group is that of Clayton Yeutter, former USTR. He writes that:

> On numerous occasions they [the Cairns Group] have provided a balance wheel to the ideological tiffs between the European Community and the United States over agriculture, nearly always

with a constructive outcome. The Cairns Group has been catalytic, sensible and pragmatic. Without question their input was critical to the launching of the Uruguay Round agricultural negotiations, and to bringing them to a successful conclusion years later.[21]

This was strong endorsement of approach taken by the Cairns Group and understandable also given that it had aligned itself almost completely with the US on agricultural trade issues. Yet, the Cairns Group did not particularly distinguish itself in the negotiations. Indeed, it could have played a more noteworthy role if it had been more pragmatic and less dogmatic in arguing the near absolutist position on free trade, which might have allowed it to broker a compromise deal between the US and the EU. To rephrase a maxim, the role of the Cairns Group reflected why the perfect is the enemy of what is probable. The final Uruguay Round settlement on agriculture had no input from the Cairns Group but in the Doha Round, the Cairns Group adopted a similar extreme position. Moreover, despite strong US praise for the Cairns Group, the US singled out Brazil, a member of Cairns Group and the G-20 for blame when the Cancun trade talks collapsed in 2003.

To break the impasse between the EU and the US, the Chairperson of the Agricultural Negotiations Group, Stuart Harbinson, released a compromise draft on modalities (numerical targets for achieving the objectives of negotiations) in mid-February 2003 with the expectation that this would form the basis for further negotiations, scheduled for completion by end of March 2003. All major players rejected this and a revised draft was submitted in mid-March 2003. However, in the absence of clear guidelines on how the draft paper had to be re-worked, the revision included only minor changes.

The proposal called for a 60 percent reduction in allowable subsidies (US$19.1 billion for the US, and US$67 billion for EU). This would leave the US with allowable subsidies of US$7.6 billion while permitting the EU total subsidies of US$27 billion at the end of the transition period. This gross imbalance led the US farm lobby, The American Farm Bureau Federation, to reject the proposal as "woefully inadequate."[22] On tariffs, the chairperson offered the following suggestions:

- That for all agricultural tariffs greater than 90 percent ad valorem, the simple average reduction should be 60 percent, subject to a minimum of 45 percent per tariff line.
- That for all agricultural tariffs lower than or equal to 90 percent ad valorem and greater that 15 percent, the simple reduction rate

should be 50 percent, subject to a minimum cut of 35 percent per tariff line.

- That for all tariffs equal to or less than 15 percent, the simple reduction rate should be 40 percent, subject to a minimum of 25 percent.
- That the rate of tariff reduction for processed products should be equivalent to that for the product in its primary form multiplied, at a minimum, by a factor of 1.3.
- That all trade distorting subsidies had to be phased out completely but over a longer, ten year, transition period.

The revised draft was again rejected by both the US and EU as unacceptable and flawed. For developing countries, the draft on modalities had a mixed message. It sought to avoid one egregious deficiency in the Uruguay Round Agreement on Agriculture, namely the reliance on average reduction in tariffs (apart from back-loading the liberalization schedule). Average reduction in tariffs mean that a target of 50 percent, for example, can be met by reducing a 150 percent tariff by 1 percentage point, while eliminating a 1 percent tariff. Since the latter would be counted as a 100 percent reduction, the average of both reductions, 0 and 100, is 50 percent. John Nash points out that this "was the approach adopted in the [Uruguay Round] and allowed governments to shield their sensitive products from significant reductions." By contrast the Harbinson draft proposed a four tiered reduction in average tariffs "combined with very large minimum cuts on individual products in order to produce real liberalization."[23] Yet, alongside this creditable proposal, the draft also incorporated a lengthy phase out of trade distorting subsidies, which developing countries rejected as unacceptable and inequitable. Rangarirai Machemedze, of the Southern and Eastern African Trade Information and Negotiations Institute argued that:

> The document's contents would result in the continued dumping of agricultural products through high levels of the distortion of domestic support and export subsidies for at least 10 more years.[24]

With developed countries reluctant to offer significant concessions, pressure remained on developing countries to make further concessions. The Chief Economist of the World Bank, Nick Stern, in a speech in India in November 2002, urged developing countries like India and China to adopt unilateral free trade to provide a model to the developed countries that might also perhaps shame them into liberal practices.[25] He added that the welfare gains to developing countries from unilateral free trade would be US$116 billion over the next 12 years compared to a welfare gain of US$76 billion from removal of developed countries' import barriers. If implemented it would force developing countries to make a bigger sacrifice than developed countries because LDC tariffs are generally higher than developed country tariffs. This was also the likely net effect of an American proposal, in late 2002, to eliminate all tariffs by 2015.[26] Moreover, the reality is that lower tariff rates in developed countries do not necessarily imply a broad-based commitment to liberal trade because these countries rely extensively on non-tariff barriers and subsidies to protect domestic industries. Developed countries also frequently resort to antidumping provisions of the WTO to exclude cheaper imports from developing countries.

If developing countries expected a fair deal in the development round, proposals that were put forward by developed countries in 2002–03 were only likely to result in greater inequities. Failure to meet the March 2003 deadline for an agreement on negotiating parameters raised concerns that the 5th Ministerial Conference of the WTO in Cancun, Mexico, in September 2003, to review progress in the Doha Round would have little of any significance to report and discuss. Indeed, the lack of progress at the end of 2002 prompted the Director General of the WTO to issue a warning that failure to reach agreement "will sour an already tense atmosphere among WTO members . . . ."[27]

The missed March 2003 deadline on agreement on modalities cast an understandable pall over the future of the Doha Round but there were also speculative suggestions that the past will once again repeat itself as another tragedy for developing countries. This is because the negotiations had, to this point, played out in a manner remarkably reminiscent of the Uruguay Round negotiations on agriculture. In the final stages of the Uruguay Round, negotiations had reached an impasse between the US and EU over precisely the same issues. However, rather than be held responsible for scuttling the Round, the EU and the US reached a compromise settlement, the Blair House Accord, which ultimately left the Cairns Group and the developing countries out in the cold with little improvement in market access or penetration.

The Blair House Accords resulted in a compromise over agricultural support measures and classified these in three separate boxes: amber box measures which had substantial trade distortion effect; green box measures such as producer retirement programs and environmental protection measures which had no trade impact; and blue box measures which introduced exemptions allowing the US and EU to continue to support agriculture. In terms of commitments to reduce subsidized exports, it was agreed that developed countries would reduce export subsidies to a level that was 36 percent below the average for 1986–90 and reduce subsidized exports by 21 percent over six years, relative to the 1986–88 base period. There was no product-by-product requirement of cuts in subsidies, and compensation payments were exempt from cuts. On the positive side, the agreement required developed countries not to extend subsidies to new product lines. The French government however, still held out for a better deal and in December 1993, the EU and US agreed to substantially revise the Blair House Accords, allowing each more subsidized exports in the transition period. Thus, the changes allowed,

> the European Union to subsidize exports of an additional 8 million MT of wheat and flour, 362,000 MT of beef, and 250,000 MT of poultry above that which would have been possible under the original base-period requirement. Similarly, the United States will be able to subsidize exports of a total of 7.5 million MT of wheat and flour, 1.2 million MT of vegetable oil, and about 700,000 MT of rice more than would have been permitted under the terms of the Blair House accord.[28]

Speculation that the Doha Round negotiations might follow the earlier precedent prompted Supachai, who at the time of Uruguay Round negotiations was Minister of Commerce in Thailand, to reiterate his commitment for genuine reforms and to prevent a repeat of the unsatisfactory conclusion to agricultural negotiations in the Uruguay Round. But prospects of a side agreement between the US and EU, bypassing WTO multilateralism, again could not be ignored when it was revealed, in late April 2003, that US and EU had been negotiating a compromise deal for about two months.[29] Indeed, at the Cancun ministerial meeting, the US and EU took a united position against the liberalizing demands of the G-20 or of the Cairns Group. In interviews, one representative of the G-20 revealed that it was precisely the concern of a US–EU compact, in the manner of the Blair House Accords that prompted the formation of the G-20 to prevent the imposition of another "unfair" agricultural agreement.

The closing of EU–US ranks belied American rhetoric in support of freer agricultural trade. It signaled the collapse of the Cancun ministerial meeting but it also clarified the depth of common interests between the US and EU as providers of massive farm subsidies and their inability, in real terms, to sell liberal trade domestically to powerful farm groups. Another factor that may have contributed to this united front was the determination, perhaps, to repair the damage that had been done to the trans-Atlantic alliance by the American decision to launch pre-emptive strikes against Iraq in April 2003. The US decision had been bitterly opposed by France and Germany, and American support for the EU position at Cancun may have been designed to placate these two important countries that are also the main defenders of EU's Common Agriculture Policies. It was not improbable that USTR Zoellick would try and broker a trade deal with the EU as a way of preventing the political spat from spilling over to trade and economic relations, even if it damaged interests of other WTO members.

A side agreement became more likely when a summit meeting in Egypt in late June 2003 of trade ministers from about 30 countries failed to break the stalemate. This was not unexpected given that EU ministers had suspended talks on reforming the CAP regime. EU members did agree to initiate reforms shortly before the Cancun meeting but the EU and US also reached agreement not to make an issue of each other's agricultural subsidies at Cancun. This "non-aggression pact"[30] frustrated developed countries and firmed their resolve not to let developed countries hijack substantial liberalization. The EU insisted that farm subsidies were not necessarily evil or trade distorting, citing WTO practice of classifying subsidies variously as trade distorting (amber box), less trade distorting (blue box) and non-trade distorting (green box). The EU maintained as well that the bulk of EU support for farmers could be classified either in the blue or the green box, following reforms in 1992, 2000, and 2003, blaming the US for trade distorting agricultural policies. Developing country were unconvinced that such niceties presented a true picture of damage done to agriculture and farm communities in developing countries.

At Cancun, the EU proposed the following as a basis for negotiating further agricultural liberalization:

- Cut trade distorting farm subsidies by 55 percent from URAA (Uruguay Round Agreement on Agriculture) levels.
- Open agricultural markets by slashing tariffs by 36 percent and a minimum reduction per tariff line of 15 percent, as in the URAA.
- Scale back all export subsidies by 45 percent.[31]

The proposals were a direct extension of the Uruguay Round agreement and offered no firm timelines for removal of farm subsidies, as demanded by developing countries and the Cairns Group.

In agricultural negotiations, the Japanese government adopted a quiet and passive stance, aware that the EU was unlikely to make substantial concessions that might, in turn, put pressure on Japan's own protectionist policies. As pointed out earlier, Japan has the highest rates of protectionism among developed countries and is also among the largest provider of subsidies to its farmers. Yet, with attention focused on conflict between the US and EU, Japan had the luxury of observing from the sidelines as the EU fought to retain protection for domestic farmers. The Japanese government was aware that if the EU position prevailed, Japanese farmers would be the main beneficiaries. It had no reason to assertively stake out its own interests and invite negative commentary.

Ironically, Japan's long-term interests are perhaps best served by rapid and drastic liberalization of the agricultural sector. Japanese public policy has been hostage to the vested interests of farmers since the end of the Second World War and while it was relatively easy to carry the burden of protectionism during the high growth phase of the economy, it has become a serious burden since the collapse of the Japanese economy in the early 1990s. The Japanese economy has been stagnant for more than a decade and it has been impossible to introduce bold reform measures in order to revive the flagging economy. In particular, the ruling Liberal Democratic Party (LDP) is beholden to the farm community and has been unable to introduce structural adjustment for fear of disrupting links with the agricultural sector.

However, if the Doha Round were to substantially liberalize trade in agriculture, Japan would most likely submit to it and an astute government could even use that opportunity to implement fundamental and necessary economic reforms, even if it resulted in adverse electoral consequences for the LDP in the short term. The South Korean government was in a similar position. But one South Korean farmer, Mr Lee Kyung Hae, worried about prospects of liberalization, made his own statement of opposition by setting himself alight and committing suicide at Cancun in September 2003 as trade ministers and representatives gathered for a WTO ministerial meeting for a mid-term review of the Doha Round negotiations.

As delegates gathered in Cancun, they did not have any significant positive achievements to build upon but rather a long list of missed deadlines. The only significant positive on which they could draw upon was an American decision in late August to accept the pharmaceuticals agreement that it had rejected in December 2002. That decision cleared the path for poor African states to import generic drugs to deal with a range of health issues and epidemics.[32]

The Cancun ministerial meeting marked also the first time developing countries engaged their developed country counterparts both vigorously and vociferously. They came prepared to press their interests partly because they had been led to believe that this Round would deliver pro-development outcomes where previous rounds had failed to protect interests of developing countries. Even the poorest countries had found it fit to finalize their negotiating position. For example, more than 30 of the least developed countries had convened earlier in the year in Dhaka, Bangladesh to prepare their list of demands. West African nations similarly came prepared with specific demands on ending subsidized cotton exports by the US that had adversely affected their production and exports. According to Bernard Hoekman of the World Bank, "This was a first for the WTO—African countries coming forward with a specific demand."[33] More importantly, the larger developing countries—Brazil, India, and China—formed a coalition of developing countries with South Africa and some members of the Cairns Group of Free Traders to press for agricultural liberalization.

At Cancun, developing countries expected, or rather hoped, to gain significant concessions on agricultural trade and liberalization. There were some grounds for optimism given that EU had successfully negotiated an internal debate on subsidies reform and reached agreement on some, however modest, reforms to placate its opponents. Nonetheless it quickly became clear that the South had an exaggerated and false sense of optimism. The wide chasm that separated the developing countries, represented by the recently formed G-20[34] and the developed economies of Europe and US complicated the process of securing common grounds. The Mexican Foreign Minister Luis Ernesto Derbez distributed, on September 13, a draft ministerial text as the model for finalizing agreement. The Derbez text, however, made limited concession to developing country demands on agriculture and specified no timelines, for example, for removal of export subsidies in developed countries. For developing countries, it did provide special and differential treatment in tariff reduction and extended implementation periods but the text was criticized as overwhelmingly biased toward the interests of developed countries. The Indian and Brazilian governments were particularly critical of the Derbez text arguing that it had jettisoned the developmental goals of the Doha Round.

Delegates from the North and South essentially talked past each other and failed to find common ground. The West, for instance, wanted Cancun to affirm the inclusion of the so-called new issues flagged in the Singapore ministerial meeting of the WTO in 1996. Developing countries, however, were unprepared to accept any broadening of the negotiating agenda, fearful that such a move would dilute their ability to secure a favorable deal on agriculture and other issues of concern to them.

The Singapore issues related to trade rules covering government red tape, government procurement policies, foreign investment, and competition policy. If there was an opportunity for a *quid pro quo* deal between the developed and developing countries on the Singapore issues and agriculture, the opportunity slipped away quickly in the midst of developing country suspicion that the West was less than serious in dismantling its subsidies regime. Developing countries had good reasons to be suspicious since past deals and agreements had only resulted in less than spectacular success. Indeed, developing countries had a long history of being dudded by the West. Developing countries insisted that there had to be meaningful and actual achievement on issues at hand before they would agree to the inclusion of new issues in the negotiating agenda.

To meet developing country objections, Pascal Lamy, on the final day of the talks, proposed dropping two of the most contentious issues, investments and competition policy. But if the EU hoped to make progress by this unbundling of the Singapore issues, developing countries flatly repudiated the offer as missing the central point of no new inclusion before existing issues had been satisfactorily resolved. The EU strategy also was rejected by South Korea, backed by Japan, that all four Singapore issues had to be placed on the negotiating table. As far as developing countries were concerned, the emphasis on Singapore issues was largely a diversion from the main task and an attempt by EU and Japan to deflect attention away from agricultural liberalization. They suggested that the WTO should continue to study the issues, as agreed to at the Singapore ministerial meeting, rather than make a formal attempt to negotiate global rules and regulations.

The hardline stance can be attributed at least partly to their collective experience with the way Uruguay Round agreements on services liberalization, trade related intellectual property (TRIP), trade related invested measures (TRIM), agricultural liberalization and a phased withdrawal of the Multi-fibre Agreement (MFA) had worked to the detriment of developing countries. For instance, while developing countries had accepted and implemented, however reluctantly, the strict discipline of TRIPs, there were few, if any, meaningful reciprocal benefits to them in the area of either agriculture or textiles trade.

Another explanation for the radicalization of Southern countries is that they were plied with misleading, overly optimistic and muddle headed positions by non-governmental organizations (NGOs) that encouraged them to stand firm and refuse any compromise. *The Economist* summed up by blaming both developed and developing countries for the collapse of Cancun talks but singled out NGOs for radicalizing the public face of developing countries. It concluded that "The NGOs' main mistake, however, was to raise poor countries' expectations implausibly high. Shout loudly and long enough, they seemed to suggest, and you will get your way."[35]

In recent years, NGOs have played a prominent role in WTO negotiations. The are legitimate players in multilateral policy making processes given their many specialized skills and knowledge as well as involvement in developing countries, and it is unfortunate that these organizations have been targeted as dysfunctional and obstructionist. At the first WTO ministerial meeting in Singapore, in 1996, a total of 108 NGOs and 235 representatives participated in the talks but in Cancun the number of NGOs had swelled to 795 and their representatives to 1578.[36] It is easy to correlate the rising importance of NGOs with negotiating difficulties but it is unfair to blame NGOs either for the collapse of Cancun talks or for heightening developing country expectations. Instead, expectations were raised with the launch of the Development Round and when developed countries encouraged the developing countries to actively engage in negotiations and set aside their frustrations with earlier negotiating rounds. Developing countries were led to believe that the Round would deliver significantly improved market access but instead, developed countries seemed more intent to add to the mission creep of WTO, with the inclusion of the so-called Singapore issues.

The collapse of the mid-term review cast a gloomy shadow over the future of the Doha Round. The EU Trade Commissioner Pascal Lamy expressed disappointment that agreement had been thwarted by a group of 22 developing countries (G-20), "I wouldn't say the Doha round is dead but it certainly needs intensive care . . . An agreement on agriculture was nearly there . . . We have lost, all of us. We could have gained, all of us."[37]

Even if the stance of G-20 has not dealt a fatal blow to the Doha Round and to the WTO, there is still a danger that the West, and the US will interpret the activities of the G-20 as akin to transforming the WTO into a political forum like the United Nations (UN) rather than a serious forum for trade liberalization. US government officials were particularly upset that a western hemisphere country had taken such a strong position against the US.

However, it is unfair either to single out individual countries or to condemn developing countries as simply trying to score cheap political points in Cancun. It was the first time they had prepared themselves for negotiations in the WTO and their demands were in keeping with the WTO mandate of trade liberalization. The Brazilian Foreign Minister, a leading figure in the G-20, declared that it was "a broad-based political coalition, and a force for free and fair trade."[38] In the 1970s and 1980s the US government was vocal in demanding fair trade and a level playing field in trade with its leading trade partners, particularly Japan, and if those arguments had merit, the claim of the developing countries is even more valid and just.

Indeed, while Kofi Annan, the UN Secretary General, expressed his disappointment with the stalemate at Cancun, he also supported the hard-line stance of G-20 as a positive development in the struggle to highlight the interests of developing countries.[39] The danger is that this simple message will be lost on the Americans and they will deal with this setback just as they did in the UN Conference on Trade and Development (UNCTAD) when they lost a vote on the basis of majority rule, when the US had come to expect a consensus rule. If that happens there is real potential for serious harm to the future of the WTO and which would end up encouraging more trade bilateralism and regionalism.

When the US negotiated the North American Free Trade Agreement (NAFTA), it was seen as a major departure from trusted principles of world trade that emphasized non-discrimination in trade practices. Since the signing of the NAFTA, there is greater emphasis to conclude similar deals elsewhere, most notably in the Asian Pacific Region. In Cancun, the US government made no secret of its willingness to deal with countries on a bilateral or regional basis. It is uncertain whether the US government has embraced trade bilateralism and regionalism as genuine substitutes for failing multilateralism, or as catalysts for facilitating multilateral trade negotiations. The latter assumes that a fear of trade bilateralism will induce other countries to soften their hardline positions in order to secure completion of the WTO Round.[40] It assumes also that when the earlier Uruguay Round was similarly deadlocked, critical EU concessions to break the impasse had to await American initiatives for a NAFTA and support for the Asia Pacific Economic Cooperation (APEC). Yet, even if contemporary American bilateralism is mere posturing to secure a multilateral trade deal, it is still possible that posturing will come increasingly to define practical realities not only for the US but also for many other developed countries. This is especially the case if American trade policy is driven by a genuinely held belief that its trade interests are best served by a dual track policy that combines multilateralism and bilateralism.

Cancun and beyond

Cancun marked a sharp break in the pattern of North–South trade negotiations. It disrupted the pattern of one-sided agreements imposed by developed countries on the world community and yet there was no certainty that any subsequent agreement, assuming that deadlock could be broken, would indeed be more balanced. The disruption at Cancun could well be a momentary setback but on a positive note, Cancun at least forced negotiators back to the drawing board to devise an acceptable formula for liberalizing trade in agriculture. In terms of bargaining strategy, success for developing countries in securing a balanced agreement required some measure of unity, purpose, resolve and skill in squeezing meaningful concessions. This had to be balanced against the risk of being seen as intransigent and inflexible. Indeed, following the failed Cancun meeting, developing countries were under renewed Western pressure to be "reasonable" in their demands or risk a total collapse of the Doha Round. In the end, the Doha Round was saved when developing countries agreed on a negotiating formula that was only marginally better than the offer they had rejected at Cancun.

In the one-year period since the impasse at Cancun, a number of proposals were put forward or resurrected to resolve the disagreement over agricultural issues. These were the Uruguay Round formula, the Swiss formula, and the Harbinson formula.

The G-20 also submitted a framework proposal on agriculture shortly before the start of the Cancun Ministerial meeting. It called for substantial reduction on domestic support measures, elimination of export subsidies, enhanced special and differential treatment and the establishment of Special Products to safeguard some agricultural commodities in developing countries.[41] On tariff reduction the G-20 proposal supported the Swiss Formula, which provided the best tariff reduction outcomes for developing countries. Bernard Hoekman *et al.* write that:

> As the variance in tariffs is higher in developed countries than in developing countries, while levels of bindings are much higher in developing countries, a "Swiss-type" formula that centers on reducing the average levels of bindings can do much to both reduce tariff peaks and escalation in OECD countries *and* give credit to developing countries for past reforms.[42]

For obvious reasons, the two large agriculture exporters, the EU and US did not support the Swiss Formula. At the same time, the Cairns Group had limited bargaining strength as a result of internal splits and divisions, and breakaway membership of some in the G-20. The Cairns Group had no major impact in the final Uruguay Round settlement and few expect it to do any better in the Doha Round.

The Harbinson formula had been put forward in early 2003 and while it received little support in the lead up to Cancun, it became a serious contender with a unique, tiered approach to tariff reduction. He proposed that the higher the tariff the higher should be the level of tariff cut, so that if tariffs were above 90 percent the average cut would be 60 percent, if tariffs were between 15 and 90 percent, tariff cuts would be 50 percent. For developing countries the cuts would be lower and would be phased in over ten years while developed countries would be required to deliver cuts in five years. Interestingly, he also included provisions for countries to designate commodities as "sensitive" or "strategic," which would be exempt from tariff reduction commitments. The Harbinson formula can be located between the two extremes of the Uruguay and the Swiss formula and was not very generous to developing countries. Under the Harbinson formula, India's agricultural tariffs would have been reduced by an average of 43–80 percent whereas US would have to reduce its import tariffs by only 5 percent from the respective base year. Any agreement based on the Harbinson Formula would have limited benefit for developing countries especially the least developed countries. In the Cairns Group, the Canadian Agri-Food Trade Alliance (CAFTA), a supporter of the Swiss Formula criticized the Harbinson formula as providing limited tariff reductions and prolonged phase-out of agriculture subsidies, that might result in a back-loading of subsidy cuts as happened in the Uruguay Round.[43]

Negotiations over the various proposals led to the July Framework Agreement on agriculture and other issues. Developed country concession included dropping three of the Singapore issues from the negotiating agenda, special consideration of cotton trade in recognition of the plight of least developed countries, and a tiered reduction[44] of export subsidies and tariffs so that members with high levels of subsidy and tariffs will be required to make relatively greater reductions. The plan to make substantial cuts in domestic subsidies however may not amount to much as cuts will be based on subsidies allowed under WTO rules and not the actual amounts. The US, for instance, spends only about half its permitted US$49 billion.[45]

At the same time, developed countries protected their interests by giving themselves the right to designate an "appropriate" number of commodities as "sensitive" and exempt from liberalizing discipline.

In theory, developing countries also had access to sensitive product provisions but were expected instead to favor provisions for special product designations. However, while sensitive products were to be self-designated, the designation of "special product" was to be based on a yet to be determined approach that may include some objective criteria of food security and others, multilateral agreement, or, indeed, self-designation. Depending on the final agreed criterion, this may make it difficult to obtain special product listing. The July Framework established the broad principles and modalities but the details remain to be negotiated, including the numbers of sensitive and special products for each country, the maximum permitted deviation for these products from the general tariff cut formula, and whether there has to be an equivalent level of compensation in another product area.[46] As far as the likely impact of sensitive product provisions, Kym Anderson and Will Martin estimated the potential gains and found that if only

> 2 per cent of HS6 Agricultural tariff lines in developed countries are classified as sensitive, and are thereby subject to just a 15 per cent tariff cut, the welfare gains from global agricultural reform would shrink by three-quarters. However, if at the same time any product with a bound tariff in excess of 200 per cent had to reduce it to that cap rate, however [sic], the welfare gain would shrink by "only" one-third.[47]

A major flaw in the Framework Agreement was the decision to use bound tariffs[48] as the benchmark for negotiating tariff cuts. Bound tariffs can be much higher than applied tariffs with the result that applied tariffs might not change to any great extent, especially in developing countries. Table 6.2 illustrates the gap between bound and applied tariffs for

Table 6.2   Bound and average applied tariff for selected countries (%)

Country	Bound	Applied 1995	Applied 1997	Applied 1999
Argentina	35	na	10	na
Brazil	37	10	10	13
Colombia	87	15	14	14
Thailand	35	37	na	na
Venezuela	52	15	15	15

Source: http://www.ers.usda.gov/publications/aer796/aer796g.pdf.

selected countries and to the extent that countries are enjoined from raising applied tariffs above bound tariffs, shows that Thailand was in breach of its international commitments.

Moreover, while average bound tariffs for developed countries are lower than those for developing countries, the former have a spread of tariffs which is seven-fold that of the latter. The average bound tariff for the EU is 17.4 percent but the peak bound tariff is 456.9 percent whereas the average bound tariff for Brazil is 35.5 percent and the peak bound tariff is 55 percent. Konandreas writes also that,

> the tariff profiles of the developed countries are highly skewed with many tariff lines at zero or very low single-digit levels and another set of tariff lines bound at very high level.[49]

With basic agreement on negotiating parameters in place, tariff negotiations will now hinge around defining the threshold for the different tiers or bands and the type of tariff reduction in each band. The July Framework Agreement borrows on the Harbinson formula and unless there are very large cuts in bound tariffs, there will be only marginal impact on applied tariffs and market access for developing countries. This is also pointed out by Walkenhorst and Dihel, who write that ". . . reductions in bound rates do not necessarily translate into corresponding cuts in applied tariffs, but first merely squeeze out unused protection."[50]

Conclusion

Agriculture is critical to successful completion of the Doha Round and is of particular interest to developing countries because roughly 70 percent of the world's poor (in developing countries) engage in agricultural activities. The absolute numbers are large as well, for instance 300 million in India and 800 million in China. The quality of their lives is diminished by some of the agricultural practices in developed countries. If the Doha Round succeeds in scaling back the high and escalating tariffs as well as producer and export subsidies, such changes can be expected to make some difference to the lives of many in developing countries. Agriculture is a relatively small sector in developed country gross domestic product (GDP) but with considerable political clout and agricultural interests have vociferously defended their privileged existence. Overall, agriculture contributes only 1.8 percent to developed country GDP. Yet, developed countries have not found it easy to offer meaningful concessions. Kym Anderson and Will Martin find it ironic that such a small sector is able to hold up global trade liberalization.[51] Perhaps the answer lies in the very smallness of the agriculture sector, which has allowed producers to collude and collaborate to maximize their political influence. As Mancur Olson pointed out in his *Logic of Collective Action*, small groups are easier to organize and are consequently better positioned to extract political concessions.[52]

Despite the obstacles, successful completion of the Doha Round will require a resolution of the agricultural disputes. The July Framework Agreement (2004) has at least provided some markers and focused efforts on the issues of market access and subsidies. Whether common sense on agricultural subsidies will prevail in future is uncertain but a precedent may now exist on winding back subsidy payments. In January 2005, EU and US formally agreed to commence three-month long negotiations to eliminate all state subsidies to Boeing and Airbus. Interestingly, under terms of the agreement, EU will not be able to offer subsidies to Airbus during the three months negotiating period to hammer out details for withdrawal of subsidies.[53] This was welcome relief for the WTO, which had been asked, by the US, to adjudicate the dispute. There is no expectation that a bilateral resolution will be easy and, indeed, a day after the agreement was announced, Airbus announced that it had applied to four European government for subsidies to defray the development costs on its planned A350 jetliner.[54] But if negotiations succeed, this could open a pathway for dealing with the more complicated issue of agricultural subsidies. At least a precedent will have been set and budgetary constraints may compel governments across the Atlantic to negotiate a similar deal over agricultural production and exports.

There have been suggestions however that this focus on subsidies is misplaced. According to one estimate by Hoekman *et al.*, a 50 percent tariff cut is likely to benefit developing countries more than an equivalent reduction of domestic support and export subsidies because tariff cuts are more likely to improve price competitiveness and to boost exports. They concluded that focus in the Doha Round should be on reducing tariff levels rather than on forcing cuts to subsidy levels.[55] Tariff reduction agreements in the past have, however, failed to substantially improve market access. The July Framework Agreement may similarly provide for deep reductions but in bound rather than applied tariffs.

Developing countries have placed high hopes on agricultural liberalization but neither the EU nor the US have shown a readiness to substantially cut their farm population loose from generous governmental subsidies and import penetration. Liberalization will require a tremendous amount of political will on the part of European governments to revamp the CAP. For the moment, the US is content to shelter behind European inability to agree on CAP reforms. And alongside pressure on developing countries to be more flexible Robert Zoellick the USTR stated in late June 2003 that ". . . whether we move ahead or get stuck very much depends on the EU."[56] The US government has not yet had to face the difficult choice of ending domestic subsidies and it remains to be seen whether it will prove any more adept at deflecting the pressure of domestic farmers against liberalization.

The original deadline for agreement on agricultural negotiating parameters lapsed without any headway on the critical issue of subsidies. The issue, of course, is domestically sensitive on both sides of the Atlantic and it should be noted also that missed deadlines are not necessarily fatal in international negotiations. There were, for instance, many missed deadlines before the Uruguay Round was brought to completion. Collapse of the Cancun ministerial meeting marked an important watershed in international trade negotiations but rather than quietly abandon any hope for finalizing the Round, negotiators made fresh attempts to bridge the divide, leading ultimately to the Framework Agreement. The details remain to be finalized but domestic political difficulties may prevent a major change in the structure of international agricultural trade. The July Framework also agreed to exempt the poorest 50 countries from having to make any concessions at all.

The long negotiating hiatus meant that there was to be no final agreement to conclude the Doha Round by the end of 2005. Indeed, 2004–05 was a period of transition for the WTO, when personnel changes meant that there was little headway likely in substantial negotiations. In late 2004, EU Trade Commission Pascal Lamy left office and this was followed by the departure of his American counterpart Robert Zoellick. The first half of 2005 was also consumed by political maneuverings to replace Supachai as head of the WTO.

With energy consumed by other issues, the Doha Round negotiations were in a holding pattern. Already there are suggestions that the deadline could be extended to the end of 2007, the year Congressional Trade Promotion Authority expires. That provides trade negotiators ample time to work out acceptable compromises on the contentious issues and Supachai Panitchpakdi ventured optimistically that Cancun only represented a setback, not the failure that was Seattle, and that an agreement, when it was reached, would add to the global weight of WTO in dealing with trade issues.[57]

The Collapse of the Cancun ministerial meeting had the not unexpected effect of shifting focus away from global multilateral talks to bilateral or regional trade agreements. The resurgence in bilateralism has been evident for sometime but it would be unfortunate, especially for developing countries, if bilateralism were to become the sole policy agenda rather than an additional policy tool alongside multilateralism. Recent examples of bilateral preferential trade agreements include the US–Australia free trade agreement signed in 2004. The Australian government has signed a similar trade agreement with Thailand and is pursuing deals with several other trade partners.

Moreover, as *The Economist* observed, failure in the agricultural sector could instigate a range of new problems. For instance, in the Uruguay Round, countries had negotiated a "peace clause" to put on hold many of their farm-related trade disputes. The peace clause expired on December 31, 2003 and failure, in Cancun, to make progress on agricultural liberalization had the potential to unleash a slew of litigious actions by big agricultural exporters like, for example, Brazil. Such an outcome would have further enhanced the divide between countries that subsidize their agricultural exports (developed countries in general) and those that do not (the Cairns group and developing countries) and destabilize global multilateralism.[58]

However, efforts to revive the Doha Round began soon after the collapse of Cancun ministerial meeting. Success will require concessions on both sides of the divide. In January 2004, expectations were raised that the stalled talks could resume with possible concessions by the US. In a letter to WTO members, US Trade Representative Robert Zoellick urged members to take a commonsense approach and informed them that the US was prepared to agree to a timeline for elimination of export subsidies, the main stumbling block in the Doha Round. In addition the US agreed also to drop demands for rules on two of the Singapore issues, investments and competition policy.[59] Coming in the wake of plans to negotiate a Free Trade Agreement for the Americas, this was a clear indication that the US had not given up on multilateral trade policies but was keeping its options open. In 2005, Rob Portman replaced Zoellick as the new US Trade Representative and much will depend on his personal capacity and determination to move Doha Round negotiations forward.

US concessions, as far as genuine, will increase pressure on developing countries to be more flexible. Indeed, the likelihood is that developing country resolve and determination will crumble as they discover the difficulty of reconciling the divergent interests of the coalition members. Certainly China, for example was a member of the G-20 but it did not commit wholeheartedly to the cause of liberalizing trade in agriculture. China is no longer as dependent on agricultural exports as some of the other leaders of the G-20 and may be more prepared to break ranks, which is also what the developed countries may hope for. Moreover, China has an agricultural population of more than 70 percent, and there may be some negative consequences if the agricultural sector were to be fully liberalized, since China is a net agricultural importer. On the other hand India, Brazil and South Africa are large net exporters of agricultural products and stand to benefit from global market liberalization.[60] Developed countries have tried to exploit these divisions within the G-20. In press statements and comments following the meeting, the US was harsh on Brazil[61] but full of praise of China. USTR Robert Zoellick, for instance observed that China was a good partner and added that even though China participated in G-20 negotiations ". . . my sense is their participation was . . . well, others were the leaders of the process."[62] This was a subtle attempt to identify and reinforce a divide among the prominent members of G-20, between Brazil and India on one hand and China on the other. If criticism of China was muted, the Bush administration, however, soon infuriated the Chinese government when it imposed quotas on selected Chinese textiles in November 2003.

A common impression that is being encouraged is that Cancun talks broke down because of developing countries refusal, buttressed by false and mischievous political intrusions by NGOs, to compromise on the Singapore issues. That, however, is only a partial, even misleading, reflection of the facts. The talks failed equally because of the developed countries' refusal to offer meaningful concessions on agricultural liberalization. From the perspective of developing countries, the Singapore issues were thrown up as chaff by the EU to deflect attention away from the core concerns of the developing countries and in an attempt to portray them as intransigent. However, developing countries had reason enough to be wary of taking on additional commitments. In the Uruguay Round, they signed on to the TRIPs agreement, which has turned out to be detrimental to their interests. It was natural, therefore, that before negotiating on new issues they should want a satisfactory conclusion of existing agenda items.

The Doha Declaration had stated only that negotiations on the Singapore issues could commence with the consensus of members but the G-20 ensured that precondition was not met. Developing countries had resisted that inclusion at the Doha meeting and they refused to allow a consensus decision at the Cancun meeting without prior agreement on issues that were already on the negotiating agenda. In the

July 2004 Framework Agreement, one concession won by developing countries was that three of the four Singapore issues would not be on the negotiating agenda in the Doha Round. At Cancun, developed countries had offered to drop two of the four issues in a last-ditch and futile attempt to save the talks. The Framework Agreement is still only a partial victory for developing countries, which would have preferred to defer negotiations on all of the four issues.

7
Bilateralism in a Multilateral World

Most policy makers and trade economists acknowledge that multilateralism is a superior alternative to bilateral and regional trade agreements for all countries. Regional and bilateral agreements are best understood as preferential trade agreements (PTAs) because they assign to contracting parties certain preferences that are not available to other states. At the end of 2004, the World Trade Organization (WTO) had been notified of around 300 PTAs that had been negotiated among member countries. With the growing popularity of preferential trade agreements, a recent report on the future of the WTO lamented the reality that the most favored nation (MFN) clause, a central pillar of the WTO, was in danger of becoming Least Favored Nation clause.[1] WTO and the General Agreement on Tariffs and Trade (GATT) have accepted the inevitability of some preferential trade agreements as long as they resulted in genuine liberalization of trade among participant countries and provided such agreements did not result in higher trade barriers against external countries (Article 24). Still this was a reluctant acceptance and of the many PTAs that have been signed, few are actually consistent with multilateral trade rules, but as Jeffrey Schott points out none were actually ruled by the GATT or WTO as being inconsistent.[2]

Nonetheless, the reality is that trade policy has progressed along two tracks and most states see nothing inconsistent in pursuing the two options simultaneously. Even states that have a long history of exclusively multilateral trade policies, such as Japan, have softened their stance toward regionalism and seem keen to explore such options with major trade partners. In analyzing bilateralism and regionalism, opinion appears to cluster around the following five positions:

1. The pro-multilateralism camp is deeply cynical about bilateralist options and regards these as unnecessary distractions and detrimental to

global trade negotiations. This position is associated with Jagdish Bhagwati, a prominent economist, who insists that multilateralism should be the focus of trade policy makers. He argues that bilateral and regional policy initiatives are dysfunctional and divert attention from the central goal of global trade liberalization; so they are stumbling blocks on the path of multilateralism. Critics of bilateral and preferential trade agreements fault these as leading to undesirable trade diversion, which can exceed any benefit arising from trade creation.

2. Contrary to the above, another opinion cluster assumes that bilateralism and regionalism are stepping stones to global liberalization, especially as they progressively expand in size and membership to inevitably become global compacts, hence the European Union (EU), which began with 6 European countries, now has a membership of 25. Regionalism and bilateralism can conceivably be regarded as functional building blocks of multilateralism. That may be so in principle but the actual liberalizing achievements of regional and bilateral trade agreements have been limited. According to a World Bank report, *Global Economic Prospects 2005*, two-thirds of tariff reduction between 1983 and 2003 was a result of unilateral reforms by individual countries, a quarter as a result of Uruguay Round commitments, and only a tenth due to regional or bilateral deals.[3]

3. A third opinion cluster might be that bilateral deals are useful either in subverting some of the unacceptable provisions of WTO's trade multilateralism or in securing provisions unrealizable through the WTO process. This position is based on a particular reading of recent trade deals. For instance, the Singapore–US Free Trade agreement (FTA) includes provisions on intellectual property that are more restrictive than WTO guidelines. Similar provisions are also included in the Central American Free Trade Agreement (CAFTA) negotiated between the US and the Central American countries. If the relevant provisions of Singapore–US FTA and CAFTA assume the role of a precedent, these could inhibit the capacity of developing countries, like Thailand, which is currently negotiating a trade agreement with the US, to secure supply of cheap generic medicines to combat epidemics, like acquired immunodeficiency syndrome (AIDS). Indeed, according to Sidney Weintraub, the United States (US) selected Singapore as a FTA partner in order to establish a precedence. He writes that each "bilateral agreement that contains provisions on these themes [such as intellectual property] reinforces their inclusion in subsequent agreements."[4] This might seem inconsistent with a general perception that PTAs bring together like-minded countries and while it is true that almost all of US bilateral initiatives in recent

years have involved developing countries,[5] it would be drawing a long bow to suggest that the US and developing countries are like-minded. See opinion cluster 4 and 5 for possible explanations of why developing countries have accepted bilateral deals with developed countries.

4. It could be argued also that bilateral and regional trade deals are important learning tools for developing countries prior to engaging in more difficult multilateral negotiations. Trade negotiations at a multilateral level have become considerably complex since the Uruguay Round and it might be argued that some countries, particularly developing countries, use bilateral negotiations as useful learning devices to prepare for multilateral negotiations. Rajan *et al.* cite Sager that FTAs act as a "testing ground or pilot project for exploring complex trade issues" and may help establish benchmarks for trade negotiations involving a larger number of countries.[6] Yet, if true, it would make more sense for Thailand or Singapore, for instance, to negotiate with a less powerful country than the US, if the intention indeed was to hone bargaining skills for multilateral negotiations.

5. Finally, it is possible to regard preferential trade arrangements as insurance against future increases in trade protectionism.[7] This may be particularly attractive for developing countries that usually are supportive of multilateralism but may enter into bilateral deals to protect their interests in the event of collapse of global multilateralism.

The two instruments of trade liberalization, multilateralism and regionalism/bilateralism, have coexisted throughout the postwar period and uncertainties about the Doha Round may have created additional incentives for countries to try and secure individual gains by separate agreements that bypass the WTO. Certainly, there are advantages of adhering to a common global set of rules but in the absence of success in multilateral negotiations it is not surprising that states should try to pursue alternate strategies, even if the end result is suboptimal. Under globalization, production processes and supply chains, including the procurement of parts and labor, are becoming increasingly multilateral and the efficiency of global business accordingly depends on a common global framework rather than a web of bilaterally negotiated trade deals. Bilateral and regional PTAs are partial and resource-intensive to negotiate and to maintain. It was for this reason that China too saw fit to apply for WTO membership, which would obviate the need to negotiate separately on a bilateral basis in order to obtain MFN status. Yet, some countries, including even China, have demonstrated an interest in pursuing the option of trade bilateralism enthusiastically in recent years.

In late November 2004, China and the Association of South-East Asian Nations (ASEAN) signed a trade liberalization agreement that was considerably less comprehensive than a free trade deal but still a significant first step toward expanding trade in a regional setting. The agreement did not include trade in services, an area of relative strength for the ASEAN countries, nor did it contain any strict dispute resolution mechanism that would ensure and enforce compliance but these gaps will presumably be addressed over the coming years.

Among developed countries, the Australian and American governments have looked favorably on stand-alone trade agreements with their trade partners. In 2003, Australia concluded a FTA with Thailand and Singapore, countries in its immediate neighborhood and the following year it concluded a similar agreement with the US and began to pursue one with China as well. More significant for the future of multilateralism is the competitive push by Japan, China and India to conclude FTAs with ASEAN countries. Even if bilateralism does not displace multilateral initiatives completely it is likely that the two-track strategy of some of the key trading countries will persist for sometime.

A large-scale descent into bilateralism would be damaging to the interests of developing countries since they are likely to be left out of such deals, because their small size may not warrant special treatment. And when developed countries hold out the option of FTA with a developing country, the asymmetric bargaining position may produce a patently iniquitous agreement. For example, with the US protective of its pharmaceuticals industry, there have been suggestions that the US will pressure developing countries to cede their right to manufacture generic AIDS medicines in exchange for a free trade deal. In 2004, French officials accused the US government of precisely this form of bargaining strategy, which the French President Jacques Chirac labeled as "tantamount to blackmail."[8]

Many of the significant bilateral deals that have been concluded or which are being pursued are largely among developed countries or between developed countries and a select few of their main developing country trade partners. Those that have been established or proposed between developing countries exclusively have little global significance because developing countries, with a narrow band of export competitiveness, tend generally to be competitive rather than complementary in their economic structures and do not carry much weight in terms of global trade volumes.

The slide into bilateralism and regional FTAs predates the collapse of the Doha Round talks in September 2003. The push for bilateral trade deals is being led by a number of countries, including the US,[9] China, Australia and Singapore. Australia and Thailand, for example, started negotiating their FTA in May 2002, after both governments had committed to a joint scoping study in July 2001. And after years of acrimonious finger pointing and accusations, in July 2004, Australia and Malaysia surprised observers by declaring a commitment to explore the opportunities for a bilateral trade agreement. This came soon after Prime Minister Mahathir of Malaysia stepped aside and was replaced by his deputy.

When the GATT was established at the end of the Second World War, world leaders left open the option of regional and PTAs in order to accommodate some of the existing preferential agreements, such as British imperial preferences. More significantly, they demonstrated an optimistic faith that regional accords will over time become multilateralized and that such deals could become building blocks for a global trade accord. That faith appears to have been misplaced and instead regional trade deals compete with multilateralism for the attention of policy makers. The drift away from multilateralism received a boost in the early 1990s with the establishment of the North American Free Trade Agreement (NAFTA) and Asia Pacific Economic Cooperation (APEC). As an indication of the spread of regionalism in recent years, it is noteworthy that while 163 regional trade agreements were notified to the GATT/WTO between 1947 and 1997, 77 of these agreements were notified in only the five-year period between 1992 and 1997.[10] By one count, there are now close to 300 preferential trade agreements and, Bhagwati writes, their proliferation threatens to swallow the global trading system.[11]

Drift away from multilateralism

There are a number of reasons for the drift away from multilateralism. First, despite trade globalism the reality is that most countries trade mainly with a handful of countries. For example, in 2002, the top ten trading partners of the US accounted for 70 percent of American imports and 65 percent of its exports. The figures for Canada are more skewed. In 2000, 74 percent of Canadian imports came from the US and 86 percent of its exports were to the US. There is similar trade concentration among other developed countries. Most of Japanese trade is with the US, China, Korea and Taiwan. These four economies together account for roughly 43 percent of Japanese imports and 50 percent of Japanese exports. Similarly, Australia trades mainly with Japan, the US, China and South Korea. It is ironic indeed that in a global economy, trade is concentrated among a few countries. A handful of developed countries account for a disproportionate share of world trade. By contrast, the entire African continent has a miniscule 2 percent share of world trade, and only 1 percent if South Africa is excluded.

International trade is also regionally concentrated. For instance, in 2002, intra-EU and intra-NAFTA trade accounted for 60 percent and 46 percent of total EU and NAFTA trade, respectively. Unlike the highly regionalized trade of the European and North American countries, East Asian trade was largely extra-regional, with intra-regional trade comprising only 33 percent of their total world trade. Interestingly, as Desker observes, East Asian economies that had previously supported GATT/WTO multilateralism have begun actively to seek and conclude bilateral FTAs, not only as a result of the slowdown in multilateral negotiations but also to enhance their collective negotiating and bargaining influence in multilateral negotiations.[12]

A second reason for the seeming abandonment of multilateralism, related to the first, is that the WTO with 146 member countries (in April 2003) has become an unwieldy institution. Its precursor, the GATT was originally composed of 23 countries and negotiations and the negotiating agenda were relatively manageable. With the large number of countries and a complex negotiating agenda, the WTO may have become too costly to maintain relative to the potential benefit for the main trading partners. The difficulties encountered in the course of the Doha Round negotiations may have added to the incentives for bilateral deals that, in turn, only weaken the WTO further.

An assumed advantage of multilateralism is that it obviates the need for negotiating separate agreements with a large number of countries on an individual basis that can be both expensive and time consuming. For China, admission into WTO was attractive precisely because it had to negotiate MFN status on an annual basis with the US, which always raised tensions in their bilateral relations over issues of human rights and so on. These annual negotiations implied large transactions costs that also adversely affected other parts of their bilateral relationship. Transactions costs alone were considered a good reason to move in the direction of multilateral regulatory regimes. However, WTO may have become so large as to make negotiations unwieldy and equally costly. Moreover, with trade concentrated on a small number of countries, countries may find it attractive to bypass the WTO structure for separate long-term deals. This suggests that the very success of the WTO could now have placed it in jeopardy.

A third reason for the popularity of bilateral trade agreements is that while many economists see these as undesirable, studies by Andrew Rose point to a misguided faith in the WTO as a guarantor of liberal trade and as an instrument of trade growth. This conclusion is disputed by other studies, such as the World Bank report *Global Economic Prospects 2005* cited earlier but if the WTO really has been far less effective historically, there is less reason to continue to support it, especially now that such support is becoming increasingly costly.

Bilateralism and its impact on developing countries

Trade bilateralism has serious negative consequences. A majority of the poor developing countries will find themselves excluded and marginalized. The average developing country cannot hope to conclude more favorable trade deals on a bilateral basis than what developed countries have offered in the WTO. Following the collapse of Cancun trade talks in 2003, some developing country trade representatives rejoiced at their new-found voice and influence but the Trade Minister of Bangladesh perhaps best understood the potential negative fall-out for developing countries when he said, "I am really disappointed. This is the worst thing we poor countries could have done to ourselves."[13] Some developing country representatives were reported to be elated with the outcome and the inability of the West to have its way but that was probably no more than ill considered immediate reaction. Cancun may have been one of those rare occasions that developing countries put up a united front against Western demands but the triumph over western hegemony may yet prove to be a pyrhic victory.

Of course, the blame for failure lies equally with developed countries but developing countries are likely to suffer more than the rich countries, which trade extensively with other rich countries. Developing countries need the rich countries more than the rich countries need them for their economic growth and prosperity.

A majority of existing FTAs and PTAs are between developed countries (Australia–New Zealand Closer Economic Cooperation, EU), followed by those between developing countries (ASEAN Free Trade Agreement), and only a relatively few include both developed and developing countries (Australia–Thailand Free Trade Agreement, NAFTA). It is the last category of FTAs that are likely to be most beneficial to developing countries seeking bigger markets for their primary and labor-intensive exports. The scoping study to assess the impact of an FTA between Australia and Thailand reported the finding of the Center for International Economics that over a 20-year period an FTA would increase Thai GDP by US$25.2 billion (in 2002 net present value) and increase Australian GDP by US$6.6 billion. The estimates were based on the assumption of "overnight" liberalization and even though that is an unlikely scenario, the relative gains to Thailand are greater than the gains to Australia.

In theory, it makes little sense for a developed country to invest time and resource in negotiating a FTA with developing countries with which its trade is most likely to be of marginal significance. The reality, however, is considerably different and may relate less to economic benefit and more to the potential spillover effects, political or economic. For example, it is likely that American interests in pursuing trade deals with Oman and the United Arab Emirates include the possibility that such deals may create more propitious conditions for the spread of West-allied democracies in the Middle East.[14]

In 2002, the US signed a FTA with Singapore. With a population of 4 million Singapore is a small city-state. But it is America's twelfth biggest trade partner and could become a model for FTAs with other Asian countries. The agreement with Singapore contained conditions more restrictive than the WTO on intellectual property protection and placed limitations of Singapore's rights to access compulsory licensing agreements. The US is pursuing a similar agreement with Thailand, which would make it difficult for the latter to respond to potential public health crises, in the region and elsewhere, in the future and is contrary to the WTO agreement on pharmaceutical trade and human immunodeficiency virus (HIV)/AIDS. Bilateral FTAs, where the US can pick off countries one by one, therefore, have a real danger of eroding established conditions.[15]

Developing countries may have their own reasons for bilateral trade deals and against the backdrop of the WTO meeting in Cancun, there were suggestions within India that the government should perhaps concentrate its efforts in bilateral trade deals and withdraw from the WTO. As to whether this route might prove more profitable than tough negotiations at the WTO, the *Financial Express* observed:

> the OECD economies account for almost 50 percent of India's exports. Will any of them accept an FTA with India that is less demanding than the Doha development Agenda? Never.[16]

In the end, developing countries will have to face up to the challenge and pressure of balancing demands for an equitable outcome in the Doha Round negotiations with their interest in ensuring the success and continued viability of the WTO, if only to stave off a growing trend toward trade bilateralism. For a majority of developing countries, the best defense against exclusive bilateral or regional trade deals is a rules-based global trading system. The WTO ministerial meeting in Cancun exposed a subtle shift in the balance of power between developed and developing countries and while that may be heartening to developing countries the danger is that the West, will lose faith in the WTO and reduce it to irrelevance, in a replay of the fortunes of UN Conference on Trade and Development (UNCTAD). Developing countries therefore, will have to carefully and cleverly balance their interests with the imperative of preserving the integrity of the WTO.

In an ironic twist, the future of the WTO, established by developed countries, now rests partly with developing countries. It is inevitable that they will feel the pressure to moderate their position even if developed countries offered no more than token concessions in agriculture trade. The WTO is the guardian of rules-based trade and a collapse of the Doha Round will inevitably weaken WTO and its capacity to safeguard trade rules of national treatment and MFN. Developing countries have a stake in the principle of WTO multilateralism even if it has not served their interests in the past. The alternatives to multilateralism are more unpalatable and the basic objective should be to reform the governing principles, rules and norms so that the underprivileged are treated fairly and not denied trade and growth opportunities. Some economists, like Andrew Rose, are dismissive of the WTO, finding it to be ineffective, historically, in either liberalizing trade or in trade expansion.[17] He finds, for example, that a bulk of existing trade patterns can be explained by factors other than WTO membership or WTO liberalization, including traditional linkages like belonging to regional trade pacts, or shared language, borders and colonial histories (the so-called gravity effects).

If developing countries have a stake in protecting the WTO, so do the developed countries, including the US despite its openness to look beyond multilateral solutions. The US cannot be too confident that it will easily accomplish through bilateral and regional negotiations what it is unable to secure at multilateral talks. Nor can it afford to be complacent about the perils confronting trade mutilateralism.

Thus, although the US recently trumpeted a proposed CAFTA by highlighting that American exports to Central America were more than exports to Russia, India and Indonesia combined, the reality is that compared to Central America the latter three are fast growing economies and the US can hardly afford to be locked out of these economies by a breakdown of trade multilateralism. Moreover, if the US assumed that its initiative in securing agreement on a Free Trade Area of the Americas (FTAA) would be easy, that proved wrong when negotiations bogged down in November 2003 over disagreements between the US and Brazil. The 34 western hemisphere countries met in Miami in November 2003 to hammer out the FTAA but the US refusal to make significant concessions on farms subsidies and antidumping duties (issues of interest to Brazil) was met by a similar Brazilian refusal to negotiate investment rules, intellectual property rights and government procurement (issues of interest to the US).[18] The meeting ended with the two large economies at loggerheads with each other and the regionalist proclivities of the US government in some disarray, not unlike the WTO's Doha Round. Still, at a personal level, US Trade Representative (USTR) Zoellick appeared to have mended fences with his Brazilian counterpart which, in itself, was a significant development given the invective that had been heaped on the Brazilians a few months earlier.

In January 2004, a Summit of the Americas, bringing together 34 countries, gave grudging assent to an FTAA to be launched in 2005. However, most acknowledge that this ambitious target date is unlikely to be achieved, as there are few precise deadlines to complete negotiations on the pending issues. If successful, the FTAA will become the largest trade block, with 800 million people and total GDP of US$13 billion, with the US alone accounting for $10 billion. Latin American countries, however, remain adamant that the US has to offer major concessions on agriculture for any agreement to be possible. America's trade nemesis, the leftist President of Brazil Lula da Silva added a cautionary note, saying, "International trade can be a powerful factor in development. But it should be just and balanced, benefiting everyone equally." As a large primary exporting country, Brazil is wary of the American push for the FTAA because it is fearful that any final agreement must appease American political interests in farm protection and hence be skewed in allocating gains to the US at the cost of Brazilian primary producers.

In March 2004, after protracted and difficult negotiations, the US concluded a FTA with Australia but refused to substantially liberalize trade in sugar and beef, two industries in which Australia had hoped to achieve greater access to US markets. Still the Australian government hailed the agreement as a major breakthrough, perhaps more in terms of solidifying its alliance with the US than for its economic benefit. In 2004, South Korea finalized a FTA with Chile and the Japanese Ministry of Economy Trade and Industry doubled the size of its FTA negotiating team in order to push ahead with negotiations with Korea, Mexico and several ASEAN economies. Among developed countries,

Japan and South Korea have demonstrable interest in protecting global multilateralism but have been forced to accept bilateral FTAs in response to China's growing emphasis on networking its economy with regional countries through bilateral trade deals.[19]

Neither multilateral, nor its regionalist and bilateral alternatives, are easy but multilateral solutions are far superior to a patchwork of inconsistent and varied trade rules. The US and developed countries, like the developing countries, are best served by the WTO and any final resolution of the current impasse requires concessions by both developed and developing countries. Failure to search out a compromise solution will be damaging to all countries and reduce the WTO to a small forum for resolving trade disputes, with little influence or role in trade liberalization.

After Cancun, the G-20 was criticized by many in the West as having weakened the WTO. Among developed countries, Australia's reaction to G-20 was more nuanced. The G-20 may have jeopardized success of the Doha Round but like the G-20, Australia is committed to farm liberalization, an issue of importance to Australian farmers unable to compete against subsidized production in the US and EU countries.

Ten months after the fateful Cancun meeting, a WTO meeting in Geneva in July/August 2004 agreed to restart the stalled Doha Round negotiations based on an understanding between the developed and developing countries on agriculture and the Singapore issues, such as trade facilitation. Five days of intense negotiations produced a commitment by developed countries to eliminate export subsidies and trade distorting domestic subsidies to the agricultural sector while developing countries agreed to negotiate on informal barriers to trade, including governmental regulations and so on. Commentators acknowledged that the breakthrough reflected a realization on the part of developed countries that in a globalized economy, where components are sourced from a multitude of countries, bilateral deals are suboptimal to reducing, for instance, tariffs and other barriers at a global level. This would suggest that the developing country gamble at Cancun was worth the risk and that they were right in raising the stake in global negotiations.[20]

The reform proposals that restarted the talks were drafted by the so-called five interested parties (FIPS) or "Non-Group of Five" (NG5), consisting of US, EU, Australia, Brazil and India. The composition of the FIPS demonstrated the newfound clout and influence of the larger developing countries but this process of selection was dominated by the US, which saw other countries, such as China and Canada, excluded from the small group negotiations. Most delegates gathered in Geneva accepted the FIPS negotiations as unavoidable but criticized the lack of briefing sessions to give the minilateral talks a semblance of multilateral engagement. Switzerland, a strong critic of the FIPS process, pointed out that the agreement may have "saved the Doha Round but we might have killed the organization."[21]

At the Geneva meeting the first three days were occupied by the FIPS meeting while other delegates patiently awaited the outcome. The marathon negotiations tested the negotiating, technical and legal skills of the two developing countries involved which had considerably less resources to bring to the negotiating table compared to US, EU or Australia. The text of the draft proposal showed a shift in the right direction but skeptics pointed to textual ambiguities to suggest that the developed countries had, in fact, conceded considerably less than what they had seemingly agreed to. Not only were the end dates for elimination of subsidies left unspecified, the text also provided for special sensitive commodities that importing countries could exempt from the subsidies agreement. Depending on how extensively countries exploit the loophole on sensitive products, the final agreement has the potential to weaken trade opportunities for developing countries. But intense lobbying by Benin and other African countries, which came to Geneva much better prepared than for past meetings, led to an American commitment to give special priority to reforming trade in cotton.[22]

Conclusion

The collapse of Cancun trade talks appears to have hastened a drift toward bilateral and regional free trade deals that are at odds with multilateralism. However, while Cancun was a serious setback, it should not be seen as a fatal blow to globalization and trade multilateralism. Doha Round negotiations were revived following the July (2004) Framework Agreement and there is cautious optimism that the re-elected Bush administration will prioritize trade policy. Fred Bergsten writes:

> Most urgent is a more forthcoming offer of liberalization by the United States . . . especially in agriculture, to revive the Doha Round . . . The breakdown at Cancun proved that developing countries, united in a new G-20, can block multilateral trade progress on their own. Policymakers must recognize this fact and work constructively with the coalition, rather than trying to ignore it or dismantle it. The next administration must also revise trade policy as it related to bilateral agreements.[23]

In the July Framework Agreement, developing countries moderated and toned down demands for sweeping reform of global agricultural production and trade and conceded to terms that may ultimately deliver only modest benefits. Nonetheless, they obtained developed country concessions on export subsidies and on the Singapore issues. The G-20 can be credited with these achievements and its formation, as a loose coalition of developing countries within the WTO, raises some interesting questions about the role of lesser groups within a multilateral context. In the literature on regimes, some scholars have identified, as a more promising path for developing countries, the formation of negotiating alliances that cut across the North–South divide. Sewell and Zartman write that, "Until the North–South divide can be bridged so that countries can form coalitions and associations of only alliances of their real interests, progress in North South negotiations is not likely to be great."[24] Earlier in the Uruguay Round, developing countries had just such an association in the Cairns Group, involving both developed and developing countries.

The Cairns Group, despite achieving a high profile, was largely inconsequential to the final settlement of the Uruguay Round. This grouping had two main flaws. First, given a limited area of common interests they consequently find it hard to balance the need for flexibility and strict solidarity. While flexibility is a prerequisite for successful negotiations, this also has the potential to undermine group solidarity. Inflexibility, on the other hand, has detrimental consequences for bargaining and negotiating success but may preserve internal group solidarity. To the extent that the ultimate goal of small groups is to secure bargaining advantage, the dilemma is to balance the imperative of flexibility with solidarity. This is not easy and evidence suggests that such groups err on the side of solidarity even at the risk of becoming marginalized. Thus, the Cairns Group was committed to complete elimination of all agricultural subsidies but in the end American and European flexibility allowed for a compromise solution to which the Cairns Group made no meaningful contribution.

Second, the Cairns Group structure was that it tried to play a role as a third force in negotiations between the US and EU and quickly found itself marginalized, especially with the radical demands of countries like Australia in the Cairns Group. The success of the G-20, by contrast, can be partly attributed to its ability to transform the negotiations as a North–South issue, which became the primary divide in the Doha Round. The issues important to the South were no longer ancillary issues but the primary focus of negotiations. Whether the strategy can be sustained into the future is uncertain given that its formation also naturally invites counter-strategies of divide and rule.

The theoretical literature is unequivocal about the benefits of multilateralism, as compared to bilateralism, for small and weak states[25] but the history of GATT/WTO has negotiations have shown how meager these benefits can be for developing countries. Obvious frustration with outcomes of the Uruguay Round and inability to secure concessions on key issues from developed countries in the Doha Round were critical factors that encouraged developing countries to group together to enhance their bargaining position. In forming small groups within multilateral agencies, like-minded units, for instance the developed countries, have no real incentive to form overt coalitions but weak and small units, like developing countries, can hope to derive some bargaining advantage by presenting a united front on areas of common interests.

This minilateralization of multilateralism is not a newfound practice and takes two distinct forms. At one level, multilateral agencies were remade as minilateral bodies progressively such that by the 1960s, the GATT, for instance, had confined real negotiations to that between the principal buyers and consumers of specific commodities rather than on a pure multilateral basis, considered unwieldy and problematic. Thus, by the time of the Kennedy Round, GATT negotiations were multilateral in name only whereas what transpired was a series of bilateral and plurilateral negotiations.[26] The only concession to multilateralism was that any resulting agreement was made available to all on the basis of GATT's non-discriminatory and MFN principles.

Another form of minilateralization takes the form of issue-based coalitions with the objective of influencing negotiations and securing specific advantages. Members of such coalitions may be neither the principal buyer nor supplier of a specific tradable commodity but have clearly defined interest in ensuring certain negotiating outcomes. This type is also, in part, a reaction to the first exceptional category and the exclusion of smaller countries from the standard negotiating practices of the GATT/WTO. The G-20 belongs in this category. In the past, however, such groupings have been less than successful in securing their preferred goals.

The G-20 is likewise faced with a dilemma that flexibility will undermine group solidarity and unity but if it is to make progress in the Doha Round negotiations, it will have to display some flexibility on the negotiating issues. Absolute demands can only lead to absolute failure and that will be a tragic outcome for trade multilateralism, as some developing countries themselves are too well aware. The weak need multilateral rules of engagement more than the stronger counterparts and developing countries stand to lose more if multilateral institutions are weakened, a possibility if dispute between developed and developing countries leads the former to pick off individual developing countries through a network of bilateral agreements that weakens solidarity.

It would be stretching the truth to say that collapse of the Cancun ministerial meeting was due entirely to developing country inflexibility because the reality is that developed countries assumed an equally inflexible position. While developing countries insisted upon genuine agricultural liberalization, developed countries moved agriculture negotiations to the back burner and substituted instead "demands to open third world economies to protected foreign investment (the so-called 'Singapore issues' in trade jargon), an issue viewed as a poison pill for many developing countries."[27] By the time developing countries had walked out on negotiations, the atmosphere had degenerated to futile finger pointing but if the Round produces no tangible outcome, it will be the developing countries that will be equal losers. The practice of multilateralism may have been flawed but the principle is still worth preserving because multilateralism eschews the overt use of political power in favor of more democratic processes. Whatever the flaws that exists must be rectified by working within the system rather than by destroying the fabric of multilateralism. The protest movement in which many developing countries have become active participants should be "protest within the system" rather that "protest about the system." It is therefore of some concern that many developed countries, US, Australia and Japan, have moved aggressively to negotiate bilateral trade agreements, a pattern that is detrimental to the interests of the weak.

Both sides were inflexible in negotiations but this was the first time for developing countries and many developing country and NGO representatives celebrated this newfound strength as a triumph of negotiating competence. Phil Bloomer of Oxfam explained that:

> On paper, this meeting has failed, but the new power of developing countries backed by campaigners around the world has made Cancun turning point. In the past, rich countries made deals behind closed doors without listening to the rest of the world. They tried it again in Cancun. But developing countries refused to sign a deal that would fail the world's poorest people.[28]

Exuding confidence and optimism, the Ecuadorian Commerce Minister, stated at the end of the meeting, "It's not the end. It's the beginning . . . of a better future for everyone."[29] The future may be better but not by a whole lot. Developing countries hope for a balanced trade deal but they also want to strengthen the discipline of trade multilateralism. It is in this context that we must interpret their acceptance of the July Framework Agreement that promises marginal improvements but restores the importance of multilateralism. At Cancun developing countries were able to flex their political muscle but the reality is that no deal is possible without American consent. The US is central to both the survival of multilateralism and to a successful conclusion of the Doha Round. It is to his credit that US Trade Representative Zoellick did not pursue bilateralism at the expense of advancing multilateral solutions. His presence at the helm of US trade policies was important to the July Framework Agreement that has, at least, allowed negotiators to press forward and conclude the Doha Round. In the second Bush administration, however, Zoellick was moved from his trade role and into the State Department as deputy to the new Secretary of State. As such, trade multilateralism will lose an important campaigner but much will depend on his successor and whether that new appointee brings a commitment to trade multilateralism. In March 2005, President Bush nominated Rep. Rob Portman (Ohio) to succeed Zoellick as Trade Representative. His support for PTAs, in the past, do not necessarily mark him as predisposed to favor bilateral initiatives over multilateral strategies but he has yet to demonstrate a capacity to push forward the multilateral agenda.

8
Conclusion

Economic globalization is not easily reversible and protestors, despite some spectacular results, managed only to put up temporary obstacles rather than derail it. At a national level, even the election of a left wing candidate to the presidency in Brazil, in 2002, did not result in any radical shift in economic direction. As a relatively recent development, globalization has its supporters and detractors. It is faulted, by some, for exacerbating the economic divide between the North and the South while advocates of globalization will point out that globalization *per se* is a neutral force; any existing inequities are a result of political intervention and decisions, faulting governments for the miscarriage of globalization. Yet to the extent that inequities are present in the structure of contemporary globalization, critics have a point in their accusations. It is important to recognize that politics cannot be expunged from the process of globalization but through multilateral negotiations, it may be possible to minimize the negative consequences of political intervention in global market forces and, perhaps, even to introduce some affirmative action programs to assist developmental goals of the southern countries.

The World Trade Organization (WTO) and its predecessor, the General Agreement on Tariffs and Trade (GATT), have presided over impressive trade liberalization agreements but liberalization has not added greatly to the welfare of developing countries. This is due to the number of exclusions to the liberalization agenda. In this context, developed countries and multilateral agencies have failed developing countries quite badly. Nonetheless this has generated a myth that developing countries, in general, no longer wish to pursue any further economic and trade liberalization, and that they are interested only in more liberal access to developed country markets. A better depiction of reality is that most

161

developing countries have staked out either defensive or offensive interests. The former, such as Bangladesh, are considerably more cautious and protective of narrow interests but many in the latter category are not afraid to take on more liberal trade commitments, provided these are also balanced and fair outcomes. Moreover, mindful of past inequities, offensive liberalizers, such as South Africa, have declared their interest in rebalancing the most egregious of existing rules and structures. None of this is to suggest that trade opportunities, or the lack of them, are the only impediments to successful development in developing countries.

There exist deep-seated tensions in the global economy that run along the North–South divide. The South wants special and differential treatment but these demands have received little sympathy in the developed countries. For a long time, the United States (US) even stymied claims for access to cheap generic medicines to fight the AIDS (acquired immune deficiency syndrome) crisis in Africa, giving in only shortly before the Cancun ministerial meeting of the WTO. Judging by the history of WTO negotiations, developed states will have to make very significant concessions if the Doha Round is to fulfill its mandate as the Development Round. In the lead-up to the mid-term review of the Doha Round at Cancun in September 2003, trade negotiators missed all the important deadlines for agreement on modalities. This included intellectual property rights (end-2002), agriculture (March 2003), and even industrial tariffs (end-May 2003). In negotiations on industrial tariffs countries failed to agree on a draft proposal put forward by Pierre-Louis Girard, Chairman of Tariff Talks, that high tariff countries, mostly developing countries, be required to cut tariffs less than low tariff countries, and that tariffs on commodities of interest to developing countries, such as textiles, electrical goods and gems, be eliminated.[1] The Cancun meeting itself ended in a deadlock and negotiations resumed only following the July Framework Agreement of 2004. There is, as yet, no clear indication of outcomes and some of the key unresolved issues include agriculture and services trade, and non-agricultural market access.

However, while conflict over issues of fairness and justice in the global political economy is real and becoming more pronounced, there is little reason to be concerned about a civilizational conflict, a la Samuel Huntington. This is, at least partially, because neither side is completely united in purpose. The more numerous South has many cross cutting cleavages and the North, too, has conflicting agendas. In the Uruguay Round and the Doha Round, for example, there were serious disagreements between the US and Cairns Group of Fair Traders on the one hand and the European countries and Japan on the other, especially in terms of agricultural liberalization. The former group has been adamant in demanding an elimination of most farm subsidies and protectionist policies while the latter is equally insistent on protecting domestic agriculture from foreign competition. This nearly scuttled the Uruguay Round in its latter stages and might actually sink the Doha Round. It is possible that the Doha Round will be salvaged by the same sort of deal-making in agriculture between the US and European Union (EU) which salvaged the Uruguay Round, but at the cost of key developing country interests.

So far developing countries have received only modest benefits from global economic structures. The paucity of benefits lead, legitimately, to questions of "whose globalization?" At one level, the question is easy to dismiss with rhetorical flourishes about the benefits of free trade but which, without due concern for equity, become the imperialism of free trade. Just as other multilateral agencies, like the World Bank and the (IMF), have highlighted the importance of developing country "ownership" of anti-poverty strategies, and a consultative process, there is need for similar engagement of developing countries in the WTO. For globalization to work, developing countries must be brought in from the cold. In 2003, Supachai Panitchpakdi, Director General of the WTO, established a Consultative Board on the Future of the WTO composed of eight individuals headed by Peter Sutherland, a former Director General, to explore proposals to assist developing countries engage with the global economy. In early 2005, the Consultative Board delivered its report and recommendations, including the following.

1. Ensure the major economic institutions work together in helping developing countries implement appropriate trade policies.
2. Engage developing countries in decision making so that it is not only the rich countries that have a sense of ownership of the WTO.
3. Collaborate with non-governmental organizations (NGOs) in a creative manner to tap into their expertise.
4. Offer improved market access but also look careful at regulatory standards, such as in health and rules of origins, to remove unnecessary confusion and complexity, which in turn impede export opportunities.[2]

The US and developed countries were the primary architects of postwar liberal international economic order and, curiously, these countries also have a history of ignoring and violating rules with relative impunity whenever it has suited their purposes. Thus, while they, through the various multilateral agencies and structural adjustment programs, have forced many poor countries to cease or drastically reduce subsidy payments, they continue nonetheless to subsidize production at home and even to support subsidized exports. Daily subsidies to the agricultural sectors in the US and Europe exceed US$1 billion. Subsidized agricultural exports from developed countries have devastated the farm sector in developing countries and it remains to be seen how effectively the Doha Round negotiations will eliminate these subsidies, even though there is in-principle agreement to end export subsidies.

WTO rules also prohibit countries from exporting industrial products that have received government subsidies but rules on agricultural subsidies are somewhat ambiguous and allow subsidized exports as long as they do not displace the exports of another member country. This rule has been violated by the EU and the US to the detriment of smaller agricultural exporting countries such as Australia, and the developing countries, such as Mali but the WTO has failed to act to stop this practice. Western countries are large exporters of subsidized agricultural exports and are able to do so with complete impunity whereas any hint of subsidized industrial exports from developing countries is promptly dealt with under the antidumping provisions of the WTO.

Trade hypocrisy is rampant elsewhere as well. For instance, the original rules regarding balance of payments adjustments placed the onus on deficit countries but in later years, as the US experienced chronic balance of payments deficits, it shifted the responsibility on to the surplus countries, like for example Japan, on suggestions that the latter was an unfair trader and exporter.

Much is at stake in the Doha Round but a series of rulings by the Dispute Settlement Body (DSB) of the WTO may have dampened American interest and support for the WTO. For instance, in March 2002, the US went against its WTO obligations to impose higher tariffs on steel imports in order to protect the domestic steel industry. This prompted threats of retaliation from steel exporters and the dispute was resolved ultimately in a manner that demonstrated that the US was not entirely beyond the disciplinary powers of the WTO. Following a WTO resolution that US tariffs were WTO-illegal, the US government, in early December 2002, agreed to rescind the tariffs rather than defiantly proceed on a unilateralist trade path and trigger a tariff war with its trade partners. While this episode may be characterized as a triumph of multilateralism, there is other evidence to suggest also a seeming American distaste for multilateral organizations and multilateral solutions.[3] In recent years, for example, the US signed a number of bilateral trade deals and the attractiveness of bilateral trade agreements is that there is greater scope for the exercise of hegemony and influence. Bhagwati and Panagariya point out, for example, that in the process of negotiating the North American Free Trade Agreement (NAFTA), the United States demanded that Mexico accept provisions for protecting intellectual property rights.[4]

Another source of difficulties in the Doha Round is the stand of the corporate sector in the US and Europe. Mattoo and Subramanian of the World Bank and IMF respectively, write that historically the corporate sector was an important driver of multilateral trade liberalization but find that the Doha Round is "plagued by a private sector interest deficit. The corporate demandeurs—the traditional protagonists—of the North are conspicuous by their absence. All the focus on developing country discontent with globalization and the WTO . . . have obscured this fundamental problem afflicting the Round."[5]

The North–South conflict and the Doha Round

While the July Framework Agreement of 2004 has kept hopes alive, there is, as yet, no guarantee that the Doha Round will be completed. Failure to conclude the Round will have a larger negative impact on developing than on the developed countries. In explaining poverty and underdevelopment, dependency theorists externalized the source of the problem to an exchange relationship that was exploitative. Their advocacy of either autarky or revolutionary socialism however is not realistic in the contemporary period. The failure and collapse of socialism as an alternative economic strategy means it is no longer an alternative, and autarky too may create more disadvantages than benefits. Global engagement is the best course of option for developing countries and, indeed, in the Uruguay Round developing countries have actively participated in the negotiations. In the past, developing countries had placed greater faith in UN Conference on Trade and Development (UNCTAD)[6] than on the GATT processes.

It is clear that the many privileges that developed countries have arrogated to themselves will not be easily surrendered. Developing countries did not derive much benefit from the Uruguay Round and the same may recur in the Doha Round. Negotiating agenda is far more diverse and complex and developing countries are on a steep learning curve and will have to play smart in order to produce a more balanced agreement. Active participation may not be immediately rewarded but developing countries have to be prepared to sustain their efforts over the long term in order to bring about systemic changes and a more just international political economy.

Failure of the Doha Round will have a less deleterious effect on the developed countries. The US, in particular, will be free to pursue bilateral deals more to its liking and without having to bend to the collective will of a large number of countries inside the WTO. This is not to suggest that the US is disinterested either in the Doha Round outcomes or the WTO but simply that it has alternative fallback strategies. At a trade meeting in Egypt in 2003, US Trade Representative Robert Zoellick bluntly acknowledged that if the Doha Round failed to deliver acceptable outcomes, the US would turn to bilateral and regional trade agreements.[7] For developing countries however, multilateralism offers the best prospects for obtaining a favorable trade deal.

The developing countries are more numerous but, as might be expected, developed countries have several advantages in monopolizing the process to their advantage. With their superior power position, bargaining skills and negotiating strategies, they have considerable advantages in structuring rules to their benefits. The impasse on the leadership of the WTO was eventually resolved when Thailand conceded and suggested the eventual compromise solution. It had become obvious to the Thai government that Supachai was unacceptable to the West and the compromise was put by the Thai Prime Minister to the US Secretary of State. It was publicly articulated and explained by the Australian Deputy Prime Minister Tim Fisher, as a neutral third party.

For developing countries, the issue is not whether, but how, to engage with globalization. Certainly the external dimension of inequity is a constant presence as are opportunities to help shape more equitable international structures. Developing countries also have to address internal weaknesses that impede their capacity to structure exchange relationships and rules in ways that are more equitable. The two main weaknesses of developing countries in international negotiations relate to their limited technical and financial resources, and to their larger numbers.

The developing countries are simply unable to marshal technical expertise to put their views forward or, indeed, to assess the economic impact of proposals sponsored by developed countries. Thus, they have signed on to agreements that have had adverse impact on their economic interests. On trade related issues, they are disadvantaged even by the location of the WTO in Geneva, which has made it difficult for poor countries to maintain adequate representation. More than 20 of the smaller developing countries do not have offices in Geneva, which makes it difficult for them to attend meetings or contribute to decision-making. Many other developing countries that maintain representation in Geneva have relatively small and understaffed missions because of cost considerations.[8] Their missions also deal with a multiplicity of international agencies besides the WTO, such as World Health Organization (WHO), International Labor Organization (ILO) and the UNCTAD.

Alongside their inferior technical and negotiating capacity, the structure of trade negotiation is, itself, an obstacle and strains the meager capacities of developing countries. In particular, the Uruguay Round and the still to be completed Doha Round have been marathon processes, both in terms of the negotiating agenda and duration of negotiations. Poorly prepared to begin with, developing countries are liable to suffer "negotiating fatigue" much sooner than the developed countries. As mentioned, most developing countries have very small missions to the WTO. Even the South African mission, which among developing countries is one of the larger ones, is staffed by only four individuals. Easily fatigued by the intensity and scope of negotiations, developing countries are apt to give in and accept outcomes that are detrimental to their interests. This happened with the trade related intellectual property (TRIPs) negotiations in the Uruguay Round when developing countries were slowly pressured or bought off to abandon their hardline stance and ultimately, India, which alone remained steadfast in resisting developed countries' proposals on patent protection succumbed to negotiation fatigue and abandoned its defense of a more liberal regime on intellectual property rights (IPRs). The Uruguay Round then "adopted texts to protect IPRs, liberalize services and prohibit trade-related investment measures."[9]

For developing countries to achieve more propitious outcomes, it is necessary to develop appropriate negotiating capacities. In recent years there has been considerable discussion about enhancing state capacity but frequently this is framed in reference to implementation of internationally negotiated agreements. It is necessary also to enhance capacity in order to strike more favorable bargains, which in turn are less likely to face the implementation problems that developing countries currently encounter. This refers to the "ownership" problem but the WTO has a very small budget of SFr30 million for technical assistance purposes, including short courses on trade matters. Even with minimal technical assistance, one informed source commented how a Western representative to the WTO had, following the collapse of the Cancun talks, remarked that capacity building was a bad idea.

Nonetheless, it is important to give developing countries "ownership" of the emerging rules. Ownership, in turn, will facilitate implementation of, and adherence to trade rules, as the IMF has discovered in relation to structural adjustment programs, as well as help to silence the protest movement against globalization. At present, this is a serious deficiency in the trade regime but to effectively rectify this, developing countries will require assistance to develop their bargaining capacity and knowledge. In February 2003 the German Marshall Fund, a US policy group, set up the Trade and Poverty Forum (TFP) bringing together prominent individuals and representatives from developed and developing countries to assist in spreading the benefits of trade to the poorer countries and to make an impact on WTO negotiations. Rahul Bajaj, an Indian industrialist and leader of the TFP said that "There is a feeling of helplessness, even some anger in the developing world, that the developed world . . . only look after their own interests."[10] It is clear also that unlike many NGOs, groups and individuals that coalesced to defeat the Multilateral Agreement on Investments (MAI), based on a philosophical rejection of globalization and liberalization, governments in developing countries cannot afford to adopt a similar position of rejecting *a priori* negotiations on economic liberalization. Rather they have to be better prepared to participate in multilateral fora with a good understanding of the issues and likely consequences.[11]

The inequities in the system, however, can only be partially addressed through capacity building measures[12] because structural handicaps are not easily overcome by simply being better prepared. Making the system fairer will not be an easy task but to the extent that many of the rules and structures are currently being negotiated, there is an opportunity to shape their final design. In that context, it is all the more important that developing countries actively engage in negotiations as best as structures permit and develop effective negotiating and bargaining strategies.

The WTO is only able to provide limited assistance to another possibility for developing countries is to collaborate more closely with international non-governmental agencies, which have been active in preventing flawed international bargains, such as the MAI. Just as the US and developed countries tend to respond favorably to interests of big business, developing countries should make better use of expertise and technical know how of established NGOs in the fields of development and poverty alleviation. WTO provisions allow extensive collaboration between member states and NGOs but a survey of 30 states found that only three governments involved NGO representatives effectively in trade negotiations.[13]

There are, however, some prominent success stories, most notably the campaign for access to cheaper medicines. The campaign was spearheaded by prominent NGOs like Oxfam and MSF and according to Drahos, these NGOs "had analytical resources, a track record of credible public policy work, international networks extending into developing countries and experience in running international campaigns. In the post-Seattle environment government officials listened to the policy voice of such NGOs with greater attentiveness."[14] The alliance of NGOs and developing countries was effective not only because of the issue of AIDS but also because NGOs, in particular, were able to marshal evidence and provide convincing analysis to include medicines on the negotiating agenda.

Alongside negotiating fatigue and lack of capacity, strangely enough, developing countries are also made to feel responsible for breakdown in negotiations and, subsequently, for compromise and concession. Thus, many Western governments were quick to blame the South for the collapse of the Cancun meeting.

Structural disadvantages facing the South

Although the WTO does not follow the weighted voting strategy of the IMF,[15] WTO rules do not necessary benefit developing countries. The WTO operates on the basis of unity and consensus but these principles have failed to protect the interests of developing countries primarily because developing countries face enormous pressure to not hold out on agreements even if their interests have not been addressed. It also has given the US, as an example, a virtual veto over WTO proceedings and agreements. This became evident in early 2003 when the US rejected a TRIPs agreement on pharmaceuticals, overriding consensus among all the other member states of the WTO.

WTO decision-making is not transparent and there are many informal decision-making structures that exclude developing countries. In 2003, One World Trust, a British charitable NGO, prepared a report on accountability in intergovernmental organizations and multinational corporations (MNCs) and observed that although the WTO officially permitted all members to "add items to the agenda of governing body meetings, there is evidence that much of the agenda is set behind closed doors in private meetings. These meetings, known as 'Green Room' meetings, are rarely publicly announced in advance. Attendance is subject to invitation by the Director General and developing countries are routinely excluded."[16] The Green Rooms however, are frequently used to coerce developing countries to give their assent to a "consensus" decision. Drahos writes "developing country leaders might be invited to participate in the Green Room process in order to win them over to the consensus group. In the case of the TRIPs negotiations, the pressure of these Green Room meetings became so great that developing country delegates began to refer to them as the 'Black Room' consultations."[17]

Similarly, at WTO's first Ministerial Conference in Singapore all ministers were "allocated time to make speeches at the open plenary meetings, but most developing countries were never even invited to the really important discussions on issues where there were disputes and which took place in 'informal groups'." For most of the Conference, their Ministers and senior officials were kept in the dark as to what was going on. "Lack of transparency" was the term used by most delegates, NGO representatives, and journalists alike to describe the Conference's manner of operations.[18] The presence of informal decision-making structures impedes the capacity of small developing countries to have influence processes and outcomes. Thus, even a decision rule of consensus can be subverted to entrench the dominant position of some of the larger countries.

A principle of majority rule would be more democratic but not likely to be supported by the dominant developed countries because it would eliminate their control of the WTO agenda. Western and US hostility to majority voting in multilateral agencies can be gleaned from the experiences of the UNCTAD. The UNCTAD had been established in the early 1960s to advance the interests of developing countries but lost favor with the US, especially after events in the early 1980s. It then proceeded to subvert it and render it impotent. In 1982, the developing countries used their overwhelming majority to vote through a Board resolution despite strong opposition from the developed countries.

The resolution established the principle of the UNCTAD Secretariat servicing meetings devoted to trade negotiations among developing countries and did not invoke any major substantive issue but the US took exception to this exercise of majority rights. Nassau Adams, a former Head of UNCTAD's Division for Data Management says, it is difficult to say whether this was the final straw for the US but that American actions thereafter served only to undermine the role and significance of UNCTAD.[19] For example, even though UNCTAD had been established on the premise that developing countries required special and differential (preferential) treatment, in an UNCTAD Board meeting in 1984 the US began reengineering its role by stressing that notions of a world polarized between the core and the periphery were antiquated and did not reflect the new realities of interdependence, in which the rich and the poor and the strong and the weak should be treated equally. The US also indicated that the UNCTAD should be a forum for discussion, a talk-shop, rather than decision-making and by the early 1990s the nature of the organization had been completely transformed. UNCTAD was no longer in a position to influence trade policy and developing countries were left without their support organization.

Multilateral institutions are at the core of the global political economy and also the instruments of American domination and influence. These institutions were established after the Second World War to give more stability to a liberal trade structure, unlike the free trade regime of the nineteenth century, which had no institutional ballast, and also to disguise the exercise of American hegemony and power. As noted in relation to the Washington Consensus, for instance, existing multilateral institutions are prominent vehicles for propagating the ideology of the dominant power and it is, in that context understandable, that the US should safeguard its dominant position in multilateral agencies. To maintain its control the US, in mid-2003, blocked attempts by developing countries to increase their voting power at the World Bank from 40 percent to 43 or 44 percent, arguing that its own voting share of 16 percent did not reflect its real weight in global GDP, which stood at 21 percent. At present European countries are over represented in the Executive Board of the World Bank and it is unlikely that they will readily vacate their position to developing countries.[20]

Southern alliance politics

To participate effectively in multilateral politics, developing countries need to coordinate their actions and policy choices. The importance of a united front in order to influence global policy-making is not lost on developing countries. There are a plethora of regional and cross-regional groupings precisely for that purpose.

In the lead-up to the Cancun ministerial meeting of the WTO in September 2003, a group of 39 of the least developed countries joined together, in late May and early June 2003, for a meeting for only the second time in Dhaka, Bangladesh. The three-day meeting brought together trade ministers and officials to develop a common response and course of action preparatory to the WTO meeting for a mid-term review of the Doha Round. At the end of the meeting, delegates issued the Dhaka Declaration expressing strong discontent with prevailing trade arrangements that have seen the marginalization of developing countries and a continuing diminution of their share of world trade since the 1960s. The Dhaka Declaration contained a set of demands for a fairer deal, including:

- Duty and quota free access for all developing country products in export markets.

- Differential and special treatment to reverse the marginalization of developing countries in world trade.
- Simplification of visa procedures and free temporary movement of skilled and unskilled service providers.
- Enhanced technical and financial assistance to developing countries.
- Exemption of LDC exports from antidumping, countervailing and safeguards (protectionist) measures.
- Mechanism to restore a system of preferences for developing country exports that had been introduced in the 1960s (Generalized System of Preferences—GSP) but which had become practically meaningless with progressive reduction of most favoured nation (MFN) tariffs. Lower MFN tariffs of around 4 percent had reduced the margin of GSP preferences (0 percent tariff) on select developing country exports.
- Protection of genetic resources.

The Bangladesh Minister for Commerce, Amir Khosru Mahmud Chowdhury, emphasized that it was necessary to "send a strong message to the international community emphasizing our interests." Unfortunately, this large gathering of trade ministers and officials from developing countries received scant media attention in the West, a fact highlighting the difficulty of breaking through the barrier of relevance. The demands were to be tabled at the 5th Ministerial Meeting of the WTO to undertake a mid-term review of the Doha Round in September 2003. The list of demands was nothing extraordinary although the inclusion of easier movement for temporary workers might be seen to be at odds with the greater focus on border protection in developed countries following recent terrorist activities. After the September 11, 2001 terrorist attacks, movement of people across border has become more tightly controlled than ever before. In some respects if an "iron curtain" had descended across Europe at the end of the Second World War to prevent the exit of people from the socialist countries, today a new "iron curtain" has descended around developed countries to prevent the entry of people from outside.[21]

However, temporary movement of labor is one of the four recognized modes of services delivery and included in the General Agreement on Trade in Services (GATS) that was negotiated during the Uruguay Round. While Mode 4 delivery of services constituted only 1 percent of total world trade in services, for developing countries, remittances from temporary and permanent workers contributed about US$71 billion to their foreign exchange earnings in 2001. According to one source if "temporary movement of labor up to 3 percent of the total labor force in rich countries were permitted, developing countries would stand to gain as much as US$160 billion in additional incomes."[22] Labor mobility has other advantages in technology and skill transfer to developing countries and, as observed by Shahid Yusuf of the World Bank:

> The Overseas Chinese diaspora, which commands a huge volume of capital and can draw upon detailed market information as well as a wide range of expertise, has contributed significantly to the growth of south-east Asian economies. Similarly, as India has liberalized its economy, the overseas Indian community has become far more active in launching business ventures in the subcontinent and supporting the development of skills in ICT and high tech industries.[23]

Coming from a group of the least developed countries, the Dhaka Declaration did not have any noteworthy impact on actual negotiations in Cancun. But even though this attempt at demonstrating collective resolve was less than a spectacular success, it was remarkable still that such a large number of countries had been able to agree to a consensus declaration. This is because all large groups suffer from the tyranny of numbers.

The developing countries are more numerous but they are also more diverse and it has been difficult for them to develop and adhere to common positions in international negotiations. According to Mancur Olson, for example, small groups are both more efficient and effective because they are easier to organize whereas large groups find it harder to agree to a common position and to coordinate their actions. It is a well-worn adage that there is strength in numbers but extremely large groups suffer coordination failures even though coordination in trade negotiations is essential to the development of positive outcomes.

Thus while the Dhaka Declaration of 2003 was a consensus document, African countries were unhappy with Bangladesh's determination to include the removal of travel restrictions as one of the 16 points in the list of demands because it would benefit only a few countries.[24] The African countries were primarily interested in removal of subsidies on all farm and agricultural products.

At other times, a few of the larger developing countries have been outspoken in rejecting western domination of the trade agenda and decision making but their activities have been labeled as obstructionism, which is unlikely to be rewarded and easy to dismiss as irrelevant. In the Uruguay Round negotiations, Egypt, Yugoslavia, Brazil and India were united in their opposition to yet another round of liberalization of areas sensitive to developing countries, especially as the Tokyo Round agreements had not yet been fully implemented. This "obstructionism" was quickly dismissed and the four countries pejoratively labeled the "gang of four." This gave the impression that these four countries were engaged in negative attempts to destabilize negotiations. This deliberate ploy to ridicule the genuinely held beliefs of certain developing countries was unfair but the reality is that negotiations always entail an element of discrediting the opposition to protect one's position. The same principle can also be seen in the US' attempt to ridicule the demand for cheaper drugs and liberal licensing requirement as a poorly masked attempt by developing countries to obtain Viagra. In this propaganda war, developing countries have not been very successful in getting across their points of view, given western domination of the media and the knowledge machinery.

In 2003, India and China, two of the largest developing countries and rivals for leadership, also agreed to work together and coordinate their trade policies in some of the key areas of concern to developing countries, such as intellectual property rights.[25] These two countries are large producers of generic drugs and stand to gain considerably from an improved regime on compulsory licensing.

None of these alliances proved very effective in raising the profile of developing countries in multilateral negotiations. A simple majority-based decision-making rule may have improved their bargaining position but that is unlikely to find favor with the developed countries. In its present structure, the WTO is ostensibly democratic but has marginalized the views and opinions of a majority of its members through an opaque and inaccessible decision-making structure. Moreover, being weak, dependent on aid and largesse of developed nations, developing countries are susceptible to blackmail and pressure, especially the smaller and the least developed countries.

As such, coordinating policies among this very diverse group of countries is fraught with difficulties but it is still possible for some of the larger developing countries to take a leadership role and articulate general policy preferences of the larger group. The formation of the Group of Twenty (G-20) just prior to the Cancan ministerial meeting of the WTO owed less to a perceived need to coordinate response than to the immediate threat of having an unfavorable agreement on agriculture outcome imposed on them by the US and EU. The G-20 is led by the triumvirate of India, China and Brazil and represents more than half the world's population. The main demand of this group is greater market access for agricultural commodities and it engaged in extensive lobbying at the Cancun ministerial meeting. It also received the support of Australia and Cairns Group, which was formed during the Uruguay Round to press for agricultural liberalization. The G-20 has been reasonably effective in terms of its immediate concerns but its continuation beyond the Doha Round is uncertain and will depend on an understanding to maintain policy coordination.

When the WTO convened its ministerial meeting in Cancun in September 2003 to review progress in the Doha Round, the G-20 grouping of developing countries played an important role in rejecting the inclusion of new agenda items until developed countries agreed to deliver more equitable access to their agricultural markets. With a sense of purpose and determination based on a view that developing country interests had for too long been denied a fair hearing, the G-20 maintained its stiff resistance and ultimately the meeting ended without any firm conclusion. The collapse of the Cancun meeting marked a new chapter in the evolution of the WTO. It is true that the Uruguay Round too was protracted and encountered many missed deadlines; the Doha Round is the first instance of failed negotiations because of developing country rejection of Western agenda. In the months ahead there will no doubt be many attempts to restart negotiations and attempts to destroy unity of the G-20 group and much of eventual outcomes will depend on whether or not developing countries are able to sustain unity in the face of hostile pressure. But regardless of what happens, it is clear that developed countries will not be able to ignore the interests of developing countries. In that sense, at least, the formation of the G-20 must be regarded as a success even though as a grouping it has not presented a coherent and comprehensive list of demands against which we might measure its success more accurately when and negotiations produce a final agreement.

The success to date of the G-20 can be attributed to its determination to make the North–South dimension the primary focus of WTO negotiations instead of letting outcomes be subject to negotiations between the US and EU. Contrary to suggestions that developing countries have more to gain by forming alliances across the developmental divide, the G-20 has achieved more than the Cairns Group, composed of both developed and developing countries, in the Uruguay Round. Whether the G-20 will survive beyond the Doha Round is, however, uncertain. When the G-20 was formed in 2003, parallels were drawn to an earlier grouping of Latin American countries that was formed to resist American and European moves to exclude agriculture from the Uruguay Round of trade talks. That refusal to countenance duopolistic decision making led to the collapse of the 1988 Montreal mid-term review of the Uruguay Round but the announcement that followed alluded only to a temporary adjournment rather than a break down of talks. This ensured that no "big headlines ensued."[26] In the end, however, this group of five Latin American countries led by Brazil caved in to external pressure and was disbanded.[27] For the G-20 to defy the weight of history, coercion and the inherent centrifugal forces within this diverse community of states will require considerable skill and determination. One advantage that the G-20 possesses is that it is composed primarily of developing countries that might be called the "offensive liberalizers." That gives it some unity of purpose.

Whose globalization?

Every economic system and every policy decision inevitably entails trade-offs. Benefits are not always equitably distributed and, indeed, some are disadvantaged. Alongside the advocates and beneficiaries of globalization there are a large number of dissidents and disadvantaged groups. These may range from those that fear a race to the bottom in the developed countries and individuals in threatened industries. More fundamentally, however, globalization of the form that is unfolding has systematically disadvantaged the poor and developing countries, even as they are enticed to participate under false and misleading promises.

In a perfectly globalized world, conflict between the North and the South would not be a serious issue since absolute free trade can be theoretically demonstrated to be in the interest of all countries regardless of differences in the stages of development. That is not the case and the inevitable intrusion of political considerations mean that globalization will be manipulated and engineered in ways that are beneficial primarily to the more powerful members of the global economy. In an ideal world, countries would collectively declare unconditional acceptance of liberal economic principles but that is unlikely in present circumstances. Instead, we witness a process of constitutional engineering, efforts to establish rules and codes of conduct for an imperfect world of economic globalization. Absolute globalization is not in the realm of possibilities and it, therefore, becomes material to discuss issues of costs allocation and benefits arrogation.

Economic exchange has always been marked by inequities but developing countries have been promised and led to believe that participation in the global economy is crucial to their economic development. However, the structure of rules that have been proposed by developed industrial countries do not inspire confidence that they are willing to share the bounty of globalization in a fair and equitable manner. To prevent egregious exploitative behavior, developing countries will have to negotiate smarter and not take claims and promises for granted. A historical parallel already exists. In the 1980s, the US pioneered arguments for results oriented trade in negotiations with Japan. The strategy was not an unambiguous success for the US and developing countries, too, should carefully weigh claims rather than accept them in good faith. Certainly power asymmetries will not make bargaining easy but that can be partially overcome through strategies designed to maintain unity and discipline among developing countries. Moreover, they can also enlist the support of international NGOs and civil society groups to press their claim for a more equitable distribution of benefits from the global economy.

Developing countries in multilateral negotiations

Developing country involvement in the Doha Round stands out in sharp contrast to their participation in GATT negotiating rounds. These countries relied more on the UNCTAD and through it managed even to get GATT acceptance and introduction of special and differential treatment (SDT). In early 1970s GATT approved the GSP giving developing countries easier access to markets in developed countries. That principle of SDT, differentiated expectation and commitment, continued through the Tokyo Round of the GATT but began to be eroded in the Uruguay Round. The Uruguay Round offered no less onerous conditions to developing countries and instead embraced the principle of uniform commitments. The only concession was extended transition period that would lead eventually to common standards.

The interests of the developing countries are varied and include liberalization of trade in their export products, elimination of subsidies and SDT. They have also indicated interest in recovering privileges lost through progressive erosion, as happened when GSP preference was eroded with lowering of MFN tariff rates. This position, however, is often criticized as misplaced, that developing countries should focus on negotiated bargains that will provide better access in return for similar reciprocal commitments. Indeed, that is the true meaning of negotiations where privileges are traded. In interviews for this monograph it was frequently pointed out that developing countries should not expect privileged access unless they were prepared to lower their own protectionist barriers. Yet, if some form of affirmative action is acceptable in a domestic context, there is no reason why similar schemes cannot be implanted at the international level.

Negotiations between the North and South are not negotiations among equals but developing countries have an expectation that the development round will lead to outcomes that will enable them, ultimately, to bridge the economic divide separating the two groups. This is unlikely if the pressure is on them to make reciprocal liberalizing commitments, even if that is how most negotiations are structured. This is also the position of many NGOs that have demonstrated an interest in international trade and economic issues but advocacy by NGOs is easily dismissed as unrealistic and biased. For developing countries to make real progress that advocacy role should be assumed by multilateral agencies that have a special commitment to promoting global development. That would be seen as serious and constructive contribution rather than as the radical outburst of unaccountable NGOs.

While developing countries want a fairer structure of rules with in-built "affirmative action" programs to assist their developmental goals, this should not be seen as necessarily leading to a fundamental redistribution of the cost–benefit matrix of the global trade regime. It would be futile to try and achieve a step-level change in existing economic regimes nor indeed, is there any need to do so. Developing country claims are not necessarily antithetical to interests of developed countries, although it is probable that some domestic groups will be made worse-off. These groups have been able to survive because of protection extended to them and, at a general level, welfare will be greater if such protectionist measures were eliminated and developing countries given fair access to foreign markets for their products, or even some preferential treatment. Unfortunately the latter is made harder by the fact that the principle of affirmative action at the domestic level is being questioned in some of the larger Organization for Economic Cooperation and Development (OECD) countries.

Developing countries have actively participated in Doha Round negotiations with the purpose of achieving a more balanced distribution of the benefits of liberal international trade. And they have to achieve this without undermining developed country support for global multilateralism, a prospect that seemingly was high following the establishment of the G-20 bargaining coalition and collapse of the Cancun ministerial meeting.

If expectation were high for the development round, experience in the first couple of years pointed to yet another round where developing country interests would be sacrificed in order to preserve the privileges enjoyed by the West. In the lead up to Cancun mid-term review of the Doha Round, many of the key negotiating deadlines were missed and concern mounted that US and EU might again try to replicate another Blair House Agreement to maintain their trade distorting subsides and agricultural protection. This was instrumental to the establishment of the G-20, a grouping of developing countries led by the Brazil and a few of the larger developing countries.

The G-20 refused to accept the flawed agreements that were placed on the negotiating table and chose instead to walk away. At Cancun, developing countries pushed for major concessions on agriculture but it was actually the Singapore issues that led to an impasse and ultimate failure of the meeting to produce agreement on negotiating modalities. The activities of the G-20 shattered the comfort zone of developed countries and introduced into the WTO a real sense of multilateralism. According to Ambassador Rubens Barbosa, Brazil's Ambassador to the US, "What the G-20 really did—and this is probably the reason for such great discomfort in Brussels and Washington—was question for the first time the duopoly of the European Union and the United States in the WTO system."[28] However, whether this early sign of a multilateralization of processes will translate into real and positive outcomes will depend on a number of factors including the capacity of developing countries and of the G-20 to maintain negotiating unity and purpose.

A key expectation from the Doha Round was that developing countries would regain their SDT that had been progressively eroded as well as bargained away in the Uruguay Round. If successful, they will not have to commit to the same standards of economic liberalism. SDT goes beyond the equity concerns for equal opportunity and introduces notions of affirmative action in international trade practices. The claim for SDT is a demand that developed countries acknowledge the particular situation of developing countries. Developed countries, by contrast, are committed to trade liberalization that adheres to a common formula and uniform outcomes. They must also be aware of the downside to SDT—that protection of any form, once granted to a particular sector, is extremely difficult to retract. Still, SDT was an accepted principle of the GATT and it may not be unreasonable to seek its restoration as long as developed countries find an acceptable graduation strategy that will progressively wind it down for beneficiaries that can no longer be classified as developing.

The Doha ministerial declaration underscored the expectation of developing countries that "provisions for special and differential treatment are an integral part of the WTO agreements." Nonetheless, the dominant view among analysts appears to be that chasing SDT is unnecessary and irrelevant to developmental prospects in developing countries, that, as observed by Hoekman *et al.* the "primary determinant of the benefits from trade is a country's own policies—the principle that 'what you do is what you get'."[29] The disputed position on SDT is not easy to resolve but at least from the perspective of capacity and resources, developing countries have not found it easy to meet obligations that are on par with commitments assumed by developed countries. This was the lesson of the Uruguay Round, that simply extending the implementation phase for developing countries is insufficient. Thus there is a good case for linking liberalizing commitments to capacity and resources and not to some arbitrarily determined, and binding, phase-in period.

Critics of SDT, Hoekman *et al.*, argue that exempting developing countries from principles of reciprocity is the reason why they have not been able to negotiate a better deal in trade talks, that their inability to make offers has limited their capacity to demand concessions from developed countries, such that products of interest to developing countries are given high protection in OECD countries. This is an argument that turns SDT on its head, to suggest that it is the very reason why developing countries are subject to unfair treatment in the global trading regime. This was not why developing countries have pushed for SDT and if negative discrimination is the practical result, it suggests a breakdown in the implementation of SDT, not in its value as a principle of trade-led development. It is true that SDT will not automatically elevate developing countries out of their plight, or that problems of corruption and national trade policy are irrelevant, but the essential argument is that developing countries should receive concessional terms in addition to MFN treatment.

At Doha, the poorest 50 developing countries were exempt from making any concessions and no doubt there will be considerable analysis to show how their failure to liberalize will have jeopardized their chances of maximizing gains from the global economy. That may indeed be so but the logic of picking out the poorest 50 countries is not clear nor why the principle could not be extended to all developing countries, especially as a bulk of the world's poor people live not in the least developed countries but in countries like India and China. Moreover, the SDT gained by the least developed countries is insignificant to the SDT that developed countries have arrogated to themselves through provision that make it possible for them to designate some commodities as "sensitive" and therefore exempt from liberalizing discipline. Developing countries also have the option of identifying special products from exemption, partial or complete, from liberalizing disciplines but bound tariff peaks in developing countries is considerably less than similar tariff peaks in developed countries, for instance rice in Japan. As such, actual market liberalization in developed countries will be less than for developing countries, if developed countries designate products with high bound tariffs as sensitive.

In the modalities established thus far, emphasis has been on finding a single formula for both developed and developing countries, rather than consider a favorable formula for all developing countries. The only concession, as in the Uruguay Round, is to allow extended time lines for developing countries to implement the accords. This means developing countries will have failed to achieve one of their major demands.

On pharmaceuticals, developing countries obtained a significant breakthrough with US concession on trade in generic medicines. Pharmaceuticals may appear to be more a public health issue than a development issue but, in fact, uncontrolled epidemics have a direct bearing on lost productivity, labor supply, and on meager health resources of developing countries. Still, the critical issues for developing countries are agriculture and access to non-agricultural markets. The agreement on the modalities of agricultural negotiations will most likely produce mixed results for developing countries but there may be some special consideration given to the cotton producing countries of Africa. The original *Agriculture—Framework Proposal* that was tabled by the G-20 before Cancun in 2003 demanded elimination of export subsidies but did not include any specific time lines as to when and how this should be achieved. In 2005, however, the G-20 fleshed out its proposal and demanded that export subsidies be eliminated as fast as possible and no later than five years.[30] It remains to be seen whether developed countries will accept such an ambitious timeline but the past practice of longer phase-in and back-loading of liberalization commitment does not offer much hope for radical change. In terms of market access, the provision on sensitive products could negate much of the claimed benefits from liberalization.

Developing countries have extracted some concessions but the regime has not been so drastically changed as to undermine developed country support for multilateralism. After Cancun, there has been some drift toward bilateral preferential trade agreements (PTAs) but there have been no major defections from the global trade regime. The US has, for instance, completed a number of bilateral PTAs, but none of these involve a major trading partner. Indeed, the total trade weight of all PTAs entered into by the US is a small fraction, 4.75 percent of total American trade.[31]

The strategy adopted by developing countries at Cancun of holding out for a better deal always had the potential to lead to defections and that made it imperative for them to carefully calibrate the length of time they could hold out. After a one-year period of relative inactivity, negotiations resumed following the July Framework Agreement of 2003. In that agreement, developing countries won promises from the EU to phase out export subsidies and most importantly were able to defer negotiations on three of the four so-called Singapore issues that had been responsible for the stalemate at Cancun.

The goal of equity and fairness is not a finished business but bargaining a redistribution of relative benefits is always a complicated task, not because it will necessarily make developed countries worse off than before but because some groups will lose and be made worse off. It is logical that such groups will resist and governments will advocate their interests to the extent that these groups are politically influential.

Notes

1 Introduction

1. Bhagwati, J. *In Defense of Globalization* (New York: Oxford University Press, 2004), p. 5.
2. *Global Monitoring Report 2005* (Washington, DC: World Bank, 2005), p. 133.
3. Hoekman, B., "Developing Countries and the WTO Doha Round: Market Access, Rules and Differential Treatment," in Basudeb Guha-Khasnobis (ed.), *The WTO, Developing Countries and the Doha Development Agenda* (Houndmills: Palgrave Macmillan, 2004), p. 29.
4. Waltz, K., "Globalization and Governance," James Madison Lecture, 1999, in *PS Online* (December 1999).
5. Kratochwil, F., "Globalization: What It Is and What It Is Not. Some Critical Reflections on the Discursive Formations Dealing with Transformative Change," in Doris A. Fuchs and Friedrich Kratochwil (eds), *Transformative Change and Global Order: Reflections on Theory and Practice* (Hamburg and London: Lit Verlag, 2002), p. 33.
6. At one extreme, Anne Krueger of the World Bank asserts that the process of globalization "has been going almost throughout recorded history . . . ." See "Krueger Makes Case for Globalisation," in *IMF/World Bank Daily* (September 29, 2002), p. 13.
7. Fukuyama, F. *The End of History* (New York and London: Avon Books, 1992).
8. However, according to estimates by the Japan External Trade Organization, FDI in 86 countries was about US$695 billion in 2001, a decline of 52 percent over the previous year. See, "A Triple Dip in Global Economic Activity," *Japan Focus* (October 2002), p. 8.
9. Helleiner, E., "From Bretton Woods to Global Finance: A World Turned Upside Down," in Richard Stubbs and Geoffrey R.D. Underhill (eds), *Political Economy and the Changing Global Order* (Houndmills: Macmillan Press Ltd, 1994), p. 172.
10. Mandle, Jay R. *Globalization and the Poor* (Cambridge: Cambridge University Press, 2003), pp. 58ff.
11. See Lescent-Giles, I., "Globalization as a Long-Term Process: A Case Study of British Manufacturing Since 1700," *Enterprises Et Histoire*, no. 32 (2003), p. 17.
12. The so-called gray area measures were not GATT authorized but preferred by the US government because of procedural simplicity and ability to respond to protectionist sentiment with targeted measures.
13. See Hatch, W. and Kozo Yamamura *Asia in Japan's Embrace: Building a Regional Production Alliance* (Cambridge: Cambridge University Press, 1996).
14. Ibid., p. 6.
15. Ibid., p. 10.
16. Schaeffer, Robert K. *Understanding Globalization: The Social Consequences of Political, Economic, and Environmental Change* (Lanham, MD: Rowman and Littlefield Publishers, 2003), pp. 19ff.

17. Moore, M. *A World Without Walls: Freedom, Development, Free Trade and Global Governance* (London: Cambridge University Press, 2003).
18. Huntington, Samuel P. *The Clash of Civilizations and the Remaking of World Order* (New York: Simon and Schuster, 1996).
19. "India Fears Impact of Bid to Curb Jobs Export," *Financial Times* (June 4, 2003), p. 6.
20. See *Time* (March 1, 2004), p. 26.
21. Bergsten, C. Fred., "A Renaissance for US Trade Policy?," *Foreign Affairs*, vol. 81, no. 6 (November/December 2002).
22. Bacchetta, M. and Marion Jansen *Adjusting to Trade Liberalization: The Role of Policy, Institutions and WTO Disciplines*, Special Studies No. 7 (World Trade Organization, Geneva: WTO Publications, 2003), p. 26.
23. Stiglitz, Joseph E. *Globalization and its Discontents* (New York: W.W. Norton & Company, 2003), p. 104.
24. Tanzi, V., "Globalization Without a Net," *Foreign Policy* (July/August 2001), p. 78.
25. Bacchetta, M. and Marion Jansen *Adjusting to Trade Liberalization: The Role of Policy, Institutions and WTO Disciplines*, Special Studies No. 7, WTO Publications, World Trade Organization, Geneva, 2003, pp. 49–50.
26. Madeley, J. *Hungry for Trade: How the Poor Pay for Free Trade* (London and New York: Zed Books, 2000), p. 23.
27. Moore, M. *A World Without Walls: Freedom, Development, Free Trade and Global Governance* (London: Cambridge University Press, 2003), p. 98.
28. Madeley, J. *Hungry for Trade: How the Poor Pay for Free Trade* (London and New York: Zed Books, 2000), pp. 16–17.
29. Sampson, G.P. *Trade, Environment, and the WTO: The Post-Seattle Agenda*, Policy Essay No. 27 (Washington, DC: Overseas Development Council, 2000), p. 3.
30. Bello, W., "Learning from Doha: A Civil Society Perspective from the South," *Global Governance*, vol. 8, no. 3 (July–September 2002).
31. Gilpin, R. *The Challenge of Global Capitalism: The World Economy in the 21st Century* (Princeton, NJ: Princeton University Press, 2000), p. 13.
32. Deardorff, Alan V. and Robert M. Stern, "What the Public Should Know about Globalization and the World Trade Organization," paper prepared for the conference on *Globalization: Trade, Financial, and Political Economy Aspects*, Delphi, Greece, May 25–27, 2000, pp. 20–1.
33. Faini, R., "Trade Liberalization in a Globalizing World," paper prepared for the *Annual World Bank Conference on Development Economics*, Washington DC, May 3–4, 2004, p. 1.
34. Lairson, T. and David Skidmore *International Political Economy* (Toronto: Wadsworth, 2003), chapter 3.
35. This is not to assert however that the developing country debt crisis is manufactured entirely by exogenous forces. Developing countries also have themselves to blame for mismanaging capital flows and for corrupt practices.
36. Werlin, H.H., "Poor Nations. Rich Nations: A Theory of Governance," *Public Administration Review*, vol. 63, no. 3 (May/June 2003).
37. See Diane Coyle, "Benefiting the Entire World," *Australian Financial Review* (May 24, 2004), p. 23.
38. In the US, at least, radical agitation against globalization is markedly less prominent following the September 11, 2001 terrorist attacks. For example,

the annual World Bank/IMF meeting in late September 2002 attracted far fewer protestors than had been anticipated. In the streets of Washington DC security personnel had greater visibility than protestors. The anticipation of major and violent demonstrations still managed to shut down parts of the city.

39. Fukuyama, F. *The End of History and the Last Man* (New York: Avon Books, 1992).
40. Stiglitz, Joseph E. *Globalization and its Discontents* (New York and London: W.W. Norton & Co., 2003), pp. 20–1.
41. Cardoso, F.H. *Charting a New Course: The Politics of Globalization and Social Transformation*, edited and introduced by Mauricio A. Font (Lanham, MD: Rowman and Littlefield Publishers, Inc., 2001).
42. Cardoso, F.H. and Enzo Faletto *Dependency and Development in Latin America* (Berkeley, CA: University of California Press, 1979), p. 174.
43. On Washington Consensus see Christian Comeliau, "The Limitless Growth Assumption," *International Social Science Journal*, no. 166 (December 2000). See also Branislav Gosovic, "Global Intellectual Hegemony and the International Development Agenda," *International Social Science Journal*, no. 166 (December 2000).
44. Stiglitz, Joseph E. *Globalization and its Discontents* (New York and London: W.W. Norton & Co., 2003), p. 78.
45. See Lloyd, V. and Robert Weissman, "How International Monetary Fund and World Bank Policies Undermine Labor Power and Rights," *International Journal of Health Services*, vol. 32, no. 3, pp. 435–6.
46. See, Maswood, J. *International Political Economy and Globalization* (Singapore: World Scientific Publishing Co., 2000), pp. 177–8.
47. See *Reforming Public Institutions and Strengthening Governance: A World Bank Strategy*, Poverty Reduction and Economic Management Network, World Bank (November 2000), pp. 85–6.
48. Broad, R. and John Cavanagh, "The Death of the Washington Consensus?," in Bello, W., Nicola Bullard and Kamal Malhotra (eds), *Global Finance: New Thinking on Regulating Speculative Capital Markets* (London and New York: The University Press, Dhaka and Zed Books, 2000), p. 91. Rawls, J., *A Theory of Justice* (Cambridge: Belknap Press, 1971).
49. Williamson, J., "From Reform Agenda to Damaged Brand Name: A Short History of the Washington Consensus and Suggestions for What to do Next," *Finance & Development* (September 2003), pp. 10–13.
50. See Karliner, J., "Grassroots Globalization: Reclaiming the Blue Planet," in Lechner, F.J. and John Boli (eds), *The Globalization Reader* (Malden, MA: Blackwell Publishers, 2001), p. 36.
51. The viability of a Tobin tax depends, however, on whether a universal agreement can be reached to eliminate the incentive for capital relocating to international tax havens. Without such a comprehensive agreement, it will be impossible to return the globalization genie back in the bottle.
52. See Bruno Jetin and Suzanne De Brunhof, "The Tobin Tax and Regulation of Capital Movements," in Bello, W., Nicola Bullard and Kamal Malhotra (eds), *Global Finance: New Thinking on Regulating Speculative Capital Markets* (London and New York: The University Press, Dhaka, and Zed Books, 2000).
53. Keynes quoted in Helleiner, E., "From Bretton Woods to Global Finance: A World Turned Upside Down," in Richard Stubbs and Geoffrey R.D. Underhill (eds),

Political Economy and the Changing Global Order, Macmillan Press Ltd (1994), p. 164.

54. Eichengreen, B. *Toward a New International Financial Architecture* (Washington, DC: Institute for International Economics, 1999), pp. 88ff.
55. *Globalization, Growth and Poverty* (Washington, DC: The World Bank, 2001).
56. Anderson, K., "The Challenge of Reducing Subsidies and Trade Barriers," paper presented at a Roundtable in Copenhagen, May 24–28, 2004, p. 5.
57. Dollar, D. and Aart Kraay, "Trade, Growth and Policy," Development Research Group, The World Bank (March 2001), p. 2.
58. Bairoch, P. *The Economic Development of the Third World Since 1900* (Berkeley, CA: University of California Press, 1977), p. 192.
59. *Poverty Reduction in Bangladesh: Building on Progress* (New York: Poverty Reduction and Economic Management Sector Unit, South Asia Region, World Bank (Report No. 24299-BD), December 2002), p. 7.
60. *Poverty in Bangladesh: Building on Progress* (Washington, DC: The World Bank (Report No. 24299-BD), December 2002), p. iv.
61. See Ravallion, M., "The Debate on Globalization, Poverty and Inequality: Why Measurement Matters," *World Bank Policy Research Working Paper 3038* (April 2003), p. 8.
62. Deaton, A., "Is World Poverty Falling?," *Finance & Development*, vol. 39, no. 2, June 2002.
63. Srinivasan, T.N., "Comment on 'Counting the World's Poor,' by Angus Deaton," *The World Bank Research Observer*, vol. 16, no. 2 (Fall 2001).

2 Governing Globalization

1. Raghavan, C., "MAI Not Dead Yet," *Third World Network* (http://www.twnside.org.sg/title/dead-cn.htm).
2. Woods, N., "Global Governance and the Role of Institutions," in D. Held and Anthony McGrew (eds), *Governing Globalization* (Cambridge: Polity Press, 2002), pp. 30–1.
3. "UNDP Calls for New Globalization Rules," *China Daily* (North American ed.) (July 14, 1999), p. 4.
4. It is necessary to add however that the blight of terrorism in the contemporary period is unconnected to systemic inequities or politics of envy.
5. Mandle, J. R. *Globalization and the Poor* (Cambridge: Cambridge University Press, 2003), pp. 122–3.
6. Michalopoulos, C. *Developing Countries in the WTO* (Houndmills: Palgrave, 2001), p. 199.
7. The list was based on several indicators, including environment, migration and labor policies, openness to trade and aid. It found that 80 percent of US foreign aid, for instance, was tied to purchases in the US. See Alan Beattie, "Japan, US 'least helpful to poor nations'," *Financial Times* (April 29, 2003), p. 6.
8. Even as the GSP facilitated developing country exports, it was not a unilateral concession and was usually predicated on recipient countries fulfilling certain conditionalities. Moreover, being outside the GATT system, the GSP privilege could be, and was, readily revoked when it suited the granting country.

9. Kindleberger, C.P. *The World in Depression, 1929–1939* (London: Allen Lane, 1973).

10. Goldstein, J., "Creating the GATT Rules: Politics, Institutions, and American Policy," in John G. Ruggie (ed.), *Multilateralism Matters: The Theory and Praxis of an International Form* (New York: Columbia University Press, 1993), p. 223.

11. Ibid., p. 204.

12. Downs, George W., David M. Rocke and Peter N. Barsoom, "Managing the Evolution of Multilteralism," *International Organization*, vol. 52, no. 2 (Spring 1998), p. 397.

13. See Stairs, D., "Global Governance as a Policy Tool: The Canadian Experience," in Raimo Vayrynen (ed.), *Globalization and Global Governance* (Lanham, MD.: Rowman & Littlefield Publishers, Inc., 1999), p. 68.

14. Hoekman, B, "Developing Countries and the WTO Doha Round: Market Access, Rules and Differential Treatment," in Basudeb Guha-Khasnobis (ed.), *The WTO, Developing Countries and the Doha Development Agenda* (Houndmills: Palgrave Macmillan, 2004), p. 10.

15. Wilkinson, R., "Global Governance: A Preliminary Interrogation," in Rordan Wilkinson and Steve Hughes (eds), *Global Governance: Critical Perspectives* (London and New York: Routledge, 2002), p. 3.

16. Khor, M., "Transparency and Participation in the WTO Decision-Making Process and Procedures," *Third World Resurgence*, no. 153/154 (2004).

17. It is necessary to add the caveat that liberal rules are rarely ever the result of hegemonic imposition. Even after the Second World War, the US did negotiate with its European allies on the structure of the emerging liberal international economic order although the outcomes were more in line with US interests. The advantage of negotiated rule-making is that it is easier to implement rules through voluntary compliance than through coercion.

18. Short, C., "Dangers to Doha," *The World Today*, London, vol. 59, no. 8/9 (August/September 2003).

19. Keck, A. and Patrick Low, "Special and Differential Treatment in the WTO: Why, When and How?," World Trade Organization, Economic Research and Statistics Division, Staff working Paper ERSD-2004–03 (May 2004), p. 8.

20. Kahler, M., "Multilateralism with Small and Large Numbers," in John G. Ruggie (ed.), *Multilateralism Matters: The Theory and Praxis of an Institutional Form* (New York: Columbia University Press, 1993), p. 298.

21. See Finger, J. Michael and L. Alan Winters, "What Can the WTO Do for Developing Countries," in Anne O. Krueger (ed.), *The WTO as an International Organization* (Chicago: University of Chicago Press, 1998), p. 384.

22. Before the Uruguay Round, developing country participation in trade multilateralism was channeled through the UNCTAD which they, indeed, hoped would eventually replace the GATT. See Cohn, Theodore H. *Governing Global Trade* (Aldershot: Ashgate), p. 72.

23. Oyejide, T. Ademola, "Development Dimensions in Multilateral Trade Negotiations," in Mike Moore (ed.) *Doha and Beyond: The Future of the Multilateral Trading System* (Cambridge: Cambridge University Press, 2004), p. 79.

24. Rawls, J. *A Theory of Justice* (Cambridge: Belknap Press, 1971).

25. There is, however, considerable debate as to the irreversibility of globalization. First of course, there is the historical experience of "globalization" in the late nineteenth century, which unraveled quickly in the early twentieth century

and second, there is, according to Dani Rodrik, a "political trilemma" that may lead to a retreat from globalization. He points out that there is a basic incompatibility between the nation-state system, deep economic integration, and democracy and that we "can have at most two out of these three. If we want to push global economic integration much further, we have to give up either the nation state or mass politics. If we want to maintain and deepen democracy, we have to choose between the nation state and international economic integration. And if we want to keep the nation state, we have to choose between democracy and international economic integration." The simple message is that globalization is neither irreversible nor immutable. See Rodrik, D., "Feasible Globalization," NBER Working Paper Series, Working Paper 9129, Cambridge, MA (September 2002), pp. 13–14.

26. Desker, B. and Margaret Liang, "Trade Facilitation: The Road Ahead," *Trends in Southeast Asia Series, No. 1* (Singapore: Institute of Southeast Asian Studies, 2003), p. 4.

27. Woolcock, S., "The Singapore Issues in Cancun: A Failed Negotiation Ploy or a Litmus Test for Global Governance," *Intereconomics*, vol. 38, no. 5 (September/October 2003).

28. Desker, B. and Margaret Liang, "Trade Facilitation: The Road Ahead," *Trends in Southeast Asia Series No. 1* (Singapore: Institute of Southeast Asian Studies, 2003) p. 7. In his paper, Desker and Liang argue that developing country concerns can be easily allayed by a lengthy implementation period and an initial grace period during which developing countries might be exempt from disputes arising from non-compliance.

29. See "Developments Since the Fourth WTO Ministerial Conference," *Doha Round Briefing Series*, The International Centre for Trade and Sustainable Development and the International Institute for Sustainable Development, vol. 1, no. 6 (February 2003).

30. Stiglitz, Joseph E. and Andrew Charlton, "A Development Round of Negotiations?," paper presented at the Annual Bank Conference on Development Economics (May 11, 2004), p. 10.

31. The G-20 was formed on August 20, 2003 and in 2005 its members were Argentina, Bolivia, Brazil, Chile, China, Cuba, Egypt, Guatemala, India, Indonesia, Mexico, Nigeria, Pakistan, Paraguay, Philippines, South Africa, Tanzania, Thailand, Venezuela and Zimbabwe. The Group is led by Brazil.

32. The IMF is typically headed by a European but as an institution, its policies are heavily influenced by the US government.

33. Germain, Randall D., "Reforming the International Financial Architecture: The New Political Agenda," in Rorden Wilkinson and Steve Hughes (eds), *Global Governance: Critical Perspectives* (London and New York: Routledge, 2002), p. 21.

34. See Warkentin, C. and Karen Mingst, "International Institutions, the State, and Global Civil Society in the Age of the World Wide Web," *Global Governance*, vol. 6, no. 2 (April–June 2000), pp. 213–36.

35. Mallaby, S., "NGOs: Fighting Poverty, Hurting the Poor," *Foreign Policy* (September/October 2004), p. 52.

36. Abbott, Frederick M., "The Doha Declaration on the TRIPS Agreement and Public Health: Lighting a Dark Corner at the WTO," *Journal of International Economic Law*, vol. 5, no. 2 (July 2002), p. 471.

37. Alger, C., "The Emerging Roles of NGOs in the UN System: From Article 71 to a People's Millennium Assembly," *Global Governance*, vol. 8, no. 1 (January–March 2002).
38. Jan Aart Scholte, Robert O'Brien and Marc Williams, "The WTO and Civil Society," *Journal of World Trade*, vol. 33, no. 1 (February 1999), p. 118.
39. Wilkinson, R., "The Contours of Courtship: The WTO and Civil Society," in Rorden Wilkinson and Steve Hughes (eds), *Global Governance: Critical Perspectives* (London and New York: Routledge, 2002), p. 204.
40. Walter, A., "NGOs, Business, and International Agreement: The Multilateral Agreement on Investment, Seattle, and Beyond," *Global Governance*, vol. 7, no. 1 (January–March 2001), p. 57.
41. Young, Oran R. *Governance in World Affairs* (Ithaca, NY and London: Cornell University Press, 1999), p. 20.

3 Foreign Investments and the Multilateral Agreement on Investments

1. Drabek, Z., "A Multilateral Agreement on Investment: Convincing the Sceptics," World Trade Organization, Staff Working Paper ERAD-98-05 (June 1998), p. 3.
2. Downs, G.W., David M. Rocke and Peter N. Barsoom, "Managing the Evolution of Multilateralism," *International Organization*, vol. 52, no. 2 (Spring 1998), pp. 413–14.
3. *The Multilateral Agreement on Investments*, OECD Policy Brief, no. 2 (1997), p. 3 (http://www.oecd.org/publications/Pol_brief/9702_Pol.htm).
4. Transfer pricing usually occurs in the process of intra-firm trade and is intended to minimize tax payments in host countries. The potential for transfer pricing is considerable since about 40 percent of global trade is intra-firm trade. The presumption however is that the incidence of transfer payment has diminished considerably compared to the past but data for the late 1970s suggests that 92 percent of US, 73 percent of Japanese, 85 percent of Canadian, and 79 percent of British MNC had engaged in transfer pricing. See Woodward, David, *The Next Crisis? Direct and Equity Investment in Developing Countries* (London and New York: Zed Books, 2001), pp. 72–3.
5. Fukase E. and Will Martin, "Free Trade Area Membership as a Stepping Stone to Development: The Case of ASEAN," *World Bank Discussion Paper No. 421* (Washington, DC: World Bank, 2001), p. 154.
6. See for example, Zdenek Drabek, "A Multilateral Agreement on Investment: Convincing the Sceptics," World Trade Organization, Staff Working Paper ERAD-98-05 (June 1998).
7. Mandle, Jay R. *Globalization and the Poor* (Cambridge: Cambridge University Press, 2003), p. 61.
8. Woodward, D. *The Next Crisis? Direct and Equity Investment in Developing Countries* (London and New York: Zed Books, 2001), p. 138.
9. Other observers to the MAI negotiations were Hong Kong, Argentina, Brazil, Chile and Slovakia.
10. Braunstein, E. and Gerald Epstein, "Creating International Credit Rules and the Multilateral Agreement on Investment: What are the Alternatives?," in

Jonathan Michie and John Grieve Smith (eds), *Global Instability: The Political Economy of World Economic Governance* (London and New York: Routledge, 1999), p. 118.

11. Walter, A., "NGOs, Business, and International Investment: The Multilateral Agreement on Investment, Seattle, and Beyond," *Global Governance*, vol. 7, no. 1 (January–March 2001), p. 58.

12. Barlow, M. and Tony Clarke *MAI: The Multilateral Agreement on Investment and the Threat to American Freedom* (New York: Stoddart Publishing Co. Ltd, 1998), p. 98.

13. Ibid., p. 39.

14. Beattie, A., "World Bank Cuts Estimate for Global Economic Growth," *Financial Times* (December 12, 2002), p. 7.

15. Braunstein, E. and Gerald Epstein, "Creating International Credit Rules and the Multilateral Agreement on Investment," in Jonathan Michie and John Grieve Smith (eds), *Global Instability: The Political Economy of World Economic Governance* (London: Routledge, 1999), p. 123.

16. Mandle, Jay R. *Globalization and the Poor* (Cambridge: Cambridge University Press, 2003), p. 68.

17. Ibid., p. 55.

18. Braunstein, E. and Gerald Epstein, "Creating International Credit Rules and the Multilateral Agreement on Investment: What are the Alternatives?," in Jonathan Michie and John Grieve Smith (eds), *Global Instability: The Political Economy of World Economic Governance* (London and New York: Routledge, 1999), p. 124.

19. Khorr, M., "The World Trade Organization and the South: Implications of the Emerging Global Economic Governance for Development," in Jomo, K.S., and Shyamala Nagaraj (eds), *Globalization versus Development* (Houndmills: Palgrave, 2001), p. 73.

20. "Geneva Battle Resumes on WTO Accord," *Financial Times* (June 10, 2003), p. 3.

21. Mandle, Jay R. *Globalization and the Poor* (Cambridge: Cambridge University Press, 2003), p. 70.

22. Drabek, Z., "A Multilateral Agreement on Investment: Convincing the Skeptics," World Trade Organization, Staff Working Paper ERAD-98-05 (June 1998), p. 8.

4   Developing Countries and the World Trade Organization

1. Finger, J. Michael and Julio J. Nogues, "The Unbalanced Uruguay Round Outcome: The New Areas in Future WTO Negotiations," *Policy Research Working Paper 2732*, Development Research Group, The World Bank (December 2001).

2. Ibid., p. 13.

3. Ismail, F., "Mainstreaming Development in the WTO," undated typescript, p. 5.

4. The consensus rule of the GATT was strengthened in the WTO and in dispute resolution, for example, panel decisions and recommendation are final unless all member countries agree to set it aside. This is sometimes referred to as "reverse consensus" to distinguish it from decisions which require a consensus in the affirmative.

5. As of April 2003, the WTO had 146 members with another 30 governments, including the Russian government, participating as observers.

6. Petras, J. and Henry Veltmeyer *Globalization Unmasked: Imperialism in the 21st Century* (London and New York: Fernwood Publishing/Zed Books, 2001), pp. 18–19.

7. "Proposal to End Tariffs on Textiles is Decried," *The Washington Post* (December 14, 2002), p. A5.

8. Francois, Joseph F., Bradley McDonald and Hakan Nordstrom *A User's Guide to Uruguay Round Assessments* (May 1996), p. 12 (http://www.intereconomics.com/francois/text9603.pdf).

9. Hiebert, M., "Getting Ready for Free Trade," *Far Eastern Economic Review* (July 31, 2003), p. 19.

10. "China Textles Stretch Free Trade," *Australian* (April 6, 2005), p. 8.

11. "$400 billion in Textile Trade Set to Change," *Washington Post* (November 17, 2004), p. A1.

12. "US Textile Manufacturers Sceptical over China's Proposed Export Curbs," *Financial Times*, US edition (December 14, 2004), p. 1.

13. King, N. Jr, and Dan Morse, "Bush Sets Quotas on Some Imports of Chinese Goods; Action Targeting Textiles Knocks Value of Dollar on Fears of Protectionism," *Wall Street Journal* (November 19, 2003), p. A1.

14. Hutzler, C. and Rebecca Buckman, "The Economy: China Makes Sharp Response to New U.S. Textile Restrictions," *Wall Street Journal* (November 20, 2003), p. A2.

15. Claire Short, then British Minister for International Development, suggested that the round be a "development round" in view of strong disenchantment felt by developing countries with the outcomes and implementation of Uruguay Round agreements. There was also no doubt an expectation that, by raising developing country expectations of a more favorable set outcomes, these countries could also be persuaded to add new issues to the negotiating agenda that was of interest to developed countries.

16. Crispin, S.W. and Shada Islam, "Crossing Swords," *Far Eastern Economic Review*, vol. 162, no. 19 (May 13, 1999).

17. Deardorff, Alan V. and Robert M. Stern, "What the Public Should Know about Globalization and the World Trade Organization," Discussion Paper No. 460, School of Public Policy, The University of Michigan (July 20, 2000), pp. 24–5.

18. Bella, W., "Learning from Doha: A Civil Society Perspective from the South," *Global Governance*, vol. 8, no. 3 (July–September 2002).

19. This was still an unfair question since the mandate of the WTO is neither to protect cows nor the poor people in developing countries. Its mandate is simply to liberalize trade but it has so far been unable to impose the standards uniformly and equitably across its member countries.

20. "Race on for New WTO Chief," see http://www.finance24.com/Finance/Economy/D1518-25_1628008,00.html.

21. Beattie, A., "Lamy Leads a List of Four Candidates to Head WTO," *Financial Times* (January 6, 2005), p. 5.

22. Beattie, A. and Raphael Minder, "Lamy 'has Stature and Knowledge' to Head WTO," *Financial Times* (USA) (December 9, 2004), p. 7.

23. "Brazil Reacts Angrily to Amazon Proposal," *Mercopress* (February 26, 2005) (http://www.Falkland-malvinas.com/Datalle.asp?NUM=5177).

24. Boyer, M.C. *et al.*, "Who Gets to Run the WTO?," *Foreign Policy* (February 2005) (http://foreignpolicy.com/story/files/story2776.php).
25. "Cuttaree says EU Should'nt Vie for WTO Post," *BusinessWeek Online* (March 10, 2005).
26. "Race for Leadership of WTO Heats Up," *Financial Times* [European Edition] (January 27, 2005), p. 6.
27. Oberthur, S. and Hermann E. Ott *The Kyoto Protocol: International Climate Policy for the 21st Century* (Berlin: Springer-Verlag, 1999), pp. 84–5.

5   The Doha Round and Pharmaceutical Trade

1. Industrial tariffs were also part of the agenda but not a controversial item. The main disagreement seemed to be between the US and EU, with the US proposing to scrap all industrial tariffs below 5 percent whereas the EU proposed to scraps tariffs only below 2 percent.
2. Subramanian, A., "Medicines, Patents, and TRIPS," *Finance & Development* (March 2004), p. 22.
3. Abbott, Frederick M., "The Doha Declaration on the TRIPS Agreement and Public Health: Lighting a Dark Corner at the WTO," *Journal of International Economic Law*, vol. 5, no. 2 (July 2002), p. 472.
4. "AIDS out of Global Control, says UN," *The Australian* (November 27, 2003), p. 7.
5. Ibid.
6. Zutshi, B.K., "Bringing TRIPS into the Multilateral Trading System," in Bhagwati, J. and Mathias Hirsch (eds), *The Uruguay Round and Beyond: Essays in Honor of Arthur Dunkel* (Michigan: The University of Michigan Press, 1998), see pp. 44ff.
7. Michalopoulos, C. *Developing Countries in the WTO* (Houndmills: Palgrave, 2001), p. 134.
8. This is a very controversial aspect of TRIPS and has allowed Western firms to procure patent rights over biological resources of developing countries. Moreover, this aspect of TRIPS may also be in contravention of the UN Convention on Biological Diversity, which grants nations sovereign rights over biological resources.
9. Michalopoulos, C. *Developing Countries in the WTO* (Houndmills: Palgrave, 2001), pp. 144–5.
10. Smith, G., "Drugmakers Feel the Heat in Mexico," *BusinessWeek* (August 11, 2003).
11. Abbott, F.M., "Study Paper for the British Commission on the Intellectual Property Rights on the WTO TRIPs Agreement and its Implications for Access to Medicines in Developing Countries," Study Paper 2a (February 2002), p. 16.
12. "US Attacked Over Attempt to Boost Drug Patents Protection," *Financial Times* (May 23, 2003), p. 3.
13. "WHO to Gain Advisory Role on Pharmaceutical Patents," *Financial Times* (May 28, 2003), p. 8.
14. Dyer, G., "GSK Cuts Price of Top Aids Treatment," *Financial Times* (April 28, 2003), p. 15.
15. Pearlstein, S., "Absurd Report on Drug Prices Clouds the Issue," *Washington Post* (December 29, 2004), p. E1.

16. Carter, T., "Use of DDT Urged in Malaria Fight," *The Washington Times* (September 16, 2004), p. A17.
17. "Health Care in the Developing World," *PhRMA* (http://world.phrma.org/ip.access.aids.drugs.html.html).
18. Abbott, Frederick M., "The Doha Declaration on the TRIPS Agreement and Public Health: Lighting a Dark Corner at the WTO," *Journal of International Economic Law*, vol. 5, no. 2 (July 2002), p. 485.
19. Hooper, E. *The River: A Journey to the Source of HIV and AIDS* (Boston, MA: Little, Brown and Company, 1999), p. 92.
20. Funding was formally approved by the US Congress in mid-May 2003.
21. Frase-Blunt, M., ". . . And the Help AIDS Needs Now," *Washington Post* (March 9, 2003), p. B2.
22. Serwadda, D., "Beyond Abstinence," *Washington Post* (May 16, 2003), p. A29.
23. "As the Pandemic Spreads, Developed Nations Must Respond to a New Challenge from the White House," *Financial Times* (June 2, 2003), p. 11.
24. Bilmes, L., "A Poor Start for Bush's Aids Programme," *Financial Times* (July 7, 2003), p. 13.
25. Bhagwati, J., "Don't Cry for Cancun," *Foreign Affairs* vol. 83, no. 1 (January/February 2004).

6   The Doha Round and Agricultural Liberalization

1. Merlinda D. Ingco and John D. Nash, "What's at Stake? Developing-Country Interests in the Doha Development Round," World Bank Seminar, Washington DC, 2002.
2. See, *Agricultural Policies in OECD Countries: Monitoring and Evaluation 2003* (OECD, 2003).
3. See David Orden, Rashid S. Kaukab and Eugenio Diaz-Bonilla, *Liberalizing Agricultural Trade and Developing Countries*, Carnegie Endowment for International Peace, Issue Brief (November 2002).
4. Watkins, K., "Reducing Poverty Starts with Fairer Farm Trade," *Financial Times* (June 2, 2003), p. 13.
5. Dalton, R., "Snouts in Trough for Cash Crop," *The Australian* (September 8, 2003), p. 17.
6. Anderson, K., "The Challenge of Reducing Subsidies and Trade Barriers," paper presented at a Roundtable in Copenhagen (May 24–28, 2004), p. 27.
7. Eccleston, R., "Lining Up for Trade Talks . . . and all with a Barrow to Push," *The Australian* (September 8, 2003), p. 13.
8. The flip side of agricultural liberalization is that the net food importing developing countries will be worse off than before because they will have to pay higher prices for their imports.
9. CAP became official European policy in January 1992 and its main objectives are to balance supply and demand both within and outside the European Community; to provide farmers with a fair income; to stabilize agricultural markets by protecting farmers from activities of price speculators; and to ensure equitable supplies to consumers. See Gionea, J., *International Trade and Investment: An Asia-Pacific Perspective* (Sydney, Australia: McGraw-Hill, 2003), p. 183.

10. Wiener, J. *Making Rules in the Uruguay Round of the GATT: A Study of Internal Leadership* (Aldershot: Dartmouth Publishing Company, 1995), pp. 88–9.
11. Mason, J., "France Renews Strong Opposition to Reform of EU Agricultural Policy," *Financial Times* (January 8, 2003), p. 4.
12. In February 2003, at the Franco-Africa Heads of State Meeting in Paris, the French President proposed a temporary halt to subsidized agriculture exports to Africa but this only raised new fears that surplus production will be diverted elsewhere. Critics also questioned the "WTO compatibility" of such targeted trade preference. See Faizel Ismail, "On the Road to Cancun: A Development Perspective on EU Trade Policies and Implications for Central and East European Countries," *The Journal of World Investment*, vol. 4, no. 4 (August 2003), p. 579.
13. Buck, T., "EU Farm Subsidy Reform Hopes Grow," *Financial Times* (May 13, 2003), p. 4.
14. "A Contemptible Deal," *Financial Times* (June 13, 2003), p. 12.
15. Tarditi, S., "CAP Pseudo-Reforms: A Penelopean Web," *Intereconomics* (September/October 2002) (http: . . . /pqdweb?Did=000000239099831& Fmt=3&Deli=1&Mtd+1&Idx=2&Sid=!&RQT=30).
16. "EU Deal on Farm Reforms to Boost World Trade Talks," *Financial Times* (June 27, 2003), p. 1.
17. "Fischler's New Era for Europe's Farmers: Now the Argument Over Agriculture Moves to the WTO," *Financial Review* (June 27, 2003), p. 11.
18. Nash, J., "Issues and Prospects for Agricultural Trade Liberalization in the Doha Development Agenda," seminar paper presented at the World Bank, Washington, DC (April 2003).
19. Zoellick, R. and Ann Veneman, "No Half Measures in the Quest for Free Trade," *Financial Times* (April 7, 2003), p. 13.
20. Fischler, Franz and Pascal Lamy, "Free Farm Trade Means an Unfair Advantage," *Financial Times* (April 1, 2003), p. 13.
21. Yeutter, C., "Bringing Agriculture into the Multilateral Trading System," in Bhagwati, J. and Mathias Hirsch (eds), *The Uruguay Round and Beyond: Essays in Honor of Arthur Dunkel* (Michigan: The University of Michigan Press, 1998), pp. 65–6.
22. "US Producers on the Defensive," *Financial Times* (June 27, 2003), p. 11.
23. Nash, J., "Issues and Prospects for Agricultural Trade Liberalization in the Doha Development Agenda," seminar paper presented at the World Bank (April 2003), p. 9.
24. "WTO Rejects Draft Document on Agricultural Trade," *The Daily News* (Harare) (March 3, 2003).
25. Luce, E., "Poor Nations Urged to End Trade Barriers," *Financial Times* (November 29, 2002), p. 6.
26. That proposal, as expected, alarmed American textile and apparel manufacturers. Some Congressional representatives of the southern states, the main textile producers, also expressed concerns that they had been hasty in granting the administration Trade Promotion Authority (formerly fast track authority) to conclude the Doha Round of the WTO.
27. Panitchpakdi, S., "World Trade Must Not be Tripped Up by Drugs," *Financial Times* (December 16, 2002), p. 13.
28. Schott, Jeffrey J., *The Uruguay Round: An Assessment* (Washington, DC: Institute for International Economics, November 1994), p. 48.

29. "US and EU Push 'Positive Agenda' for Talks," *Financial Times* (April 30, 2003), p. 9.
30. See Lindsey, B., "Americas: The Miami Fizzle—Where Else but Cancun Redux?," *Wall Street Journal* (November 28, 2003), p. A9.
31. See *EU Agriculture and the WTO: Doha Development Agenda, Cancun—September 2003*, Agriculture and Rural Development, European Commission (September 2003).
32. In hindsight, it has been suggested that it was a mistake for the US to have given up an important bargaining tool prior to Cancun, which instead could have been used to extract developing country concessions on agriculture and the Singapore issues.
33. Hoekman, B., "Cancun: Crisis or Catharsis?," The World Bank (September 20, 2003) mimeo, p. 2.
34. The G-20 is made up of Asian, Latin American and African countries and together represents 60 percent of the world population, 70 percent of world"s farmers and 26 percent of world trade in agriculture. See Clodoaldo Hugueney Filho, "The G-20: Passing Phenomenon or Here to Stay?" (www.focusweb.org/popups/articleswindow.php?id=426) (April 19, 2004).
35. *The Economist* (September 20, 2003).
36. Wood, A., "Dangerous Spaghetti Bowl of Bilateralism," *The Australian* (November 25, 2003), p. 11.
37. "World Trade Blow Makes US the Hope," *The Australian* (September 16, 2003), p. 1.
38. "Giants Fear the Mice that Roared," *The Australian* (September 16, 2003), p. 8.
39. "Positive Side to Trade Row: UN," *The Australian* (September 17, 2003), p. 9.
40. See for example, Gordon, Bernard K., "A High-Risk Trade Policy," *Foreign Affairs*, vol. 82, no. 4 (July/August 2003), p. 105.
41. "Agriculture—Framework Proposal," joint proposal by Argentina, Bolivia, Brazil, Chile, China, Colombia, Costa Rica, Cuba, Ecuador, El Salvador, Guatemala, India, Mexico, Pakistan, Paraguay, Peru, Philippines, South Africa, Thailand and Venezuela, World Trade Organization WT/MIN(03)/W/6 (September 4, 2003).
42. Hoekman, B., Constantine Michalopoulos and L. Alan Winters, "More Favorable and Differential Treatment of Developing Countries: Towards a New Approach in the WTO," *World Bank Policy Research Working Paper 3107* (August 2003), p. 9.
43. See http://www.cafta.org/Response_to_Harbinson_Feb_2003.html.
44. The number of bands and the thresholds for defining the bands is to be decided following further negotiations.
45. "Now Harvest it; World Trade," *The Economist* (August 7, 2004).
46. Konandreas, P., "Implementing the Special Products (SPs) Provision on the Basis of an Aggregate Deviation from the General Tariff Cut Formula," unpublished paper (December 3, 2004) and Konandreas, P., "Implementing the Sensitive Products Provision on the Basis of an Additional Pro-Rated TRQ Commitment for Non-Compliance with the General Tariff Cut Formula," unpublished paper (December 3, 2004).
47. Anderson, K. and Will Martin, "Agricultural Trade Reform and the Doha Development Agenda," paper prepared for a workshop prior to the Annual

Conference of the Australian Agricultural and Resource Economics Society, Coffs Harbour (February 8, 2005), pp. 10–11.

48. A bound tariff is a tariff in respect of which there is a legal commitment not to raise it beyond that level. There can be a large gap between applied tariffs and bound tariffs but the principle of tariff binding is still considered important as a commitment not to increase applied tariffs beyond that level. As part of the Uruguay Round agreement, non-tariff barriers were converted into tariff equivalents (bound tariffs) and developed countries agreed to bind 99 percent of tariff lines while developing countries increased their binding of tariff lines from 22 percent to 72 percent. The practice of converting NTBs to bound tariffs was not properly administered and resulted in bound tariffs being set much higher than tariff equivalents of NTB. This led to "dirty tariffication." See Walkensorst, P. and Nora Dihel, "Tariff Bindings, Unused Protection and Agricultural Trade Liberalization," *OECD Economic Studies*, no. 36, 2003/1, p. 234.

49. Konandreas, P., "Incorporating Constrained Flexibility in Tariff Reductions: A Dynamic Formula," unpublished paper (July 9, 2004) p. 6.

50. Walkenhorst, P. and Nora Dihel, "Tariff Bindings, Unused Protection and Agricultural Trade Liberalization," *OECD Economic Studies*, no. 36, 2003/1, p. 242.

51. Anderson, K. and Will Martin, "Agricultural Trade Reform and the Doha Development Agenda," paper prepared for a workshop prior to the Annual Conference of the Australian Agricultural and Resource Economics Society, Coffs Harbour (February 8, 2005), p. 1.

52. Olson, M. *The Logic of Collective Action: Public Goods and the Theory of Groups* (Cambridge: Harvard University Press, 1965).

53. Blustein, P., "U.S., Europe Agree To Negotiate Over Airplane Subsidies," *Washington Post* (January 12, 2005), p. E1.

54. "Airbus Seeks Launch Aid for A350," *Financial Times*, US Edition (January 13, 2004), p. 1.

55. Hoekman, B., Francis Ng and Marcelo Olarreaga, "Agricultural Tariffs or Subsidies: Which are More Important for Developing Countries," *The World Bank Economic Review*, vol. 18, no. 2 (2004), p. 186.

56. "Ministers Fail to Break Deadlock on Farm Trade," *Financial Times* (June 23, 2003), p. 7.

57. Panitchpakdi, S., "Moving Beyond Cancun," *The OECD Observer*, no. 240/241 (December 2003).

58. "The Doha Squabble—World Trade; World Trade," A Special Report, *The Economist* (London, March 29, 2003).

59. Chong, F., "Hopes High for Trade Talks as US Recommits," *The Australian* (January 16, 2004), p. 22.

60. In 2001, China agricultural trade deficit was US$3,401 million whereas India had a surplus of US$1220 million, South Africa a surplus of US$1039 million, and Brazil a surplus of US$12,851 million. See www.g-20.mre.gov.br/statistics.asp.

61. Less than two months later however, the US and Brazil had patched up their differences at a ministerial meeting in Miami to negotiate the Free Trade Area of the Americas (FTAA). At that meeting USTR Robert Zoellick and the Brazilian Foreign Trade Minister Celso Amorim spoke of a "personal chemistry" and of "dancing to the same tune."

62. Murphy, D. Murray Hielbert and Margot Cohen, "The Fine Art of Failure," *Far Eastern Economic Review* (September 25, 2003).

7 Bilateralism in a Multilateral World

1. Sutherland, P., Jagdish Bhagwati *et al*. *The Future of the WTO: Addressing Institutional Challenges in the New Millennium* (Geneva: World Trade Organization, 2004), chapter 2.
2. Schott, J.J., "Free Trade Agreements: Boon or Bane of the World Trading System?," in Jeffrey J. Schott (ed.), *Free Trade Agreements: US Strategies and Priorities* (Washington, DC: Institute for International Economics, 2004), p. 4.
3. See *The Economist* (November 20, 2004), p. 78.
4. Weintraub, S., "Lessons from the Chile and Singapore Free Trade Agreements," in Jeffrey J. Schott (ed.), *Free Trade Agreements: US Strategies and Priorities* (Washington, DC: Institute for International Economics, 2004), p. 83.
5. Schott, J.J., "Free Trade Agreements: Boon or Bane of the World Trading System?," in Jeffrey J. Schott (ed.), *Free Trade Agreements: US Strategies and Priorities* (Washington, DC: Institute for International Economics, 2004), p. 8.
6. Rajan, Ramkishen S., Rahul Sen and Reza Siregar *Singapore and Free Trade Agreements: Economic Relations with Japan and the United States* (Singapore: Institute of Southeast Asian Studies, 2001), p. 8.
7. Bouzas, R., "Regional Trade Arrangements: Lessons from Past Experiences," in Mendoza, M.R., Patrick Low and Barbara Kotschwar (eds), *Trade Rules in the Making: Challenges in Regional and Multilateral Negotiations* (Washington, DC: Brookings Institution Press, 1999), p. 182.
8. "France Accuses U.S. of HIV Drug Blackmail," *CNN.Com* (July 13, 2004) (http://www.cnn.com/2004/HEALTH/07/13/aids.conference/).
9. The US is a late convert to regionalism and bilateralism. In the 1980s it concluded two bilateral agreements with Israel (1985) and Canada (1988) but these were explained as "special cases." In the new millennium FTAs have become a legitimate part of American trade policy, with new agreements concluded with Jordan (2000), Singapore (2002) Chile (2003) and Australia (2004).
10. Gionea, J. *International Trade and Investment: An Asia-Pacific Perspective* (Sydney, Australia: McGraw-Hill, 2003), p. 177.
11. Bhagwati, J., "The Truth about Trade," *Wall Street Journal* (January 18, 2005), p. A16.
12. Desker, B., "In Defence of FTAs: From Purity to Pragmatism in East Asia," *The Pacific Review*, vol. 17, no. 1 (March 2004).
13. *The Economist* (September 20, 2003).
14. *The Economist* (November 20, 2004), p. 78.
15. "Thai and U.S. Activists Against Bilateral Trade Deal: Access to Affordable Generic Medicines in Jeopard," Health Global Access Project Press Statement (October 19, 2003) (www.healthgap.org).
16. "Slower Track WTO Vs Fast Track FTAs," *The Financial Express* (http://fecolumists.expressindia.com/full_column.php?content_id=41375).
17. See the two studies by Andrew Rose *Do We Really Know that the WTO Increases Trade?*, NBER Working Paper No. 9273, and *Do WTO Members Have a More Liberal Trade Policy?*, NBER Working Paper No. 9347, 2003.

18. Lindsey, B., "Americas: The Miami Fizzle—Where Else but Cancun Redux?," *Wall Street Journal* (November 28, 2003), p. A9.
19. "Everybody's Doing it," *The Economist* (February 28, 2004), p. 31.
20. Peter Wilson, "Poor Nations Flex Trade Muscles," *The Australian* (August 2, 2004), p. 14.
21. See http://www.wto.org/english/news_e/news04_e/dda_package_sum_28_29 july04_e.htm.
22. Wilson, P., "Farmers Hail WTO Talks Deal," *The Australian* (August 2, 2004), p. 1.
23. Bergsten, C. Fred, "Foreign Economic Policy for the Next President," *Foreign Affairs*, vol. 83, no. 2 (March/April 2004).
24. Sewell, John W. and I. William Zartman, "Global Negotiations: Path to the Future or Dead-End Street?," in Jagdish N. Bhagwati and John Gerard Ruggie (eds), *Power, Passions, and Purpose: Prospects for North-South Negotiations* (Cambridge, MA: The MIT Press, 1984), p. 121.
25. See, for example, Miles Kahler, "Multilateralism with Small and Large Numbers," in Ruggie, John G. (ed.), *Multilateralism Matters: The Theory and Praxis of an Institutional Form* (New York: Columbia University Press, 1993).
26. Kahler, M., "Multilateralism with Small and Large Numbers," in Ruggie, John G. (ed.), *Multilateralism Matters: The Theory and Praxis of an Institutional Form* (New York: Columbia University Press, 1993), p. 302.
27. Ross, J., "WTO Collapses in Cancun: Autopsy of a Fiasco Foretold," *CounterPunch* (September 20, 2003).
28. Yerkey, Gary G., "Support for WTO in Congress, Private Sector Wanes After Collapse of Cancun Trade Talks," *International Trade Daily* (September 16, 2003), p. 1.
29. Yerkey, Gary G., "Support for WTO in Congress, Private Sector Wanes After Collapse of Cancun Trade Talks," *International Trade Daily* (September 16, 2003), p. 1.

8 Conclusion

1. "Negotiators Miss Deadline for Accord on Industrial Tariff Cuts," *Financial Times* (May 29, 2003), p. 4.
2. Sutherland, P., "The Real Trade Barriers that Hinder Poor Countries," *International Herald Tribune* (January 29–30, 2005), p. 6.
3. It should be noted, however, that a win for John Kerry and the Democrats in the 2004 presidential elections in the US would probably have had a more deleterious impact on the future prospects of the Doha Round.
4. Bhagwati, J. and Arvind Panagariya, "Bilateral Trade Deals are a Sham," *Financial Times* (July 14, 2003), p. 15.
5. Mattoo, A. and Arvind Subamanian, "Multilateralism and the Doha Round: A Stock-Taking," typescript, 2005.
6. The UNCTAD (United Nations' Conference on Trade and Development) was established in 1964 in response to developing countries' disillusionment with GATT as serving interests primarily of the developed countries. UNCTAD's main achievement was the Generalized System of Preferences (GSP) which accorded developing country exports favorable access to developed countries. GSP tariffs initially were considerably lower than

average industrial country tariffs but the system was voluntary and its beneficial effects were rapidly eroded as the differential between GSP tariffs and MFN tariffs was reduced by successive trade liberalization rounds of the GATT.

7. "Drops on Parched Soil," *The Economist* (July 5, 2003), p. 65.

8. The average number of trade officials at the WTO headquarters in Geneva from OECD countries is about seven.

9. Khorr, M., "The World Trade Organization and the South: Implications of the Emerging Global Economic Governance for Development," in Jomo, K.S. and Shyamala Nagaraj (eds), *Globalization versus Development* (Houndmills: Palgrave, 2002), p. 64.

10. "Group to Help Poor Benefit from Trade," *Financial Times* (February 28, 2003), p. 4. Key individuals within the TFP have urged industrialized countries to demonstrate leadership in the Doha Round to ensure positive outcomes for developing countries. See, Robert Rubin, Dominique Strauss-Kahn and Shoichiro Toyoda, "Sharing the Benefits of Global Trade," *Financial Times* (May 19, 2003), p. 13.

11. It should be noted that the WTO offers short-term courses on trade issues for delegates from developing countries to prepare them for multilateral negotiations.

12. Capacity building is now accepted as a useful function and the World Trade Organization, for instance, regularly runs short-term programs on the multilateral trading system and other associated topics for the benefit of senior government officials of developing countries.

13. Sampson, G.P. *Trade, Environment, and the WTO: The Post-Seattle Agenda*, Policy Essay No. 27 (Washington, DC: Overseas Development Council, 2000), p. 41.

14. Drahos, P., "When the Weak Bargain with the Strong: Negotiations in the World Trade Organization," *International Negotiation*, vol. 8 (2003), p. 94.

15. Weighted voting has ensconced the privileged position of the advanced countries, particularly the United States, and disadvantaged the developing countries. This imbalance is justified on the ground that the United States and developed countries provide the necessary funding, but this is a fallacy since developing countries repay all loans provided by the IMF.

16. Kovach, H., Caroline Neligan and Simon Burall, *Power Without Accountability?*, The Global Accountability Report 1, 2003 (London: One World Trust, 2002/2003), p. 15.

17. Drahos, P., "When the Weak Bargain with the Strong: Negotiations in the World Trade Organization," *International Negotiation*, vol. 8 (2003), p. 86.

18. Khorr, M., "The World Trade Organization and the South: Implications of the Emerging Global Economic Governance for Development," in Jomo, K.S., and Shyamala Nagaraj (eds), *Globalization versus Development* (Houndmills: Palgrave, 2002), pp. 74–5.

19. Adams, N.A. *Worlds Apart: The North South Divide and the International System* (London and New Jersey: Zed Books, 1997), pp. 181ff.

20. "US Opposes Bigger Say for Poorer Countries," *Financial Times* (June 27, 2003) p. 7.

21. See Hayter, T. *Open Borders: The Case Against Immigration Controls* (London: Pluto Press, 2000), p. 151.

22. *Global Economic Prospects 2004: Realizing the Development Promise of the Doha Agenda* (Washington, DC: The World Bank, 2003), p. xxiii.
23. Yusuf, S., "Globalization and the Challenge for Developing Countries," Development Economics Research Group (DECRG) Paper, World Bank (June 2001), p. 23.
24. For the South Asian countries, removal of travel restrictions was significant because expatriate remittances to these countries is a significant portion of total annual foreign exchange earnings. Remittances account for more than half of Bangladesh's development budget and most of Pakistan's foreign exchange earnings. See "Expatriate Remittances to Asia Exceed Western Aid," *Financial Times* (June 24, 2003), p. 6.
25. "India and China Co-ordinate Trade Policy," *Financial Times* (July 1, 2003), p. 7.
26. Ostry, S., "Canada in a Changing Trade Environment" (http://www.utoronto.ca/cis/Canada_in_a_Changing_Trade_Environment-Stats_Can.doc).
27. See TWN: Third World Network (twnside.org.sg/title/5413a.htm).
28. Barbosa, Rubens Antonio, "Why the Group of 20 was 'Suddenly' Formed," remarks made at the Cordell Hull Institute, Washington, DC, November 25, 2003 (http://www.sice.oas.org/Tunit/barbosa03_e.asp).
29. Hoekman, B., Constantine Michalopoulos and L. Alan Winters, "More Favorable and Differential Treatment of Developing Countries: Towards a New Approach in the WTO," *World Bank Policy Research Working Paper 3107* (August 2003), p. 1.
30. "G-20 Urges End to Farm Subsidies," *BBC News World Edition* (March 19, 2005) (http://news.bbc.co.uk/2/hi/business/4361109.stm).
31. Total trade with the 19 countries with which US has preferential trade agreements was US$138,337.8 million in 2004 against total US trade that year of US$2,910.0 billion. Data is compiled from *Foreign Trade Statistics*, US Census Bureau (http://www.census.gov/foreign-trade/balance/c3550.html).

Bibliography

Books and monographs

Adams, N.A. *Worlds Apart: The North South Divide and the International System* (London and New Jersey: Zed Books, 1997).

Bairoch, P. *The Economic Development of the Third World Since 1900* (Berkeley, CA: University of California Press, 1977).

Barlow, M. and Tony Clarke *MAI: The Multilateral Agreement on Investments and the Threat to American Freedom* (New York: Stoddart Publishing Co. Ltd, 1998).

Basudeb Guha-Khasnobis (ed.) *The WTO, Developing Countries and the Doha Development Agenda* (Houndmills: Palgrave Macmillan, 2004).

Bello, W., Nicola Bullard and Kamal Malhotra (eds) *Global Finance: New Thinking on Regulating Speculative Capital Markets* (London and New York: The University Press, Dhaka and Zed Books, 2000).

Bhagwati, J. and Mathias Hirsch (eds) *The Uruguay Round and Beyond: Essays in Honor of Arthur Dunkel* (Ann Arbor, MI: The University of Michigan Press, 1998).

Bhagwati, J. *In Defense of Globalization* (New York: Oxford University Press, 2004).

Bhagwati, J.N. and John Gerard Ruggie (eds) *Power, Passions, and Purpose: Prospects for North–South Negotiations* (Cambridge, MA: The MIT Press, 1984).

Capling, A. *Australia and the Global Trade System: From Havana to Seattle* (Cambridge: Cambridge University Press, 2001).

Cardoso, F.H. and Enzo Faletto *Dependency and Development in Latin America* (Berkeley, CA: University of California Press, 1979).

Cardoso, F.H. *Charting a New Course: The Politics of Globalization and Social Transformation*, edited and introduced by Mauricio A. Font (Lanham, MD: Rowman and Littlefield Publishers, Inc., 2001).

Cohn, Theodore H. *Governing Global Trade* (Aldershot: Ashgate, 2002).

Eichengreen, B. *Toward a New International Financial Architecture* (Washington, DC: Institute for International Economics, 1999).

Fuchs, D.A. and Friedrich Kratochwil (eds) *Transformative Change and Global Order: Reflections on Theory and Practice* (Hamburg and London: Lit Verlag, 2002).

Fukuyama, F. *The End of History and the Last Man* (New York: Avon Books, 1992).

Gilpin, R. *The Challenge of Global Capitalism: The World Economy in the 21st Century* (Princeton, NJ: Princeton University Press, 2000).

Gionea, J. *International Trade and Investment: An Asia-Pacific Perspective* (Sydney, Australia: McGraw-Hill, 2003).

Hatch, W. and Kozo Yamamura *Asia in Japan's Embrace: Building a Regional Production Alliance* (Cambridge: Cambridge University Press, 1996).

Hayter, T. *Open Borders: The Case Against Immigration Controls* (London: Pluto Press, 2000), p. 151.

Held, D. and Anthony McGrew (eds) *Governing Globalization* (Cambridge: Polity Press, 2002).

Hooper, E. *The River: A Journey to the Source of HIV and AIDS* (Boston, MA: Little, Brown and Co., 1999).

Huntington, Samuel P. *The Clash of Civilizations and the Remaking of World Order* (New York: Simon and Schuster, 1996).

Jomo, K.S. and Shyamala Nagaraj (eds) *Globalization versus Development* (Houndmills: Palgrave, 2002).

Kindleberger, C.P. *The World in Depression, 1929–1939* (London: Allen Lane, 1973).

Kovach, H., Caroline Neligan and Simon Burall *Power Without Accountability?*, The Global Accountability Report 1, 2003 (London: One World Trust, 2002/2003).

Krueger, Anne O. (ed.) *The WTO as an International Organization* (Chicago: University of Chicago Press, 1998).

Lairson, T. and David Skidmore *International Political Economy* (Toronto: Wadsworth, 2003).

Lechner, F.J. and John Boli (eds) *The Globalization Reader* (Malden, MA: Blackwell Publishers, 2001).

Madeley, J. *Hungry for Trade: How the Poor Pay for Free Trade* (London and New York: Zed Books, 2000).

Mandle, Jay R. *Globalization and the Poor* (Cambridge: Cambridge University Press, 2003).

Maswood, J. *International Political Economy and Globalization* (Singapore: World Scientific Publishing Co., 2000).

Mendoza, M.R., Patrick Low and Barbara Kotschwar (eds) *Trade Rules in the Making: Challenges in Regional and Multilateral Negotiations* (Washington, DC: Brookings Institution Press, 1999).

Michalopoulos, C. *Developing Countries in the WTO* (Houndmills: Palgrave, 2001).

Michie, J. and John Grieve Smith (eds) *Global Instability: The Political Economy of World Economic Governance* (London and New York: Routledge, 1999).

Moore, M. *A World Without Walls: Freedom, Development, Free Trade and Global Governance* (London: Cambridge University Press, 2003).

Moore, M. (ed.) *Doha and Beyond: The Future of the Multilateral Trading System* (Cambridge: Cambridge University Press, 2004).

Oberthur, S. and Hermann E. Ott *The Kyoto Protocol: International Climate Policy for the 21st Century* (Berlin: Springer-Verlag, 1999).

Olson, M. *The Logic of Collective Action: Public Goods and the Theory of Groups* (Cambridge: Harvard University Press, 1965).

Petras, J. and Henry Veltmeyer *Globalization Unmasked: Imperialism in the 21st Century* (London and New York: Fernwood Publishing/Zed Books, 2001).

Rajan, Ramkishen S., Rahul Sen and Reza Siregar *Singapore and Free Trade Agreements: Economic Relations with Japan and the United States* (Singapore: Institute of Southeast Asian Studies, 2001).

Robb, Caroline R. *Can the Poor Influence Policy? Participatory Poverty Assessments in the Developing World* (Washington, DC: International Monetary Fund, The World Bank, 2002).

Ruggie, John G. (ed.) *Multilateralism Matters: The Theory and Praxis of an International Form* (New York: Columbia University Press, 1993).

Schaeffer, Robert K. *Understanding Globalization: The Social Consequences of Political, Economic, and Environmental Change* (Lanham, MD: Rowman and Littlefield Publishers, 2003).

Schott, J.J. (ed.) *Free Trade Agreements: US Strategies and Priorities* (Washington, DC: Institute for International Economics, 2004).

Schott, Jeffrey J. *The Uruguay Round: An Assessment* (Washington, DC: Institute for International Economics, November 1994).

Stiglitz, Joseph E. *Globalization and its Discontents* (New York: W.W. Norton and Company, 2003).

Stubbs, R. and Geoffrey R.D. Underhill (eds) *Political Economy and the Changing Global Order* (Houndmills: Macmillan Press Ltd, 1994).

Sutherland, P. Jagdish Bhagwati *et al. The Future of the WTO* (Geneva: World Trade Organization, 2004).

Vayrynen, R. (ed.) *Globalization and Global Governance* (Lanham, MD: Rowman and Littlefield Publishers, Inc., 1999).

Wiener, J. Making *Rules in the Uruguay Round of the GATT: A Study of Internal Leadership* (Aldershot: Dartmouth Publishing Company, 1995).

Wilkinson, R. and Steve Hughes (eds) *Global Governance: Critical Perspectives* (London and New York: Routledge, 2002).

Woodward, D. *The Next Crisis? Direct and Equity Investment in Developing Countries* (London and New York: Zed Books, 2001).

Young, Oran R. *Governance in World Affairs* (New York and London: Cornell University Press, Ithaca, 1999).

Articles

Abbott, Frederick M., "The Doha Declaration on the TRIPS Agreement and Public Health: Lighting a Dark Corner at the WTO," *Journal of International Economic Law*, vol. 5, no. 2 (July 2002).

Alger, C., "The Emerging Roles of NGOs in the UN System: From Article 71 to a People's Millennium Assembly," *Global Governance*, vol. 8, no. 1 (January–March 2002).

Bella, W., "Learning from Doha: A Civil Society Perspective from the South," *Global Governance*, vol. 8, issue no. 3 (July–September 2002).

Bergsten, C. Fred, "A Renaissance for U.S. Trade Policy?," *Foreign Affairs*, vol. 81, no. 6 (November/December 2002).

Bergsten, C. Fred, "Foreign Economic Policy for the Next President," *Foreign Affairs*, vol. 83, no. 2 (March/April 2004).

Bhagwati, J., "Don't Cry for Cancun," *Foreign Affairs*, vol. 83, no. 1 (January/February 2004).

Boyer, M.C. *et al.*, "Who Gets to Run the WTO?," *Foreign Policy* (February 2005) (http://foreignpolicy.com/story/files/story2776.php).

Comeliau, C., "The Limitless Growth Assumption," *International Social Science Journal*, no. 166 (December 2000).

Deaton, A., "Is World Poverty Falling?," *Finance & Development*, vol. 39, no. 2 (June 2002).

Desker, B., "In Defence of FTAs: From Purity to Pragmatism in East Asia," *The Pacific Review*, vol. 17, no. 1 (March 2004).

Downs, George W., David M. Rocke and Peter N. Barsoom, "Managing the Evolution of Multilteralism," *International Organization*, vol. 52, no. 2 (Spring 1998).

Drahos, P., "When the Weak Bargain with the Strong: Negotiations in the World Trade Organization," *International Negotiation*, vol. 8 (2003).

Gordon, Bernard K., "A High-Risk Trade Policy," *Foreign Affairs*, vol. 82, no. 4 (July/August 2003).

Gosovic, B., "Global Intellectual Hegemony and the International Development Agenda," *International Social Science Journal*, no. 166 (December 2000).

Hoekman, B., Constantine Michalopoulos and L. Alan Winters, "More Favorable and Differential Treatment of Developing Countries: Towards a New Approach in the WTO," *World Bank Policy Research Working Paper 3107* (August 2003).

Hoekman, B., Francis Ng and Marcelo Olarreaga, "Agricultural Tariffs or Subsidies: Which are More Important for Developing Countries," *The World Bank Economic Review*, vol. 18, no. 2 (2004).

Ismail, F., "On the Road to Cancun: A Development Perspective on EU Trade Policies and Implications for Central and East European Countries," *The Journal of World Investment*, vol. 4, no. 4 (August 2003).

Khor, M., "Transparency and Participation in the WTO Decision-Making Process and Procedures," *Third World Resurgence*, no. 153/154 (2004).

Llyod, V. and Robert Weissman, "How International Monetary Fund and World Bank Policies Undermine Labor Power and Rights," *International Journal of Health Services*, vol. 32, no. 3 (2002).

Mallaby, S., "NGOs: Fighting Poverty, Hurting the Poor," *Foreign Policy* (September/October 2004).

Panitchpakdi, S., "Moving Beyond Cancun," *The OECD Observer*, no. 240/241 (December 2003).

Scholte, J.A., Robert O'Brien and Marc Williams, "The WTO and Civil Society," *Journal of World Trade*, vol. 33, no. 1 (February 1999).

Short, C., "Dangers to Doha," *The World Today*, London, vol. 59, no. 8/9 (August/September 2003).

Srinivasan, T.N., "Comment on 'Counting the World's Poor', by Angus Deaton," *The World Bank Research Observer*, vol. 16, no. 2 (Fall 2001).

Subramanian, A., "Medicines, Patents, and TRIPS," *Finance & Development*, vol. 41, no. 1 (March 2004).

Tanzi, V., "Globalization Without a Net," *Foreign Policy* (July/August 2001).

Tarditi, S., "CAP Pseudo-Reforms: A Penelopean Web," *Intereconomics* (September/October 2002) (http: . . . /pqdweb?Did=000000239099831&Fmt=3&Deli=1&Mtd+1&Idx=2&Sid=!&RQT=30).

Walkensorst, P. and Nora Dihel, "Tariff Bindings, Unused Protection and Agricultural Trade Liberalization," *OECD Economic Studies*, no. 36 (2003/1).

Walter, A., "NGOs, Business, and International Agreement: The Multilateral Agreement on Investment, Seattle, and Beyond," *Global Governance*, vol. 7, no. 1 (January–March 2001).

Walter, A., "NGOs, Business, and International Investment: The Multilateral Agreement on Investment, Seattle, and Beyond," *Global Governance*, vol. 7, no. 1 (January–March 2001).

Waltz, K., "Globalization and Governance," James Madison Lecture, 1999, in *PS Online* (December 1999).

Warkentin, C. and Karen Mingst, "International Institutions, the State, and Global Civil Society in the Age of the World Wide Web," *Global Governance*, vol. 6, no. 2 (April–June 2000).

Werlin, H.H., "Poor Nations. Rich Nations: A Theory of Governance," *Public Administration Review*, vol. 63, no. 3 (May/June 2003).

Williamson, J., "From Reform Agenda to Damaged Brand Name: A Short History of the Washington Consensus and Suggestions for What to do Next," *Finance & Development*, vol. 40, no. 3 (September 2003).

Woolcock, S., "The Singapore Issues in Cancun: A Failed Negotiation Ploy or a Litmus Test for Global Governance," *Intereconomics*, vol. 38, no. 5 (September/October 2003).

Others

Abbott, F.M., "Study Paper for the British Commission on the Intellectual Property Rights on the WTO TRIPs Agreement and its Implications for Access to Medicines in Developing Countries," Study Paper 2a, February 2002, p. 16.

Agricultural Policies in OECD Countries: Monitoring and Evaluation 2003, OECD, 2003.

Anderson, K., "The Challenge of Reducing Subsidies and Trade Barriers," paper presented at a Roundtable in Copenhagen, May 24–28, 2004.

Anderson, K. and Will Martin, "Agricultural Trade Reform and the Doha Development Agenda," paper prepared for a workshop prior to the Annual Conference of the Australian Agricultural and Resource Economics Society, Coffs Harbour, February 8, 2005.

Bacchetta, M. and Marion Jansen *Adjusting to Trade Liberalization: The Role of Policy, Institutions and WTO Disciplines*, Special Studies no. 7, WTO Publications, World Trade Organization, Geneva, 2003.

Barbosa, Rubens Antonio, "Why the Group of 20 was 'Suddenly: Formed'," remarks made at the Cordell Hull Institute, Washington, DC, November 25, 2003 (http://www.sice.oas.org/Tunit/barbosa03_e.asp).

Deardorff, Alan V. and Robert M. Stern, "What the Public Should Know about Globalization and the World Trade Organization," paper prepared for the conference on "Globalization: Trade, Financial, and Political Economy Aspects," Delphi, Greece, May 25–27, 2000.

Desker, B. and Margaret Liang, "Trade Facilitation: The Road Ahead," *Trends in Southeast Asia Series, No. 1*, Institute of Southeast Asian Studies, Singapore, 2003.

"Developments Since the Fourth WTO Ministerial Conference", *Doha Round Briefing Series*, The International Centre for Trade and Sustainable Development and the International Institute for Sustainable Development, vol. 1, no. 6, February 2003.

Dollar, D. and Aart Kraay, "Trade, Growth and Policy," Development Research Group, The World Bank, March 2001.

Drabek, Z., "A Multilateral Agreement on Investment: Convincing the Sceptics," World Trade Organization, Staff Working Paper ERAD-98-05, June 1998.

EU Agriculture and the WTO: Doha Development Agenda, Cancun—September 2003, Agriculture and Rural Development, European Commission, September 2003.

Faini, R., "Trade Liberalization in a Globalizing World," paper prepared for the Annual World Bank Conference on Development Economics, Washington, DC, May 3–4, 2004.

Finger, J. Michael and Julio J. Nogues, "The Unbalanced Uruguay Round Outcome: The New Areas in Future WTO Negotiations," *Policy Research Working Paper 2732*, Development Research Group, The World Bank, December 2001.

Francois, Joseph F., Bradley McDonald, and Hakan Nordstrom *A User's Guide to Uruguay Round Assessments*, May 12, 1996 (http://www.intereconomics.com/francois/text9603.pdf).

Fukase E. and Will Martin, "Free Trade Area Membership as a Stepping Stone to Development: The Case of ASEAN," *World Bank Discussion Paper No. 421*, World Bank, Washington, DC, 2001.

Global Economic Prospects 2004: Realizing the Development Promise of the Doha Agenda, The World Bank, Washington, DC, 2003.

Global Monitoring Report 2005, World Bank, Washington, DC, 2005.

Globalization, Growth and Poverty, The World Bank, Washington, DC, 2001.

Hoekman, B., "Cancun: Crisis or Catharsis?," The World Bank, September 20, 2003, mimeo.

Ismail, F., "Mainstreaming Development in the WTO," undated typescript, p. 5.

Keck, A. and Patrick Low, "Special and Differential Treatment in the WTO: Why, When and How?," World Trade Organization, Economic Research and Statistics Division, Staff Working Paper ERSD-2004–03, May 2004.

Konandreas, P., "Incorporating Constrained Flexibility in Tariff Reductions: A Dynamic Formula," unpublished paper, July 9, 2004.

Konandreas, P., "Implementing the Special Products (SPs) Provision on the Basis of an Aggregate Deviation from the General Tariff Cut Formula," unpublished paper, December 3, 2004.

Konandreas, P., "Implementing the Sensitive Products Provision on the Basis of an Additional Pro-Rated TRQ Commitment for Non-Compliance with the General Tariff Cut Formula," unpublished paper, December 3, 2004.

"Krueger Makes Case for Globalisation," in *IMF/World Bank Daily*, September 29, 2002.

Mattoo, A. and Arvind Subamanian, "Multilateralism and the Doha Round: A Stock-Taking," typescript, 2005.

Merlinda D. Ingco and John D. Nash, "What's at Stake? Developing-Country Interests in the Doha Development Round."

Nash, J., "Issues and Prospects for Agricultural Trade Liberalization in the Doha Development Agenda," Seminar paper presented at the World Bank, Washington, DC, April 2003.

Orden, D. Rashid S. Kaukab and Eugenio Diaz-Bonilla *Liberalizing Agricultural Trade and Developing Countries*, Carnegie Endowment for International Peace, Issue Brief, November 2002.

Poverty Reduction in Bangladesh: Building on Progress, Poverty Reduction and Economic Management Sector Unit, South Asia Region, World Bank, New York (Report No. 24299-BD) December 2002.

Raghavan, C., "MAI Not Dead Yet," *Third World Network* (http://www.twnside.org.sg/title/dead-cn.htm).

Ravallion, M., "The Debate on Globalization, Poverty and Inequality: Why Measurement Matters," World Bank Policy Research Working Paper 3038, April 2003.

Reforming Public Institutions and Strengthening Governance: A World Bank Strategy, Poverty Reduction and Economic Management Network, World Bank, November 2000.

Rodrik, D., "Feasible Globalization," NBER Working Paper Series, Working Paper 9129, Cambridge, MA, September 2002.

Rose, A. *Do We Really Know that the WTO Increases Trade?*, NBER Working Paper No. 9273, October 2002.

Rose, A. *Do WTO Members Have a More Liberal Trade Policy?*, NBER Working Paper No. 9347, 2003.

Ross, J., "WTO Collapses in Cancun: Autopsy of a Fiasco Foretold," *CounterPunch*, September 20, 2003.

Sampson, G.P. *Trade, Environment, and the WTO: The Post-Seattle Agenda*, Policy Essay No. 27, Overseas Development Council, Washington, DC, 2000.

Stiglitz, Joseph E. and Andrew Charlton, "A Development Round of Negotiations?" paper presented at the Annual Bank Conference on Development Economics, May 11, 2004.

The Multilateral Agreement on Investment OECD Policy Brief, No. 2, 1997, p. 3 (http://www.oecd.org/publications/Pol_brief/9702_Pol.htm).

Yusuf, S., "Globalization and the Challenge for Developing Countries," Development Economics Research Group (DECRG) Paper, World Bank, June 2001.

Newspaper and magazines

Australian Financial Review
Far Eastern Economic Review, Hong Kong
Financial Times
International Herald Tribune
The Australian
The Economist, London
The New York Times
The Washington Post

Index